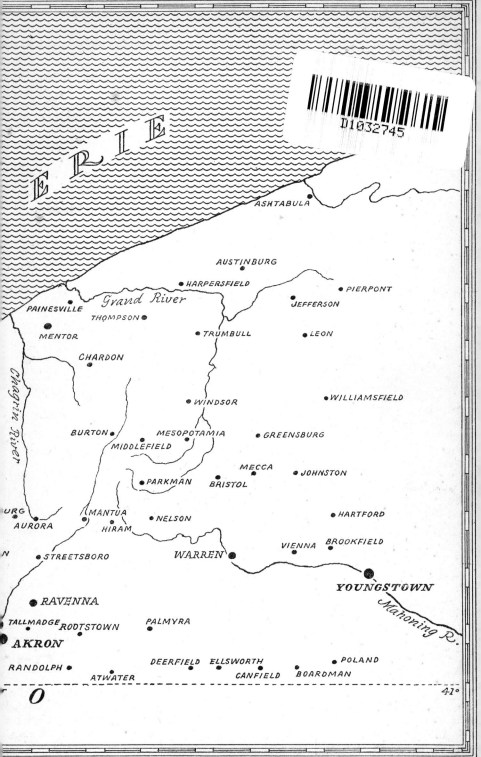

ERIE

ASHTABULA

AUSTINBURG

HARPERSFIELD

PIERPONT

Grand River

JEFFERSON

PAINESVILLE

THOMPSON

TRUMBULL

LEON

MENTOR

CHARDON

WINDSOR

WILLIAMSFIELD

Chagrin River

BURTON

MESOPOTAMIA

GREENSBURG

MIDDLEFIELD

MECCA

JOHNSTON

PARKMAN

BRISTOL

URG

MANTUA

NELSON

HARTFORD

AURORA

HIRAM

VIENNA

BROOKFIELD

N

STREETSBORO

WARREN

RAVENNA

YOUNGSTOWN

TALLMADGE

ROOTSTOWN

PALMYRA

Mahoning R.

AKRON

RANDOLPH

DEERFIELD

ELLSWORTH

POLAND

ATWATER

CANFIELD

BOARDMAN

O

41°

J. MAC DONALD

THE WESTERN RESERVE

Books by HARLAN HATCHER

LAKE ERIE

THE GREAT LAKES

THE BUCKEYE COUNTRY: *A Pageant of Ohio*

CREATING THE MODERN AMERICAN NOVEL

THE VERSIFICATION OF ROBERT BROWNING

THE OHIO GUIDE (Editor)

TUNNEL HILL

PATTERNS OF WOLFPEN

CENTRAL STANDARD TIME

LANTERMAN'S FALLS—LANDMARK OF YOUNGSTOWN

The old grist mill, built in 1803 and replaced shortly after the Civil War, is now a natural history museum and part of Mill Creek Park

THE
WESTERN
RESERVE

The Story of New Connecticut in Ohio

by

HARLAN HATCHER

THE BOBBS-MERRILL COMPANY, INC.

INDIANAPOLIS   *Publishers*   NEW YORK

THE WESTERN RESERVE AND
ITS SAVINGS BANK

THE hardy pioneers from the Eastern states who poured into this "Western Reserve" early in the last century brought with them not only their kettles and their cattle—they brought also their institutions.

Not many years after their homes and farms had been established, produce of the fields and forests was flowing east to pay for the manufactured goods that this region did not yet provide for itself. Money began to circulate. The Western Reserve felt the need of banks. Commercial banks at first to help the interchange of goods and money. When there began to be here a small surplus of money, a savings bank was needed.

The "Society for Savings in the City of Cleveland" was in form and in name an Eastern institution transplanted to the Midwest. The mutual savings-bank idea was born, as one might expect, in Scotland in 1810. It took root in Philadelphia and in Boston in 1816, in New York in 1819. Through the 1820's and 1830's many of these mutual savings banks were organized in the Atlantic seaboard states from Maryland northward.

Patterned after these Eastern savings banks, named for the "Society for Savings" in Hartford, this Cleveland savings bank began business in 1849. Through the century it has survived and grown, a reservoir of finance for the people of Cleveland and the northeastern Ohio counties where its New England founders planted it.

On this hundredth anniversary, the Society for Savings in the

City of Cleveland is proud to present a history of this Western Reserve. The author, Harlan Hatcher, is a professor of English and Vice-President of Ohio State University and author of several distinguished books on Ohio and the Great Lakes region.

Society for Savings
FOUNDED 1849
IN THE CITY OF CLEVELAND

TABLE OF CONTENTS

LIST OF ILLUSTRATIONS

THE WESTERN RESERVE

CHAPTER ONE

THE RESERVE

W<small>HEN</small> you stand on the quiet green of Hudson, Ohio, looking through the trees toward the church and the library, you feel that you are in eighteenth-century New England, not in twentieth-century Ohio. On the eastern edge of Akron, almost engulfed by that tumultuous, discontented, and crowded rubber center of the world, is the lovely village of Tallmadge. Its handsome white New England Congregational Church, calm, spiritually poised on the village green, is an oasis of peace in the clattering desert of modern industry. It is so perfect an example of New England church architecture that *Life* chose it for a Thanksgiving-issue cover as the symbol of "the devout spirit of the New England Puritans who celebrated the first Thanksgiving on Dec. 13, 1621 (O.S.)."[1] The churches at Twinsburg and Streetsboro overlooking the village greens are likewise transplanted to Ohio from their native New England. The Congregational Church at Kinsman was copied after the Old North Church at New Haven.

Gates Mills, secluded in the lush Chagrin River Valley, a few miles east of Cleveland, embodies twentieth-century man's dream of early nineteenth-century Connecticut graciousness and peace. It lies just south of U.S. 322, reached by a winding valley road. The river is as narrow and intimate as the Concord. The gleaming white New England-style houses, arranged along the village roads and on the landscaped slopes above the river, suggest quiet luxury in a restrained country-club atmosphere. The spire of one of the Reserve's finest old churches rises above the trees in its clipped churchyard enclosed by a white paling fence. Only with

---

[1] *Life* Magazine, November 20, 1944.

effort do you realize that sprawling, industrial, traffic-jammed Cleveland is hardly ten miles to the west.

Fifteen miles to the southeast of Cleveland, on the old Aurora Road (Route 43) that runs past the Cranwood, Thistledown, and Randall race tracks, you come upon the village of Aurora. In most parts of the continent it would be just another crossroads town with a garish filling station and chain grocery store. But even if you are hurried and are not historical-minded, the chances are that you will pause to admire this neat example of a passing era. For, like Hudson, Tallmadge, and Gates Mills, it retains a dignified but homelike New England quality in its white houses along its triangle of tree-shaded roads.

The scarred, white fishing boats putting out from Huron or Sandusky for Lake Erie might well be shoving off from New London, Connecticut, for the Sound. Towns south of Lake Erie bear New England names: Dorset, Andover, Norwalk, New Haven, Greenwich. Everywhere in northern Ohio are to be found the unmistakable signs of the New England origin of its settlement. Most of them are now faint or obscure, and must be carefully sought out; a few are dramatic and assertive. For this is the region known throughout the land as the Western Reserve of Connecticut.

No other five thousand square miles of territory in the United States, lying in a body outside of New England, ever had, to begin with, so pure a New England population. No similar territory west of the Allegheny Mountains has so impressed the brain and conscience of the country.[2]

The Western Reserve, however, is not a miniature New England. Hinsdale rightly added the observation that "the southern shore of Lake Erie is not the northern shore of Long Island Sound; New Connecticut is not a reproduction of Old Connecticut." It is a region of arresting contrasts of which Akron and Tallmadge are appropriate symbols. Descendants of the Puritan Mathers share the Reserve with the Slovenian Lausches, only one generation removed from the mountains of Yugoslavia. The campus of West-

---

[2] These are the considered words of B. A. Hinsdale in his scholarly and painstaking study, *The Old Northwest*, New York, 1888, p. 388.

ern Reserve University, with its strong New England tradition, has for its neighbor the Cleveland Cultural Gardens wherein fifteen foreign nationality groups pay respect to their unique cultures with formal gardens and statues honoring Goethe and Schiller, Virgil, Liszt, Shakespeare. The extensive and rich greenhouses and truck farms of the Hungarians, Slavs, Czechs, and Italians on the west slopes of the Cuyahoga River, almost in the heart of the city of Cleveland, face across the booming, industrial plants in the Flats, toward the wealthy more or less Anglo-Saxon suburb of Shaker Heights on the east. The New England campus of Lake Erie College and the wooded public green of Painesville look down the slope of Grand River to crowded Fairport Harbor where the big ore ships from Duluth put in to be serviced by the Finns who settled here a generation or two ago. Lorain, with its heavy concentration of Poles, Slovenes, Hungarians, and Italians around the giant works of the American Ship Building plant and U. S. Steel's National Tube Company plant, is only fifteen miles away from the spacious square which serves as the central campus for Oberlin College, steeped in an intellectual tradition redolent of New England.

The southeast corner of the Reserve is dark with the massive labors of Little Steel, which gears Youngstown, Niles, and Warren in the Mahoning River Valley with Pittsburgh and Cleveland to form the steel center of the world. A few miles away to the north is the unhurried New England village of Jefferson, once the home of Senator Ben Wade and William Dean Howells. Chardon, on its eminence in Geauga County, surrounded by its miles of maple groves, carries on the New England tradition of sugar and sirup making. The art has been cultivated through the generations ever since the first settlers arrived, and each year (except in bad seasons) a colorful Maple Festival is held in Chardon in the spring when the sap runs. Giant freighters put in at Huron to unload ore among the crowded docks under the massive but nimble Hulett machines, and at Sandusky receive the endless procession of coal from the railroad cars into the ship's hold for transshipment up the Lakes. A few miles away the legended Blue Hole of Castalia bubbles up its immemorial fountain as it did when astonished Indians first set eyes upon it, and to the south, along the terraces of the ancient Erie beaches, are the long fields of oats, the peach orchards, and the graceful streets of the Firelands towns of Milan, Berlin Heights, Norwalk, Monroeville, and New London.

No, Connecticut's Western Reserve in Ohio is not a reproduction of old Connecticut. It is too original, too engrossed in its own problems, too mobile and vibrant with its own life to be a reproduction of anything; but, like a gifted son of a gifted father, it wears the stamp of its progenitor without sacrificing its singular personality. It was Connecticut and New England long enough and exclusively enough to establish a distinctive atmosphere and style of living and culture that set it apart from the other regions of Ohio. When the flood of immigrations from Europe and from other portions of America swept over it, its basic pattern held firm. The Reserve changed, of course, but there was no revolution. It "contained" the invasion. In spite of all that has happened at Youngstown, Akron, Cleveland, and Lorain to amalgamate through modern industry the peoples of the earth, the Reserve is still different from the rest of Ohio. When you enter its villages with their greens and their white churches after passing through the Pennsylvania and Maryland towns in eastern Ohio and along the old National Road (U.S. 40), or from the Virginia towns of Chillicothe or Mount Vernon, you will sense this difference, this New England heritage, even though you are unfamiliar with the history of this land lying south of Lake Erie.

Why did the people of Connecticut in particular tear up their established homes, load a selection of their goods on wagons, and make the two or three months' journey of anguish through the wilderness of Upper New York and Pennsylvania into the Ohio country—often losing their goods and cattle while fording or swimming the creeks and rivers, often burying one or more of their children on the hard way among the trees? How did this small state on Long Island Sound get title to this valuable strip of land along Lake Erie west of both New York and Pennsylvania?

We shall find several parts to the complex answer, but the central point here and now is simply that Connecticut for good reason claimed ownership of this Ohio land, and her title was sustained amid controversy by the newly developed authority of the colonies organized into the United States of America. The details of this story are involved in devious legal technicalities. The significant facts, however, may be detached without damage to the truth of the whole. They also have a special interest for us because of their comment on the nature of our forefathers and the process by which our country was expanded and developed.

When the first settlements were made on the Atlantic coast, no man knew what lay to the west; no one had the haziest idea of the nature or extent of the continent upon whose eastern coast they had intruded. The best supposition was that somewhere beyond this eastern shore, perhaps not too far beyond the wall of trees, was the Great South Sea and the fabulous wealth of the Indies. But, regardless of extent, whether it ended behind the next hill or continued a thousand miles, everything to the west belonged either by right of discovery or by right of conquest to the English Crown. The Crown, therefore, had power to deed all of it or any part thereof to any person or company it might choose. Since nobody had ever surveyed or mapped it, or even laid eyes on it, the King's experts could define the boundaries of his grants only in the most casual terms. Such loose and vaguely conceived grants were made to Virginia, Delaware, Pennsylvania, New York, Massachusetts, Connecticut, and elsewhere. The Connecticut grant, like some of the others, had an indefinite western boundary. The original phrasing of 1630, conveying title to the land to the Earl of Warwick's corporation known as the Council of Plymouth, is worth reading again.

This is the way the conveyance described the territory:

All that part of New England, in America, which lies and extends itself from a river there called Narragansett river, the space of forty leagues upon a straight line near the sea shore, towards the south-west, west by south, or west, as the coast lieth, towards Virginia, accounting three English miles to the league, all and singular, the lands and hereditaments whatsoever, lying and being within the bounds aforesaid, north and south in latitude and

breadth, and in length and longitude, and within all the breadth
aforesaid throughout all the main lands there, from the western
ocean to the South Seas.

Such a description of a piece of valuable property is magnifi-
cently puzzling and inadequate. Much the same lordly disregard
of precision was used in the charters of conveyance of the grants
to Connecticut's neighbors. No reasonably cautious man would
erect a fence on such a boundary. Here, indeed, were the seeds
and the soil for litigation, wrangling, and even bloodshed. All,
alas, were reaped. Rufus Choate, commenting on the attempts to
clarify the boundaries, summed up the chaos created by these conflicting grants by saying, "The commissioners might as well have
decided that the line between the States was bounded on the north
by a bramble-bush, on the south by a bluejay, on the west by a
hive of bees in swarming time, and on the east by five hundred
foxes with firebrands tied to their tails."

The present map of the state of Connecticut will indicate how
these crude generalities were finally pinned down to exactitude on
the land fronting on Long Island Sound. The interpretation was
that the boundary should extend for 120 miles along the coast, and
from the 41st parallel (the southwest corner of the state) to 2
minutes north of the 42nd parallel. That agreement hemmed Connecticut in between Rhode Island, Massachusetts, New York, and
the Sound. But what about her western domain "throughout all
the main lands there . . . to the South Sea"? New York's recognized territory cut across the extension of these lines to the west,
and the Pennsylvania grant also overlapped them. The New York
border was finally fixed after long negotiations and hot disputes
short of war. The Pennsylvania conflict was settled only after
bloody and cruelly heartless warfare between Pennsylvania men
and Connecticut settlers in the beautiful Wyoming Valley on the
Susquehanna River. It is one of the wretched chapters in our
early history.

Connecticut colonists, firm in their belief that this was their
land, settled in the region in the 1750's and 1760's. The country

was beautiful, the soil was fertile, the climate was mild, there were
no rocks in the fields to be piled into fences, and the enthusiasm
for the Susquehanna Valley reached epidemic proportions in Moses
Cleaveland's country of Windham, Connecticut. At the outbreak
of the Revolution, three thousand or more colonists were engaged
in making a paradise of "New Connecticut" in William Penn's
domain.[3] They had their own towns, laws, tax collections, and
levies for a Connecticut regiment in the Continental Army. The
aggressive spirit of these pioneers is reflected in the words of a
Connecticut man writing of this period:

> The sordid, grasping, long-leasing policy of the Penns had never
> been able to stand a moment before the oncoming wave of Con-
> necticut democracy, with its individual land ownership, its liberal
> local government, and the personal incentive offered to individuals
> by its town system. So far as the Penns were concerned, the Con-
> necticut town system simply swept over them, and hardly thought
> of them as it went. But for the Revolution, the check occasioned
> by the massacre, and the appearance of a popular government in
> place of the Penns, nothing could have prevented the establish-
> ment of Connecticut's authority over all the regions embraced in
> her Western claims.

The massacre referred to was the black and barbaric extinction
of the frontier Wyoming colony by the British and Indians on
July 3, 1778. On that morning 230 "enrolled men" of the colony
and 70 old men and boys marched out to meet the 1,200 invaders
along the west bank of the Susquehanna. The Connecticut men
were flanked, engulfed, and overwhelmed by the British and the
Indians. They were shot down, tomahawked, scalped; a few escaped across the river, but others were murdered as they swam
toward their wives and children who watched the horror from the
opposite bank. One Tory killed his own brother. Captives were
bound, tortured, and their skulls knocked in with axes during the
orgy that followed. Nearly 300 men were killed, leaving 150
widows and 600 orphans. Survivors fled in a death march over

---

[3] This is the region which excited Shelley and his romantic colleagues to plan an
ideal colony in America.

mountain and through swamp, and some reached safety among the Delaware and Lehigh settlements. The old and the sick died on the way. One child was born and survived; one mother carried her dead baby twenty miles through the wilderness. The Indians ravaged and burned the village and laid the beautiful valley in waste.[4]

This tragic experience of brave Connecticut men and women was publicized throughout the world, and was certainly considered by the courts when they attempted to quiet the conflicting claims to western territory north of the 41st parallel. The Trenton Federal Court in 1782 ruled that "the State of Connecticut has no right to the lands in controversy," and that the territories claimed by her "do of right belong to the State of Pennsylvania."

Connecticut accepted this decision regarding Pennsylvania, as she had accepted New York's claim to land that jumped her charter. She did not, however, yield her title to the land *west* of Pennsylvania's fixed western boundary. Her claim was, indeed, strengthened by her wounds in Wyoming, and by the grace with which she extinguished her title to overlapping Pennsylvania territory. She still claimed her title to the strip of the continent from Pennsylvania westward between the 41° and 42°2' parallels; that is to say, the projection of her own north and south lines. In Ohio that strip lay between Lake Erie and a line about three miles south of present U.S. 224, just below Youngstown, Akron, New London, and Willard. If extended to the ocean, according to the charter, it would have touched the Great South Sea in northern California, and would have included parts of Nevada, Utah, Wyoming, Nebraska, Iowa, Illinois, Indiana, and Michigan—a considerable appendage indeed to little mother Connecticut. Benjamin Franklin was obviously right when he remarked that "the from 'sea to sea' colonies, having boundaries three or four thousand miles in length to one or two hundred in breadth, must in time be reduced to domains more convenient for the common purposes of government."

---

[4] For a comprehensive account of the Wyoming massacre see Alfred Mathews, *Ohio and Her Western Reserve,* New York, 1902, pp. 53-101.

The reduction was inevitable. The western lands had to be pooled under the jurisdiction of the confederation, to belong to the public domain, and be at the disposal of the United States for the general welfare. The statesmen of the colonies understood this necessity. It was vital to the very existence of the Republic itself, and until the hate-breeding conflicts were resolved there could be no genuine union. The Congress called upon the colonies to yield their claims. They responded. New York relinquished her title in 1780. Virginia did likewise, after reserving enough land north of the Ohio, between the Scioto and Miami rivers, to pay her officers and men to whom she was delinquent for their services and sacrifices during the Revolution. Massachusetts ceded in 1785. And by a deed of cession, September 14, 1786, Connecticut gave up to the Congress

all the right, title, interest, jurisdiction, and claim of the State of Connecticut to certain western lands beginning at the completion of the forty first degree of north latitude one hundred and twenty miles west of the western boundary line of Pennsylvania as now claimed by said Commonwealth; and from thence by a line drawn parallel to and one hundred and twenty miles west of said west line of Pennsylvania, and to continue north until it comes to forty two degrees and two minutes north latitude.[5]

That is to say, Connecticut, in ceding her claims, "reserved" this valuable 120-mile strip of territory south of Lake Erie for herself. The Congress accepted the "reservation," and recognized Connecticut's full right to the soil and the jurisdiction thereof. For several years it was a colony of the mother state, not a part of the Northwest Territory. It was, indeed, almost an independent state until, in 1800, legal jurisdiction was relinquished by Connecticut to the Congress. The territory was called by many names, "New Connecticut," "The Connecticut Reserve," "The Connecticut Western Reserve," etc., but it was soon designated in legal and historical records as The Western Reserve of Connecticut, and in Ohio simply as The Western Reserve.

---

[5] No one knew at this time that this line would run into Lake Erie and include a portion of Canadian possessions.

CHAPTER TWO

THE CONNECTICUT LAND COMPANY

O<small>N THE</small> Fourth of July, 1796, General Moses Cleaveland with a party of fifty men reached the western border of Pennsylvania. They had been traveling through the wilderness from eastern New York since April 28, and for the last eight days through woods and along the Lake Erie shore from Buffalo. They were weary with the struggle. At three o'clock in the afternoon, Seth Pease, astronomer and surveyor, casting about for a landmark, stumbled on the northwest cornerstone of Pennsylvania a short distance back of the high Lake Erie shore. It was clearly marked, he recorded in his journal, "on the north side, and on the south, Pennsylvania forty-two degrees north latitude, variation, seven minutes thirty seconds west, &c." He shouted his discovery, and those who came by land gathered round the marker. When they had assembled they "gave three cheers precisely at 5 o'clock, P.M.," says Pease.

A half hour later the entire party reached Conneaut where they pitched their tents on the east side of the creek. The party was in a spirited mood. They were in the Connecticut Reserve, the first party to arrive there, and they counted it a good omen that they had set foot on this soil for the first time on Independence Day. Cleaveland in his enthusiasm let his pen flow with an unaccustomed degree of eloquence as he wrote down in his *Journal* these words:

The day, memorable as the birthday of American Independence, and freedom from British tyranny, and commemorated by all good freeborn sons of America, and memorable as the day on which the settlement of this new country was commenced, and in time may raise her head amongst the most enlightened and improved States. And after many difficulties, perplexities and hardships were surmounted, and we were on the good and promised land, felt that a just tribute of respect to the day ought to be paid.

It is a memorable scene. The little band of fifty people, "including men, women and children,"[1] are gathered there in the early evening on the creek bank in the heart of a vast wilderness. Behind them and on both sides lies the heavy forest, in front of them stretches the wide blue expanse of Lake Erie. They fix their eyes on their chief, the stocky, heavy-set, and swarthy Moses Cleaveland, who impressed people as looking both like an Indian and a New England divine. He is obviously moved by the occasion. The men, under Captain Tinker, arrange themselves on the beach, rifles in hand. On command of the general, they raise their guns and break the stillness of the evening with a Federal salute of fifteen rounds. Then, "in honor of New Connecticut," they fired a sixteenth. Cleaveland then records that "we gave three cheers and christened the place Port Independence."

After the salute, Cleaveland caused grog to be poured for all the party. He lifted his cup and proposed a toast.

"The President of the United States!"

They drank.

"The State of New Connecticut!" Cleaveland proposed next.

They drank again and cheered the ambiguous designation.

"The Connecticut Land Company!" said Cleaveland.

They drank to their employers.

"May the Port of Independence and the fifty sons and daughters who have entered it this day be successful and prosperous!"

They joined the toast.

"May these sons and daughters multiply in sixteen years sixteen times fifty!" proposed Cleaveland, waxing more expansive with the toasts.

They drank to that.

---

[1] The children referred to were the three children of James Kingsbury and his wife who had followed the party from Buffalo, seeking a home in the west land. They settled at Conneaut, and a child born to them there in the following winter was the first white child born in the Reserve.

"May every person have his bowsprit trimmed and ready to enter every port that opens!" the general offered as a final toast. For the sixth time they drank.

Serious-minded Moses Cleaveland concludes his journal account of this ritual with the nearest approach to a touch of humor to be found in his correspondence. "Closed with three cheers. Drank several pails of grog, supped and retired in remarkable good order."

This band of surveyors had come to the Reserve to map the land for the Connecticut Land Company. We must tell a little of the story of this company and how it proposed to handle its property in Ohio. The State of Connecticut, following the release of her western claims, except for the Reserve, in 1786, worked out various schemes and proposals for disposition of her lands. At no time were the lands considered as military bounty as, for example, were the Virginia lands. As early as October 1786 the General Assembly had directed that the lands be surveyed and sold, but there was heated opposition to the methods proposed and nothing happened to put the legislation into effect. It legislated again in 1793, but encountered the same barriers and repealed its proposals. In 1795, General Anthony Wayne, after defeating the Indians in Ohio, signed with them the treaty of Greenville which removed from the Reserve the menace of Indian attack. The treaty apparently stimulated Connecticut further to formulate a workable method of sale and colonization of her Ohio territory.

The General Assembly at Hartford acted a third time in 1795. It devised an unusual scheme which, despite its weaknesses, met with general acceptance. Under this plan a committee of eight citizens[2] representing each county of Connecticut was authorized to sell the lands unsurveyed. The tract was presumed to embrace well in excess of 3,000,000 acres. Of their estimated total, 3,000,-000 acres were to be sold at a price of not less than $1,000,000. —thirty-three cents an acre. The committee was required to dispose of the entire Reserve, however, before concluding the sale

---

[2] They were John Treadwell, Marvin Wait, Thomas Grosvenor, Elijah Hubbard, James Wadsworth, William Edmond, Aaron Austin, Sylvester Gilbert. Charles Whittlesey, *Early History of Cleveland*, 1867, p. 162.

of any single portion of it, and the purchasers must assume all the risks of the unquieted title and possession. The proceeds of the sale were to be placed perpetually in a special fund, the interest to be used for the support of the Connecticut schools. (Still in effect.) The whole method of transaction was a gambling proposition. Only a company of speculators could cope with these specified conditions.

A group of thirty-five men negotiated the purchase, some of them acting not only for themselves but for other interested parties. The sale of the 3,000,000 acres was completed on September 2, 1795, for the sum of $1,200,000. The portions ranged all the way from Sylvanus Griswold's $1,683 and Daniel Holbrook's $8,750, to Moses Cleaveland's $32,600 and on up to Oliver Phelps's huge share of $168,185. The Committee of Eight thereupon granted deeds to each of the purchasers for his proportionate share of the still unsurveyed and undivided Reserve. They did not pay cash in hand, but gave bond to the state treasurer and a mortgage on the lands. The purchasers then formed themselves into a kind of syndicate under the name of the Connecticut Land Company. This partnership included other interested men who had been represented by the thirty-five, bringing the association to the number of fifty-seven.

Though the name Connecticut Land Company is a central part of the history of the Reserve, it was never officially incorporated. This company in turn deeded its purchase in trust to John Caldwell, Jonathan Brace, and John Morgan.[3] It then drew up articles of association setting forth in great detail how the company should be governed, the nature and extent of the powers of the directors of the association, and how the meetings of the company should be conducted. It also specified the plan for the surveys of the land, the partition of the shares, and the method of transfer and sale of the stock. Seven directors were chosen to manage the business. Among them were Oliver Phelps, heaviest stockholder, Roger Newberry of West Windsor, Samuel Mather, Jr., of Lynn, and Moses

---

[3] Deeds on the Reserve all rest ultimately on this trust for their title. Whittlesey, p. 166.

Cleaveland of Canterbury. Their meetings were held in Hartford in October. They immediately determined to clear away the Indian claims to the Reserve, which were still "unextinguished and unquieted," and to survey the property into townships five miles square. Moses Cleaveland himself was made general agent of the company to conduct the surveys in person.

And thus it came about that we discover him on this Fourth of July, 1796, just eight months after the first meeting of the company, celebrating the arrival of the surveying party on the soil of New Connecticut, and drinking toasts in grog to the success of the great enterprise.

CHAPTER THREE

THE FIRST SURVEYING PARTY

Moses Cleaveland and his party, whom we left drinking toasts in the wilderness by the lake shore at Conneaut, were not settlers but a staff of surveyors and their aids. They had come not to build cabins and to clear land, but to measure and divide the company's holdings. They had had a punishing and somewhat adventurous journey from Old to New Connecticut. It took them sixty-eight days to make the trip from Dover across New York to Conneaut, including annoying interruptions and delays. Thanks to the custom of our forefathers who kept rather full diaries and journals, we have a day-by-day, eyewitness account of this trip. We follow mainly the journal of young John Milton Holley, one of the surveyors.

They reached Albany on the third night out. From there they proceeded to Schenectady and up the Mohawk River. They were driving with them thirteen horses and some cattle. Some of the party with five supply boats crossed the Carrying Place to Oneida Lake and down the Oswego River to Lake Ontario. The others, including Holley and Cleaveland, continued the journey overland to Canandaigua. Holley and his group were delayed here for five weeks, apparently awaiting a rendezvous with General Cleaveland and news of the boats at Irondequoit. The *Journal* is not entirely clear at this point. It does say, however, that Holley made three trips over to Irondequoit (on the lake below present Rochester) in search of the boats; and that on June 3 Cleaveland arrived at Canandaigua with news of their hardship. We shall allow Holley to tell the story in his own words as he had it from Cleaveland:

27

June 3d.—Gen. Cleaveland at evening arrived at Canandaiqua [*sic*] and gave us information that the boats had gone from Whitestown to Fort Stanwix, and Mr. Stow got a letter from the British minister, or charge des' affaires, to the commanding officer at Fort Oswego, requesting permission for our boats to pass unmolested. This information, together with the favorable prospect of wind and weather at that time, gave us great hopes that the stores would get on safely and rapidly, but on Saturday morning there sprang up in the north-west a storm, and blew most violently on the shore of the Lake. This proved fatal to one of the boats, and damaged another very much, though we went a little forward to a safe harbor, and built several fires on the bank of the Lake as a beacon to those coming on. After the disaster had happened, the boat that was safe went on to the Gerundicut [Irondequoit] with a load, and left the other three, including the one that was stove, at Little Sodus, encamped near the Lake. . . .

All these misfortunes happened in consequence of not having liberty to pass the fort at Oswego. Such are the effects of allowing the British government to exist on the continent of America.

On June 5 the boats put out from Irondequoit for Niagara, portaged at the Falls and went on to Buffalo. The land-traveling party arrived at Skinner's tavern, Buffalo, on June 17. On Tuesday, June 21, at two o'clock in the afternoon, Red Jacket, Brant, Farmers Brother, Little Billy, Green Grass Hopper and other representatives of the Six Nations uncovered the council fire to negotiate with Cleaveland a settlement of their claims to the country which he was about to survey and appropriate.

General Cleaveland, who, according to Amzi Atwater, one of the party, had "a broad face, dark complexion very course [sic] features," and was of "slovenly dress and very vulgar in his conversation and manners," was able and shrewd in his negotiations with the Indians.[1] He had furnished himself with an Indian dress, and, with his swarthy skin, looked very much like an Indian chief himself. He gave the Indians plenty of whisky and kept the council going from Tuesday afternoon until Friday with much feasting, drinking, and dancing to mellow their attitude and their demands. They did soften, but not before Red Jacket delivered

---

[1] Observation of Judge Porter.

one of the keen and realistic speeches for which the Indians were celebrated. Holley reports it in these words:

You white people make a great parade about religion, you say you have a book of laws and rules which was given you by the Great Spirit, but is this true? Was it written by his own hand and given to you? No, says he, it was written by your own people. They do it to deceive you. Their whole wishes center here, (pointing to his pocket,) all they want is the money. . . . He says white people tell them, they wish to come and live among them as brothers, and learn them agriculture. So they bring on implements of husbandry and presents, tell them good stories, and all appears honest. But when they are gone all appears as a dream. Our land is taken from us, and still we don't know how to farm it.

Cleaveland offered them a thousand dollars as a present. Brant said they were easily satisfied, but his offer was too trifling. They got Cleaveland to agree to use his influence with the United States to procure for them an annuity of five hundred dollars; or, if this should fail, an additional present to them from the Connecticut Land Company of $1,500. Cleaveland agreed. Seth Pease sums up the meeting rather bluntly:

The council began 21 and ended Friday following—the Present made the Indians was D. 500. New York courency [sic], in Goods —this the western Indians Received—To the eastern Indians they gave 2 Beef Cattle and 100 Gall of Whisky.—the western also had Provisions to help them home—The Indians had their keeping during the council.[2]

This pacification cleared the way for white entrance to the Western Reserve as far west as the Cuyahoga River. The party immediately set out from Buffalo, some by land, most of them by boats, for the Pennsylvania line.

It was an interesting party of vigorous and enthusiastic young men. Augustus Porter of Salisbury was principal surveyor and deputy to Cleaveland. For the preceding seven years he had been surveying in the vicinity of Buffalo. He was a natural woodsman

---

[2] The *Journal* was published by the Western Reserve Historical Society as *Tract 94*.

and a man of wide experience in surveying the frontier wilderness. The third in command was Seth Pease, the astronomer of the party. His *Journal* is studded with professional observations: visiting Niagara, he noted that "it takes a stone 3 Seconds to fall from the top of the Rock to the Bottom"; that the latitude at noon on Lake Erie was "42° 50′ north"; that "on Examination of the Quadrant we found 180° measured 180° 4′, by the Cetant," at Presque Isle. He made observations on the polar star to check the accuracy of the compass needles, and observed "several stars" to determine the forty-first degree of latitude to fix the southwest corner of the Reserve. He had gone personally to Philadelphia to get the surveying instruments for Cleaveland's party from the astronomer David Rittenhouse.[3]

The surveyors were Amos Spafford, John Milton Holley, Richard M. Stoddard, and Moses Warren. Joshua Stow was in charge of the commissary, and the first building at Conneaut was named Stow's Castle in his honor. Theodore Shepard was physician to the party. Joseph Tinker, who lined up the men for the Fourth of July salute, was given the title of Boatman. James Hamilton, who, according to Holley, was sometimes "very cross and lazy," was camp cook. There were also thirty-five other men who served as axmen, chainmen, and rodmen for the party.

In addition to these members of the surveying party, there were six other people in the expedition, making a total of fifty-two. They were Nathan Perry and Nathan Chapman, who traded with the Indians and supplied fresh beef to the surveyors; Elijah Gun and his wife Anna, who took charge of the commissary cabin at Conneaut; and Job P. Stiles and his wife Tabitha Cumi, who looked after the company's stores at Cleveland as soon as the general and his party had picked out that favored location for the central town of the Reserve.

They spent the day following their celebration and getting to

---

[3] His *Journal* entries at Philadelphia show: "Hutton's Tables 4½ Dollars. Compass, 20 Doll.; Quadrant, 14 Doll. Compass, 20 Doll.; Levels 2¾ Doll.; One Compass, 26 Doll.; Repairing Compass, 11.00 D."

bed "in remarkable good order" by establishing their camp and putting in order their equipment and supplies. And on Thursday, July 7, they organized four field parties and began the historic survey in the field.

Land records are a commonplace to us. The cities, villages, and farms are all mapped and described and recorded at the county courthouses. Lawyers make abstracts of titles to show that all is in order and that the title to be conveyed is clear and unencumbered. But behind that simple transaction is the toil of the first surveyors. Their enterprise and endurance, and their skill, form one of the sagas of American life. These first surveyors on the Reserve had a major role in that saga.

The boundaries of the Reserve to be surveyed and marked with posts were fairly definite. As we have noted, the Reserve was to begin at the western border of Pennsylvania, between 41° and 42° plus two minutes north latitude, and extend westward for 120 miles. The company had instructed the surveyors to run the boundary line as far west as the Cuyahoga River and to lay off the land into townships five miles square.

Their base line, therefore, was the Pennsylvania border. It was already fixed, marked, and no longer subject to controversy. It had been scientifically surveyed and marked in 1786 by the best surveyors, mathematicians, and astronomers of the time. First they had projected the Mason and Dixon's line from the Maryland corner due west 5° from the Delaware River, as specified by the charter, and they had established the southwest corner of the present state of Pennsylvania by the most careful astronomical computations. From this corner they next ran the meridian boundary north until it reached the Ohio River. Virginia retained the panhandle strip between Pennsylvania and the Ohio River which later became a part of West Virginia. Then, just ten years before our surveyors arrived, Andrew Ellicott extended the line from the north bank of the Ohio to Lake Erie. This eastern border of the Western Reserve is still referred to as the Ellicott Line. Ellicott's men cut a swath from twenty to thirty feet wide from river to lake

and erected stone monuments at irregular intervals with the letter
P carved on the top or side.[4]

When, on this July morning, ten years after Ellicott, Cleaveland's men began their survey, the line was still discernible, though
the forest and underbrush were rapidly filling up the cleared vista.
Seth Pease had found the cornerstone at the 42nd parallel on
his way into the Reserve. He now traversed the lake shore from
this stone "to the stone at the north end of Pennsylvania line." In
the afternoon, Pease records in his field *Journal*

we began to measure the east line of New Connecticut. We run
about two miles south and encamped by a pond in a swamp. Plenty
of gnats and mosquitoes; poor water. *Friday, 8th.*—We run about
five miles. We crossed creek Independence. Land about middling.
Went back one mile to camp; poor water.

It took them just two weeks to trace the line south to the corner
—67 miles and 4,541 feet to the 41st parallel. The going was very
rugged indeed. Holley left a vivid description of the land and of
their struggle over its rocks and ridges, through its timber and its
swamps, and across its rivers and streams. We note two entries:

Monday, July 11th.—We were stopped by the rain, and encamped near an excellent brook, which we considered a very
favorable circumstance. The next morning we left this place and
went on to the end of the twenty-fifth mile, through the most
abominable swamp in the world. . . .
Tuesday, July 12.—In the morning we breakfasted in our camp
by the little brook, and left the pack horse men to come on after
us, but when we had proceeded about a mile, we sent back a hand
to tell the men to go round the swamp with the horses, but the
swamp continued, and we ran on till night. Here being a hemlock
ridge, we were in hopes the horses would be able to find us, but
alas! we were obliged to make a little camp of boughs, strike up a

---

[4] When this line was resurveyed in 1881, nineteen of these original markers were
found in the vicinity of the border, some in the foundations of houses and barns,
some on exhibit as relics. Two of them were in their original position and two were
only slightly deflected by repeated frosts. The resurvey showed that the line is not
quite straight; it bends a few seconds in two places. The accuracy was amazing,
however, considering the instruments used and the circumstances of the survey.

TALLMADGE CHURCH
A fine example of New England architecture

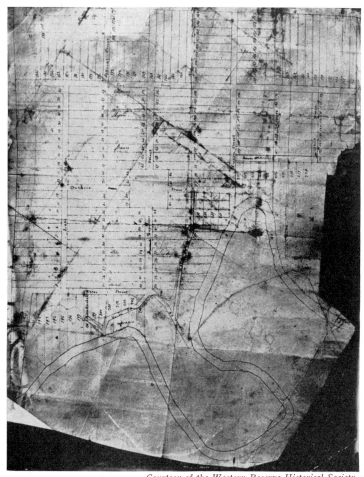

AN EARLY MAP OF CLEVELAND

A photographic copy of a map dated October 1, 1796, in the handwriting of Amos Spafford, Surveyor, found among the papers of J. Milton Holley

fire, and go to bed supperless. In the day time I had eat rasp-
berries, gooseberries, wintergreen berries and wintergreens, and in
the night I began to grow sick at my stomach, and soon after
vomited up every thing that was in me. Mr. Pease too had a turn
of the cramp, in consequence of traveling all day in the water. We
all arose early in the morning, with meagre looks and somewhat
faint for want of eating and drinking, for where we camped there
was no water, though we had a little rum.

A quite different entry occurs when, at the end of the forty-
second mile, they came out of the swamps and woods on high
ground and were able to view the land for the first time.

We encamped about 3 o'clock, and waited till morning. From
the Pennsylvania line here, we had a most pleasing prospect, a hill
at the distance of four or five miles, with the valley that lay between, covered with stately trees and herbage, which indicated
an excellent soil, altogether exhibited a delightful landscape, the
beauty of which, I suppose, was enchanced from its being the first
time we could overlook the woods.

On Thursday, July 21, they reached the corner and prepared to
make an observation of the polar star to check the variation of
the compasses. Porter and Pease

fixed the quadrant for an observation of the sun at noon. The day
was fair and their observation was good. In the evening we again
took the variation by the star, and Mr. Pease observed several of
the stars for the latitude. After comparing observations they make
the latitude to be forty-one degrees twenty seconds north. . . .
Saturday afternoon [July 23rd] Mr. Porter went down to the
corner, and set a chestnut post, sixteen inches by twelve, on the
south side is latitude forty-one degrees north, variation one minute twenty-one seconds east, west side is south-east corner New
Connecticut.—July 23d 1796, on north side, sixty-eight miles Lake
Erie; east side, Pennsylvania.[5]

With the corner now located, the four parties separated to run
the range lines from the 41st parallel back to the lake. The ranges,

---

5 There is at present no visible corner, and the true latitude is 40° 59′ 21.6″.

erected on the south base line five miles apart, were numbered
One, Two, Three, etc., to the west. The townships were numbered
from south to north. Cleveland, for example, fell in Range 12,
Township 7, i.e., fifty-five miles west of the Pennsylvania line and
thirty miles north of the 41st parallel.

If the going along the Pennsylvania line was tough, the task of
hacking out the townships into the five-mile squares which greet
the eye of the casual observer of a modern road map of the Reserve
was tougher. The party encountered all the hardships known to
men on the frontier except the blizzards of winter. They fought
off clouds of mosquitoes so thick that they looked like the fore-
warning of an August thunderstorm and so deadly that they actually killed some of the cattle. They tramped, worked, and slept in
the rain with no shelter except the branches of a beech tree. They
waded through creeks and swamps until their shoes burst from
their soles and they lost their socks. The hot sun, beating upon
them in the open spaces, raised wisps of steam from their backs.
They ran out of food and went supperless to sleep on a bed of
leaves among the whintleberries after chopping a line ten miles in
a single day through the oak timber and hemlock. They were tor-
mented by nightmares and racked by cramps from staying their
hunger with berries and quenching their thirst with rum where
there was no water to be had. They ate broiled rattlesnake when
other provisions failed. As the season wore on they fell ill with
dysentery and intermittent fever.

Still the lines pushed on behind the axmen, the rodman, the
chainmen, and the compass man through the uninhabited Reserve.
The stalwart young men got thin and haggard from excessive
labors, disease, and poor and inadequate diet, but for the most
part their morale remained high. They would come into camp wet
and cold, get a fire going, and, as Holley put it in his *Journal*, "push
about the bottle. . . . We were merry as grigs."

The journals of these men are generally matter-of-fact and impersonal and we are seldom permitted a glimpse into their hearts.
Just one entry in Holley's beautifully penned journal lets us see
his homesickness as the surveys progressed. We remember that

he was only eighteen years old and was carrying the responsibility
of one of the surveying parties. His colleague Amzi Atwater said
he was "tall, stout and handsomely built, with a fair and smiling
face, and general good appearance." One evening in late September, while he was surveying lots in the Cleveland township, he was
sitting under a tree in the Cuyahoga forest copying his field notes.
Samuel Davenport, a member of his party, had just returned from
the camp at the mouth of the river with provisions. He handed
Holley two letters which had just come in from faraway Connecticut: one was from his father and one from his brother Myron.
"This," he promptly entered in his *Journal,* "I put down as a circumstance affording me as much pleasure as anything that has
taken place since I began surveying." He does not tell us what
was in the letters, nor does he reflect on them for our benefit. But
the next entry in his *Journal* two days later is more revealing than
a page of philosophy.

Wednesday, Sept. 28th.—I carved upon a beech tree in Cuyahoga town, "Myron Holley, Jr.," and on a birch, "Milton Holley,
1796,—Sept. 26th, 1796. Friendship."[6]

---

6 Whittlesey, p. 222.

CHAPTER FOUR

AN ERROR IN THE MAPS

ON THE day the surveyors started down the Pennsylvania line, Moses Cleaveland held a council with Chief Paqua and his son Cato of a small tribe of Indians—the Massasagoes—living in the vicinity of Conneaut. They were weak and humble and Cleaveland treated them with paternal haughtiness. They smoked a pipe of peace and friendship, thanked the Great Spirit for bringing Cleaveland to their land, and then requested him to show his claim to their country. Cleaveland told them of his agreement with the Six Nations. Paqua asked what he proposed to do with his people. Cleaveland replied that they would not be disturbed in their possessions, and that he would treat them as brothers. They then presented him with the peace pipe, "a curious one, indeed," which was kept by Cleaveland's family as an heirloom. Cleaveland in return gave them twenty-five dollars' worth of wampum, trinkets, and whisky. They told him they were poor and hoped he would be liberal. Cleaveland's reply, as set down in his *Journal,* is most revealing:

I told them I acted for others as well as for myself, and to be liberal of others property was no evidence of true friendship; those people I represented lived by industry, and to give away their property lavishly, to those who live in indolence and by begging, would be no deed of charity. As long as they were industrious and conducted themselves well, I would do such benevolent acts to them as would be judged right, and would do them the most good, cautioned them against indolence and drunkeness [*sic*]. This not only closed the business, but checked their begging for more whisky.

The friendly comradeship of the party is indicated by Augustus Porter's note that thereafter the general was honored by his men with the name of Paqua.

Cleaveland shared the hardships of his men. He explored the lake shore and the creeks, noting the banks and the erosion. Two entries in his *Journal* will show the nature of his activities.

July 10th.—Went with Capt. Buckland about eight miles up the beach; wind ahead. Stopped at Jay creek, then went about three miles farther; part of the way slate rock, and trees had tumbled in; the surf high, making very hard walking on my return; lost one stocking; dined on the beach; went two miles farther and turned in, took a berth with great-coat under a hemlock.

July 11th.—Returned to Port Independence; a storm of rain coming on made it uncomfortable, and wet us very decently.[1]

The company had predetermined that a city should be laid out in the center of the Reserve on Lake Erie. Moses Cleaveland now set out with a small company by boat to find the best location. They coasted along the lake shore, scanning the forests and the underbrush which clung to the shore and overhung the banks. None of the maps in possession of the party showed the Chagrin River. The surveyors in the field thought it was the Cuyahoga when they came upon it, and they proceeded to run a traverse down its length, thinking it was the western limit of their season's assignment. Cleaveland made the same mistake. He was much chagrined, but the story that this was the origin of the name is pure legend. He coasted on another twenty miles and came to the mouth of the Cuyahoga on July 22. The river was broad as it entered the lake, but it narrowed sharply in the marshy flats through which it meandered crazily. Its low banks were overgrown with reeds and coarse grass. The high bluffs on each side of the flats were densely wooded. The river bed itself was silted over with sand, and a sand bar clogged the mouth and extended out into the lake.

Despite these drawbacks, this was a favored spot. It had al-

---

1 Whittlesey, p. 184.

ready been the scene of historic events: Major Robert Rogers had met Pontiac here when he led his Rangers to Detroit in 1760 to receive the surrender of the French fort; and the persecuted Moravians had found a temporary home on the banks of the river in 1786. Both the British and the French, and later the Americans, had noted the strategic location and had projected plans to build a fort here, but they never actually erected one. A crude cabin or two had been thrown up by the French for use in the fur trade, and a dilapidated storehouse was still standing on the west bank when Cleaveland arrived. The Lake Shore Indian trail crossed the river at this point, and the Muskingum-Cuyahoga trail from the Ohio River to Lake Erie joined it here where Cleaveland was beaching his boat. He must have noticed the trail descending the bluff as he rowed up the Cuyahoga from the lake searching for the best landing place.

Cleaveland climbed the bluff and inspected the flat land east of the river. Severe storms had damaged the forest, but a growth of young oaks had sprung up and the underbrush indicated "a lean, but dry and pleasant soil." He followed the bluff down to the lake shore, at the foot of present West Tenth Street. This serene prospect, which was to inspire many future travelers to rhapsody, must have inflamed the imagination of the superintendent of the party. Coming out of the dense forest, the spectator saw spread out before him to the north the limpid blue expanse of Lake Erie. To the west the shore line curved gracefully past present Lakewood to Bay Village, where the endless wash of the waves had cut back the brittle shore. At his feet were the river and the flat bottom offering to future ships a haven and a harbor. Thinking forward to the thousands of people for whose emigration and settlement he was preparing the way, Cleaveland must also have seen in his mind's eye the surface of the lake dotted with white sails, the harbor cleared of its sand and thriving with wharves, and the chief city of the Reserve spreading back from the river and the lake into the oak forest. He seemed to have not a moment's doubt that this was to be the site of the future city. He paced out among the trees the outline of a generous ten-acre public square, after the New England custom, and ordered his surveyors to plot the town around it. It stands to this day precisely as Cleaveland first planned it.

It is still a thrilling and rewarding experience to stand on the east end of the vast Detroit-Superior High Level Bridge and look thoughtfully to the north down upon the winding river at the spot just west of West Ninth Street at the foot of St. Clair Avenue hill where Cleaveland's boat first landed; and, as the motor traffic whirs by on top of the bridge, and the trolleys rumble across the Flats on the lower deck, and the evening sun strikes the Terminal Tower and the massive Post Office Building, to see inwardly only the little open boat on the river, the squat form of Moses Cleaveland climbing up the hill, and his men casting about under the bluff for a site for a log cabin to shelter them and their stores for the work of the summer. Nothing else but the enormous sweep of the forest, and the immense stillness broken only by the sound of the wind rustling the treetops.

They erected a cabin to shelter the surveyors, a log commissary for their supplies, and then built a cabin for Job Stiles and his wife on Superior Street (first named Broad Street) just halfway between the river and the Public Square. A replica of this cabin is on display at the Western Reserve Historical Society Museum at 10915 East Boulevard overlooking Wade Park. This was the beginning of the town which was to be called Cuyahoga, but the surveyors urged their chief to allow them to name it for him; and when the first map or plat of the city was drawn by them under date of October 1, 1796, it bore in the handwriting of Amos Spafford the legend, "Original plan of the town and village of Cleveland, Ohio."[2]

While the four parties were running the range and township lines and Moses Cleaveland was locating his city, Augustus Porter, principal surveyor and Cleaveland's deputy, was engaged in a survey of critical importance to the Connecticut Land Company.

Before the arrival of the surveyors, only the sketchiest and completely inadequate knowledge of the Lake Erie shore and the land to the south of it was available. Some of the first settlers, in fact,

---

[2] So spelled on this map. Seth Pease, who also mapped it from the field notes, spelled it Cleaveland. Moses Cleaveland always used the "a," but his men spelled it both ways. Atwater's notes on the surveyors, now at the Western Reserve Historical Society Library, spells it Cleveland.

carried with them the most authoritative work so far published on this region—the new third edition of Morse's *The American Geography*, printed in Dublin in 1792. It touched briefly and accurately, on the Ohio Valley, but neither the text nor the handsome map folded as a frontispiece showed any detailed knowledge of the Reserve. The map did locate the Grand and the Huron rivers, but, oddly enough, it did not even sketch in the Cuyahoga or the Black rivers.

The only significant information which Morse could pass on concerning this entire territory was a description of the dangerous snakes infesting the Lake Erie shore and a grim warning against them. He told his readers that the most remarkable of these venomous serpents was the "hissing snake." It is, he said, about eighteen inches long, small, and speckled.

When you approach it, it flattens itself in a moment, and its spots, which are of various colors, become visibly brighter through rage; at the same time it blows from its mouth, with great force, a subtil wind, said to be of a nauseous smell; and if drawn in with the breath of the unwary traveller, will infallibly bring on a decline, that in a few months must prove mortal. No remedy has yet been found to counteract its baneful influence.[3]

The geography was obviously not a very helpful document for the surveyors. They did not encounter the "subtil wind" with the nauseous smell, but they did find rattlesnakes. In emergencies when their stores ran short and they were without food, they killed rattlesnakes, skinned and cooked them, and declared them a delicate and savory dish.[4]

---

[3] Morse, p. 39.

[4] Holley's *Journal: "Thursday, Sept. 22d.*—Left Cuyahoga, to lot the east part of the township with Shepherd and Spafford. The day before we started from Cuyahoga, we discovered a bear swimming across the river. Porter and myself jumped into a canoe, and paddled after him, while another man went with a gun up the shore. But there was such a noise and hallooing, that the bear swam back and escaped. Munson caught a rattle snake, which we broiled and ate."

Turhand Kirtland's *Diary* while employed by the company two years later: *"Monday, June 25th.*—Being out of bread and flour was obliged to give up surveying this day. We went and explored the land for our farm to settle on . . . and cut the road two miles; on the way there killed a large rattlesnake—fifteen rattles—and carried him home and dressed him and cooked him and Notwithstanding my exclamations to the contrary, after it was cook, it was generally eat with as good a relish as any fresh meat we had eat on the road. I can say with the greatest Candor I never ate better Meat."

The old maps were not much more helpful; in fact, they were actually grossly misleading. They had all mislocated the Lake Erie shore. Henry Popple's map of about 1730 shows the lake, exaggerated in size, with shore line running due east and west. Lewis Evans, who had traveled in the territory to get firsthand information, had prepared a very serviceable map of this region in 1755. It located the "Cayohoga River" with fair accuracy, the portage at present Akron, noted that the river was "muddy and pretty gentle," and that the country immediately east of the river was "level, swamps." He also located with a star the Salt Spring near Youngstown, and mentioned the "highlands and ponds" to the north. However, he took no astronomical readings to determine the latitude of the lake shore, and, as a result, drew Lake Erie as a rectangle angled only slightly west southwest. Thomas Hutchins' map of 1778 is much more precise, but it, too, failed to note how sharply Lake Erie tilts on a northeast-southwest axis.

As the land speculators in Connecticut scanned these maps, they were convinced that the Reserve was vastly in excess of the mere 3,000,000 acres which had been purchased by the Connecticut Land Company. Oliver Phelps, himself, with several others, including General Hull who surrendered Detroit, formed the "Excess Company" to buy all of the land in the Reserve in excess of the original purchase and the Firelands, of which we shall speak in due course. People in their ignorance sought after shares in the Excess Company, and in the days immediately preceding the Cleaveland surveys the speculation was wild.

If the maps had been accurate, they would doubtless have got rich. Actually, as we now know, and as Porter was soon to find out for us, Lake Erie tilts sharply to the southwest at a rakish angle from Buffalo to the mouth of the Maumee River. Since the southern boundary of the Reserve was a fixed line on the 41st parallel, the final number of acres reserved by Connecticut would be determined by the contour of the lake shore.

Porter, having completed in record time the Fourth Range line from the 41st parallel to the lake, began his traverse of the lake shore to plat its exact location. He started at the Pennsylvania corner and surveyed the course and distance along the shore to the mouth of the Cuyahoga. Although the agreement with the Six Nations stipulated that the surveyors would not cross that river to the west, the traverse was urgent and Porter took the risk. He ran his line all the way to Sandusky Bay, i.e., until he had reached by calculation of his westings a total of 120 miles due west.[5] By the process of platting this traverse, by extending the southern line on the map to its limit of 120 miles, and then erecting the west line from the southwest corner to the lake, he could show the true limits of the land. He found it to be only 3,450,753 acres, "exclusive of the islands of Lake Erie, and including Sandusky bay, supposed to exceed the islands in quantity about 30,000 acres." He added in his report to the directors of the company that he "was not able to run the west line, on account of the Indian title not being extinguished. Owing to imperfections of the compass, there may be an error of a few thousand acres."

The errors were, indeed, considerable. The compasses, the best obtainable at the time, varied widely. Porter's and Holley's, on one observation varied fifty-three minutes east, Spafford's forty-three. These variations caused the meridian lines to converge and to diverge, and they varied as much as half a mile between the south line and the lake. The townships, therefore, were not equal and they were not square. Porter might also have added that there were errors in measurement. For the measurements were made with an old-fashioned surveyor's chain, itself subject to expansion in the heat. The chainmen were never too careful when the surveyor's eye was not upon them. They would fail to stretch the chain tight to its full length or to hold it level; they would stick the chain pins, or markers, carelessly into the ground; they would bend the chain around an obstacle or over a fallen tree; on difficult terrain, such as crossing a gorge or a swamp, they would sometimes hold the chain in the air and drop a pin approximately on the right spot. Each of these practices caused errors of a few inches in every chain length so measured, and a considerable mar-

---

[5] The formal Indian title to the lands west of the Cuyahoga was not extinguished until 1806, and the survey of this part of the Reserve was delayed until the negotiations were complete.

gin of error always crept into the surveys through these rough measurements even when the instrument work was scrupulously correct.

Later computations showed that Porter was substantially right in his estimate of the number of acres in the Reserve. Naturally his figure was questioned by those who had invested in the Excess Company. It was carefully checked by "a professor of mathematics from Yale College," but no errors were found. Years later, when all the land was fully surveyed and sold, Leonard Case patiently went through the areas of each township. He found the total acreage to be 3,333,699, of which 496,590 were in the Firelands. The Connecticut Land Company was confronted with the hard fact that, instead of 3,000,000 acres, it had for sale only about 2,500,000 acres of arable land. The Excess Company had nothing. The land which they expected to acquire was actually lying under the waters of Lake Erie, and Pelee, the largest of the islands off Sandusky Bay, though south of the 42nd parallel, belonged to Canada.

CHAPTER FIVE

RANGES AND TOWNSHIPS

THE surveying party discontinued their task in New Connecticut on a rainy Monday, October 17, 1796. Far from having completed their work, they had made only a fair beginning in the area around Cleveland and in the northeastern portion of the Reserve. Only four range lines had been run from the southern base west of Pennsylvania. Both the surveyors and the company were disappointed.

They were certainly too optimistic in ever supposing that they could map the region in a single season, but there were also good reasons why the pace was slow. Besides the difficult terrain, which we have already described, the shortage of supplies and the unorganized communications constantly harassed the field parties. Time and again they ran out of food. In September, when they were running lot lines in Cleveland, their supplies got so dangerously low that they had to stop work entirely. Holley says that at noon on September 21

we packed up everything, and embarked on board the boat for Conneaut, in consequence of not having provisions to stay any longer. We had not a mouthful of meat when we went away, part of a barrel of flour, a bag of flour and two cheeses, and some chocolate, constituted our provisions, (about 30 in number). The two boats and the bark canoe carried us. We had a fair wind, and had sailed about eight miles, when we discovered Hall & Co., on the beach with the cattle. We then went ashore, and found by them that Tinker had arrived at Conneaut with provisions. Esquire Warren also was there. He sent on two of his men with two horses loaded with flour. Himself and other hands waited to come with

44

Tinker, when the wind should be favorable. This news cheered us up exceedingly, and we returned to Cuyahoga with much lighter hearts than we left it. . . .

Began to lot the east part of Cuyahoga town . . .[1]

They lost time through illness, and on many days the rains were so heavy they could not work. They wasted valuable hours when they mistook the Chagrin for the Cuyahoga River. The lines moved slowly through the heavy forests where the surveyor and chainmen had to wait for the axmen to clear a way by chopping down trees and underbrush for the compass sights and the measuring. They got tired, sick, and bored as the season wore on. I know from personal experience in surveying in the mountains of Kentucky how, toward the end of a long season, the axmen dawdle over their chopping, how reluctant they become to attack a tree standing in the center of the line or to plunge into a dense thicket of brush and briers to clear a passage or to wade through marshlands on a cool morning. And I know how disastrous to morale the slow, illusive, intangible, and silent accumulation of homesickness of men in the field can become after three monotonous months of wilderness and bad food.

The men did not at the outset have any personal or financial interest in the company. They were enlisted for the duration, as it were, in a loose military order. General Cleaveland did, however, draw up a contract with them at their demand on the last day of September for their joint purchase of a township. They named it Euclid in honor of the geometrician. They agreed to pay one dollar per acre for the land, and to settle in the township eleven families in 1797, eighteen more in 1798, and twelve more in 1799. They were also to clear land, erect houses, and sow wheat and grass in specified numbers of acres each year. This agreement did give the men a stake in the land, but it never developed according to plan, and there is no indication that it gave more than a temporary relief to the growing discontent of the surveyors and their mounting desire to get back to Connecticut before the winter set in.

---

1 Whittlesey, pp. 220-221.

In any event, they closed camp on October 18, and, as Holley recorded, "left Cuyahoga at 3 o'clock 17 minutes for HOME. We left Job Stiles and wife, and Joseph Landon, with provisions for the winter. . . . There were fourteen men on board the boat, and never I presume, were fourteen men more anxious to pursue an object than we were to get forward." They arrived at Conneaut three days later. They tarried just long enough to take "inventory of the articles left there, and about 4 o'clock in the morning, that is, on Saturday, the 22d, we hoisted sail for Presque Isle."

Ten people were left in the Reserve to spend the long winter: Job and Tabitha Stiles and Edward Paine at Cleveland (Richard Landon, who expected to stay, could not face the dreary prospect and fled); Elijah and Anna Gun, and the first independent settlers, James and Eunice Kingsbury, with their nephew and three little children aged three, two, and one, at Conneaut.

Back in Connecticut the company was gravely concerned over the failure of the surveyors to complete their work or to report their progress, and the great expense which they were accumulating without getting their property ready to be sold. But they voted new assessments on the shareholders and laid plans for another surveying party to go back next year to carry on the work.

The little band who stayed on in the Reserve went through a desperate winter, a portent of what was in store for many of the first settlers who were to come after them. Job and Tabitha Stiles fared better than the party at Conneaut; they had the company's stores to draw upon, and the friendly Indians across the Cuyahoga augmented their supplies with fresh game. The Conneaut colony underwent a winter of suffering that has become a fixed part of the history of the Western Reserve. James Kingsbury, who became the first judge of the Court of Common Pleas just four years later, had to leave his family at Conneaut in November to make a journey back to New Hampshire. He expected to be gone about six weeks. He was stricken on the way with fever. Without waiting for full recovery he started back to Conneaut in the dead of winter. Heavy snow fell for three weeks. Between Buffalo and Conneaut it was in places over five feet deep. Haggard, sick, and worried, Kingsbury struggled back to his family through the forests and the snow with an Indian companion, covering a few miles each day. His horse died of exposure and he made the rest of the journey on foot.

He arrived at the Conneaut cabin on Christmas Eve. Mrs. Kingsbury was lying in the grim cabin ill with fever. Beside her was her newly born infant son. They had no food, and the mother was too sick and weak to nurse the child. Kingsbury dragged a sled back to the settlement at Erie, Pennsylvania, to get a bushel of wheat to keep his family alive.[2] Their cow died from browsing on oak trees. The baby son died soon after from starvation and was buried by his father in the woods in a pine box left behind by the surveyors. The mother was delirious and near death for two weeks. Kingsbury had the good luck to find and shoot a pigeon. He made some broth. Mrs. Kingsbury sipped it and revived. By some miracle they got through the remaining weeks of winter. When the new surveying party, with Seth Hart and Seth Pease in charge, arrived at Conneaut in the last week of May, they found "that Mr. Gun's family had removed to Cuyahoga & Mr. Kingsbury his wife & one child were in a low state of health—we administered what relief we could."[3] This included "one barrel of soft soap lacked 6 inches of being full," for Elijah Gun, "2 qt. Sherry Wine . . . 17½ lb Flour" and two quarts of spirits for Mr. Kingsbury, and "15 lb Cheese."[4] The Kingsburys had had enough of Conneaut. They went on to Cleveland with the surveyors. Kingsbury built a cabin east of the Public Square, then moved up on the Cuyahoga bluff southeast of the town by a good spring where he lived and prospered with the years. He died there in 1847, aged 80, lacking 17 days.

The new surveying party comprised sixty-three men, including a physician (who, as we shall see, did not help very much), eight surveyors and fifty-two axmen, chainmen, pack-horse men and

---

[2] This account follows Whittlesey. Other old residents recalled the details somewhat differently, but they are all in substantial agreement.

[3] Seth Pease's *Journal*, Friday, May 26, 1797.

[4] *Western Reserve Historical Society Tract No. 94*, pp. 64, 66.

workmen. They had learned something from the experience of the previous year about the problem of supply. They planted a garden at Cleveland, and they brought ample food. Pease recorded what he had issued to each party going into the field. It included pork, flour, tea, chocolate, sugar, ginger, spirits, vinegar, cheese, pepper, empty bags, fire steel and punk, candles, a tent, axes and hatchets, pocket compass, measuring pins, salt, soap, horses, needles, and thread. Moses Warren noted in his field book that he took out with his party of seven men

three horses; two hundred and sixty pounds of flour, one hundred and thirty pounds of pork, twelve pounds of sugar, four pounds of Chocolate, one and a half pounds of tea, six quarts of rum, one half peck of beans, one camp kettle, one frying pan, and six tin cups, for a tour of thirty or forty days, to proceed to No. 1 in Range 10.

They were swindled, however, on the pork, which they had bought packed in barrels. Pease's *Journal* read:

Sunday, 8th.—I opened the second barrel of Pork and found it very poor like the first consisting almost entirely of heads and legs except it had an old sowbelly known by the teats 2 inches long & the meat almost an inch thick.[5]

With headquarters at Cleveland, and supply depots up the Cuyahoga, the parties scattered through the south and western portions of the Reserve east of the Cuyahoga into which Cleaveland's parties had not penetrated. Pease himself crossed the Reserve on the great Indian trail from the Cuyahoga through present Stow, Kent, Ravenna, Edinburg, Palmyra, and Milton to the Mahoning to complete the south line.

They made very good progress during this second season though they had worse luck than in the previous year. On their way in, David Eldridge was drowned while attempting to swim his horse across the Grand River. Minor Bicknell fell ill and died on the trail while being carried toward Cleveland in a litter. Doctor

---

[5] *Ibid.*, p. 109.

Shepard pronounced it "putrid fever." The boatmen refused to
carry the corpse in their boat because the body had turned purple
and began to putrify; he was buried in the field. Tinker, Pierce,
and Edwards were drowned when their boat capsized in a violent
gale. William Andrews and Peleg Washburn died of dysentery.
Almost every man in the company was seriously ill of dysentery
or intermittent fever. Some of them for two weeks at a time never
had on dry clothes. It is a wonder that any of them survived.
Atwater says that he

was confined for several weeks, with several others much in the
same situation as myself, with little or no help, except what we
could do for ourselves. . . . My fits came on generally every night,
and long nights they appeared to me; in day-time, I made out to
get to the spring, and get some water, but it was a hard task to get
back again. . . .
I procured a portion of Peruvian bark and took it, it broke up
my fits. . . . I lay through the long nights of ague and fever, and
all around were much in the same situation. Oh! these were days
and nights of sorrow and affliction.

The journals and field books of Seth Pease, like the others, are
filled with sick lists, illness, and suffering. The entries in Pease's
Journal run like this:

Friday, 7th July—I was so ill as not to be able to assist I took
some Reubarb but it did not operate. in the afternoon after I had
traveled 1½ mile I took a dose of Tartar Emetic This puked me
several times. at night I felt some better.
Monday, August 28th—This morning I felt unwell. . . . I took
a puke . . . after I had done pukeing my pain gradually Sub-
sided. . . .
Tuesday, 29—This morning I took some bitters in Lieu of the
clear bark—before noon I took a dose of the bark—I feel considerable comfortable.

Nonetheless, before the autumn was over they had completed
the township lines in the Reserve east of the Cuyahoga River.
They had laid out the town of Cleveland into lots of varying sizes,

some of a hundred acres, and had staked out the principal streets. They had laid out in 160-acre lots four of the best townships which were to be sold for the general benefit of the company (Northfield, Bedford, Warrensville, and Perry). None of the townships in the Reserve was set apart for the support of churches or schools—this was a speculative land venture. By mid-September the surveying parties began to assemble at Cleveland to prepare for departure. Seth Pease left the Cuyahoga on October 3 and departed from Conneaut on the thirty-first. He made his report to the directors in December, and the company proceeded to allocate the land by lot and by shares to its stockholders.

They had devised an elaborate and cumbersome scheme for the drawing, to equalize the distribution because the land was so uneven in its worth. Parcels of land, as surveyed into lots, townships, and ranges, were numbered and classified according to value and desirability. Corresponding numbers were entered on slips of paper and placed in a box. Shareholders drew their lots according to the value of their investments. The result was that a man might find his property, not in one piece, but scattered about the Reserve. If the scheme was complicated and inconvenient, it at least guaranteed to each stockholder his rightful share of both the good land and the poor.

One important tract of 24,000 acres just west of the Mahoning River north of Youngstown was omitted from the distribution. This was the famous Salt Spring which Evans had spotted on his map of 1755. This district had been known to the Indians from ancient days. They came here to boil the waters for salt and their trails converged upon the springs. The Great Trail from present Pittsburgh to Sandusky passed through the region. Settlers in Pennsylvania came here for salt during the Revolutionary War. With good foresight, knowing how precious this commodity was on the frontier, General Samuel H. Parsons, of Middletown, Connecticut, purchased the tract under a patent dated February 10, 1788. This was the first land sale on the Reserve. He in turn sold several parcels from his extensive holdings before the surveys we have been describing were completed. Parsons, who had been appointed one of the judges in the Northwest Territory, was drowned in the late autumn of 1789 at the falls in the Beaver River after visiting the salt works. Augustus Porter inspected the works while surveying in the vicinity. He recorded:

At this place we found a small piece of open ground, say two or three acres, and a plank vat of sixteen or eighteen feet square, and four or five feet deep, set in the ground, which was full of water, and kettles for boiling salt; the number we could not ascertain, but the vat seemed to be full of them. An Indian and a squaw were boiling water for salt, but from appearances, with poor success.

The success would be even poorer now. There is a road still known as Salt Spring Road which leads out past the giant steel plants of Youngstown to the Salt Spring site. It is not a scenic drive. One lone spring continues to bubble up through a piece of drain tile. It has a feeble taste of salt and a stronger smell of sulphur.

It is pleasant to note one entry in the minutes of the company, dated at Hartford on January 23, 1798:

The Directors have given to Tabitha Cumi Stiles, wife of Job P. Stiles, one city lot, one ten acre lot, and one one hundred acre lot; to Anna Gun, wife of Elijah Gun, one one hundred acre lot; to James Kingsbury and wife, one one hundred acre lot; to Nathaniel Doan [member of both surveying parties] one city lot, he being obliged to reside thereon as a blacksmith, and all in the city and town of Cleaveland. Voted, that these grants be approved.

CHAPTER SIX

THE FIRELANDS

THE western portion of the Reserve, twenty-five miles wide, to which we have already referred, is known as the Firelands. Though it is a part of New Connecticut, it was from the outset quite distinct from the tract bought and sold by the Connecticut Land Company. In 1792 the General Assembly set aside and quitclaimed this half-million acres to the citizens of the Connecticut shore towns who had suffered property losses at the hands of British troops during the Revolutionary War. The Firelands, therefore, have their own story and have retained an individuality separate from the rest of the Reserve.

No region in the state, perhaps, is more richly colored by its past history than Erie and Huron counties. It was known in Connecticut as the Sufferers Lands, in Ohio as the Firelands, and in the official documents of the incorporation of the Sufferers as "the Half-Million Acres of Land lying south of Lake Erie." It lies entirely in Erie and Huron counties, except for irregular Danbury Township on the neck of land between Sandusky Bay and Lake Erie in Ottawa County, and the southeast township of Ruggles, which is now in Ashland County.

It is a singularly attractive region both to the eye and to the spirit. The port towns of Vermilion, Huron, and Sandusky, the charming interior towns of Milan, Norwalk, Berlin Heights, and New London, and the legended Castalia Spring are within the Firelands tract. It is a rich farming, fruit-growing, manufacturing, fishing and shipping region.

There are no hills and it is not a rolling country. Yet it does not seem flat or monotonous but pleasantly varied. The lake shore from Vermilion to Sandusky Bay and Catawba is intimate and inviting, and it has been widely publicized as Vacationland. Inland to the south of the lake the land rises gradually, then leaps up over a series of ancient beach ridges. Around Milan and Norwalk, along the Huron River, the sand is piled up in small hillocks that grace the long fields like miniature drumlins. The rows of corn and oats ride up over them and across their sides without bending their straight lines. Norwalk, apparently in a flat country, is actually built on a ridge with Main Street on its back. To the south of the fine houses with the deep lawns on wooded West Main the land falls away into a narrow valley, and the railroad passes through the town at the bottom of a ravine concealed like a ha-ha fence.

As in the other portions of the Reserve, the short rivers running north from the divide into Lake Erie have carved valleys a hundred feet or more below the prevailing level of the land. Every township in the Firelands, except Danbury, is veined with creeks and rivers. Berlin Heights is appropriately named as an eminence, for it is set on a beach that overlooks the sweep of low-lying land which stretches on to the lake at Huron. Milan is on a high bank overlooking the Huron River. The modest little red-brick cottage where Edison was born clings to the edge of the bank which falls sharply down a hundred feet to the ravine below. Monroeville clusters along the west bluff of the West Branch of the Huron River. The mitigating effect of these contours makes the Firelands, in effect, seem like a hill country when compared, for example, with the Illinois prairie land. And the towns themselves have maintained a friendly New England air that still links them in the mind with the Connecticut towns from which the Sufferers came.

The suffering began at Danbury, Connecticut, one of the great military depots of the Continental Army. On the afternoon of April 26, 1777, some 2,000 British troops swept into this town and burned it. They destroyed nineteen dwellings, the meetinghouse, twenty-two stores and barns, and the supplies that had been assembled there: 3,000 barrels of pork, 1,000 barrels of flour, 700 barrels of beef, 1,600 tents, 2,000 bushels of grain, and much rum, rice, wine, and other critical stores.

Danbury might be regarded as primarily a necessary military objective. The raids that followed were not so regarded by the citizens of Connecticut. The war in this sector was going against the British. With the collapse of their plans for a land campaign, they turned to the strategy of harassing the coast with their overwhelming naval superiority.

The coast towns were defenseless. They had no warships, they had no adequate fortifications, and they had neither soldiers nor military supplies. They were completely vulnerable to quick attack by sea whenever and wherever the British should choose. The redcoats chose to inflict three heavy blows in July 1779.

On Independence Day Commodore George Collier, commander in chief of His Majesty's ships and vessels on the coast, and Major General Tryon, commander of His Majesty's land forces, appeared off the shore at New Haven. Before they attacked they did give the citizens an opportunity to reconsider the folly of their course of resistance and rebellion. They issued a proclamation, a few sentences of which are well worth reading for the insight which they give into the attitudes and passions of those times.

The ungenerous and wanton insurrection against the sovereignty of Great Britain, into which this colony has been deluded by the artifices of designing men, might well justify in you every fear which conscious guilt could form, respecting the intentions of the present armament. Your town, your property, yourselves, lie within the grasp of the power whose forbearance you have ungenerously construed into fear, but whose lenity has persisted in its mild and noble efforts, even though branded with the most unworthy imputation. The existence of a single habitation on your defenseless coast, ought to be a subject of constant reproof of your ingratitude.

The citizens of New Haven failed to repent of their "ungenerous and wanton insurrection," and Tryon attacked on July 5. Houses were ransacked and destroyed, feather beds and personal belonging were carried off, twenty-seven people were killed, and thirty to forty were taken as prisoners. Among them was Reverend Naphtali Daggett, president of Yale, who received maltreatment at the hands of his captors. East Haven and West Haven were included in the attack.

The fleet then sailed away, only to reappear suddenly before Fairfield on the night of July 7. The British laid Fairfield in ashes; they burned 84 dwellings, 2 churches, the elegant courthouse, 55 barns, 15 stores, and 15 shops. The people fled and were left destitute. Tryon sailed unharmed away back to Huntington Bay on the Sound and appeared before Norwalk on July 11. Here he burned 80 houses, 2 churches, 87 barns, 4 mills, and 5 vessels at the wharf.

After this devastating reproof to Connecticut's ingratitude, the British left the coast towns unmolested but apprehensive until 1781. Then they singled out New London and near-by Groton across the Thames for the worst punishment in the war. This thriving seaport of New London had been threatened before because it was the harbor for the few American ships that were able to operate against the British and it had accumulated rich stores. Its daring captains had brought in prizes from the West India trade. Not long before the British attack Captain Dudley Saltonstall in the *Minerva* had brought in the *Hannah*, a treasure ship bound from London for New York and the richest taken during the Revolution. The British decided it was time for chastisement. Benedict Arnold, born only fourteen miles away, familiar with the town and many of its citizens, led the attack on his neighbors.

With 32 sail and 1,800 men, the British ran into the harbor and quickly overpowered the small garrison which guarded the town. They burned with vengeance: stores, wharves, lumber, boats, rigging, sugar, and coffee. Through the streets and gutters flowed good rum and melted Irish butter. They made of the town a desolation and a waste. Ninety-seven families were left homeless, 31 stores and warehouses, 18 mechanic shops, 20 barns, all the public buildings, and nearly all the wharves were burned to the ground. Only a few small sloops were saved when they escaped up the river where the heavier British ships could not pursue them. The landlady of the tavern on Green Street had a Tory brother fighting under Arnold and a Patriot husband withstanding the invaders. She resisted as long as she could, then fled on horseback to join her husband. She left the table set with food for her brother. He entered the inn, feasted with his men at her table, and spared the place from the general destruction.

These were, in brief, the melancholy experiences which linked the Connecticut coast with the twenty-five-mile strip of the Western Reserve known as the Firelands. The plight of the Sufferers was desperate. Many of them had lost their houses, all their worldly goods, and even the means of earning their livelihood. Neighbors took them in and were charitable, but the Sufferers needed aid on a large scale to re-establish themselves. Like good Americans, they turned to their General Assembly for relief. They sent to Hartford memorial after memorial pointing out the disproportionate share of the burdens of war which they had borne. Their petition of December 8, 1780, over a year after the New Haven, Fairfield, and Norwalk raids, is revealing, and it sounds as if it might have been written right after World War II. They wrote:

Altho many of the Sufferers have the Summer past got themselves Houses yet they out of necessity will be oblidged to live in them through this Winter without being finished for want of many materials and money to purchase others and that by means of the high prices of Materials for Buildings and the very great Demand for Labor your Honble Memorialists are very much involved and it appears to many of them as if it was impossible to ever regain their Loss. . . .

The legislature was sympathetic, and on May 10, 1792, it "released and quit-claimed to the Sufferers hereafter named, or their legal representatives, where they are dead, and to their heirs and assigns forever," the 500,000 acres roughly described on the western limits of the Reserve. But legal procedures are slow and the delays of the law are long. A list of the authentic Sufferers had to be compiled, their claims investigated and established, and an appraisal of the losses made. The General Assembly appointed "a number of Gentlemen" to estimate the losses and damage. They

did a thorough job. They concluded that the total amounted to
£294,235 16s. 1d. as of the values of 1774. According to the official record book of "The Proprietors of the half-million acres of
land, lying south of Lake Erie," in the records office of Huron
County, there were 1,866 recognized losses in the value of £175,244
4s. 6d. W. W. Williams, after examining the records, estimated
that the claims allowed amounted to $538,495.26.[1] There were
410 claims from the New Haven area, 219 from Greenwich, 289
from Norwalk, 275 from New London, 269 from Fairfield, 186
from Danbury, 93 from Groton, and 65 from Ridgefield. The
largest award was made to Jeremiah Miller of New London for
$8,845.21, and the smallest to Marah Kilby of New Haven for
41 and 2/3 cents. It would be interesting to know what possession
of Marah's the British chose to steal or destroy, but the record is
silent.

The entire list of the names of the Sufferers is published by
Williams. It is an absorbing study from many angles of interest.
The family names are all English. The baptismal names reflect the
culture of the age. Names now so common—Robert, George,
Henry, even William, James, and John—are rarities; in their place
stands a rather complete genealogy from the Old Testament:
Amos, Abijah, Ephraim, Ebenezer, Eldad, Eleazar, Hezekiah,
Gad, Eliphalet, Eliakim, Shadrach, Jabez, Shubael. The feminine
names mingle the Old Testament with Puritan custom: Abagail,
Miriam, Leah, Tirzah, Charity, Deliverance, Prudence, Temper-
ance, Thankfull. Middle names were not used.

On May 10, 1792, fifteen years after the first raid and eleven
years after the last, the General Assembly released to this list of
Sufferers, "or their legal representatives, where they are dead,
and to their heirs and assigns forever," the unsurveyed 500,000
acres which are roughly described in the instrument. This did not
mean, however, that the claimants could move into their new property. The Indians had yielded their rights to the land east of the
Cuyahoga River, but they still had a claim on all the territory west
of that line. This claim had to be legally extinguished. Moses

---

[1] W. W. Williams, *History of The Firelands*, Cleveland, 1879.

Cleaveland regarded his agreement with the Indians so scrupulously that he did not permit his surveyors even to build a cabin on the west side of the Cuyahoga, and he sent Porter along the lake shore to make the traverse only because the company had to have accurate geographical knowledge of the contour of Lake Erie. It was not until the summer of 1805 that the Indians were finally induced to give up their lands.

Representatives of the United States Government, of the Connecticut Land Company, and of the Sufferers (who had incorporated themselves in 1796 in Connecticut and in 1803 in Ohio) succeeded in meeting with the Indians at Fort Industry on the Maumee to draw up a treaty. They ceded their claims to 2,750,000 acres west of the Cuyahoga, including the Firelands, in return for $18,916.67 from the land companies, plus monetary gifts from the Government: $4,000 down and the balance in installments. The cash in specie was brought in under guard from Pittsburgh through Warren, over the trail to Cleveland and down the lake by boat. The Indians, of course, also received the usual flow of rum, tobacco, and presents. After the custom of our founding fathers, the treaty was signed on July 4. "It is said by those who attended this treaty, that the Indians in parting with and making sale of the above lands to the whites, did so with much reluctance, and after the treaty was signed, many of them wept."[2]

This treaty to the lands west of the Cuyahoga, while it cleared the title for the Sufferers, only made it possible to begin the surveys as a preliminary to sale and settlement. The survey got under way in the following spring of 1806. Seth Pease was employed by the United States Government to extend the south boundary line westward from the Cuyahoga. After finishing the surveys to the east of the river, he had surveyed in the Holland Purchase east of Buffalo and had served as Assistant Postmaster General during President Jefferson's first term. Abraham Tappan, an old and experienced surveyor, ran the township lines for the Connecticut Land Company between the Cuyahoga and the Firelands—about

---

[2] Reminiscence of Abraham Tappan. Whittlesey, p. 403.

830,000 acres. Maxfield Ludlow, a United States engineer, was engaged to fix the southwest corner of the Firelands, and, with a company of twelve surveyors, to run the west line north to the lake. After all their trouble, their survey was rejected because the corner had been set one mile too far west. The error, apparently, was not Ludlow's; it resulted from a miscalculation in the surveys east of the Cuyahoga.

Another year was wasted while the Sufferers waited for their land. In August 1807 Almon Ruggles, "well skilled in the art and mystery of surveying," was given a contract to relocate the corner and lay off the tract in townships five miles square, four sections to the township, and along the lake to shape and divide them into areas approximately equal to the others. His experiences in the field duplicated those of his predecessors which we have already noted. His field books, of large size and beautifully neat in penmanship, though now fragmented have been preserved. The entries, generally impersonal and factual, occasionally give us a glimpse of the human drama which produced them. The region west of Plymouth, now fairly well drained and made into prosperous farming country, was then a desolate swamp. Ruggles sketched it on his map and lettered it "Great Marsh," showing it as covering half of New Haven and all the south line of Cannon townships. As he struggled through the swamp, he made these entries into his field book: "117th mile west. We are in danger of our lives. 118th mile west. Sat a post in Hell. I've travelled the woods for seven years, but never saw so hideous a place as this." And he still had two miles to go to the corner.

The specifications for the survey, affirmed by the treaty with the Indians at Fort Industry, called for the north-south line of the Firelands to run parallel with the state line. Actually it bears 4°40' west of the true meridian, and the townships are not squares. This has caused speculation and given rise to legend. Ruggles noted this divergence, but his field books made no comment. Some have observed that these surveys by magnetic compass and chain were at best rather loose approximations, and that a somewhat wider variation to the west which added valuable acreage to the tract is not a cause for wonder. One legend, often repeated, has it that the line was deliberately angled to the west to include in the Firelands the famous spring at Castalia.

The truth, as usual, is quite simple. It is supplied in a letter of instruction from Albert Gallatin to the surveyor general at Marietta, April 20, 1805. He reviews the contention of the Connecticut Land Company that they were entitled to a 120-mile breadth throughout their limits from the western Pennsylvania boundary, i.e., between 41° and 42°2″ north latitude. Says Gallatin:

This is true, and they say that, as the Pennsylvania line is a true meridian, if this western boundary shall be ascertained by a meridian line drawn from a point in latitude 41°, one hundred and twenty miles west from the Pennsylvania line, they will have less than one hundred and twenty miles in breadth north of that latitude. ... [They] ought to have so much westing as will preserve throughout their limits the required breadth of one hundred and twenty miles. It appears to me that the request is just; and that it will be necessary to give instructions accordingly to the assistant surveyor you may send on the spot.[3]

Thirty years had now gone by since the Sufferers began their suffering. Many of the claimants were dead and had been in their graves for a quarter of a century. Forty-year-old men who had seen their houses burn at Norwalk were now seventy and too old to consider migration. Children too young even to remember the British sails and the swarming redcoats of the Revolution were now grown men with families. The legal problem of caring for the "heirs and assigns" was immense. And the Sufferers Company had accumulated considerable expense in prosecuting their claims. Nonetheless they went forward now with the distribution of the Firelands.

Their method, designed to equalize the lands, was complicated. They divided the proprietary rights into 120 classes each representing one one hundred and twentieth of the original loss. Four classes were then put together, each in a separate bundle marked

---

[3] MSS. of Western Reserve Historical Society, Vol. 11.

1, 2, 3, and 4, and each tied by a disinterested person. This made thirty bundles. The bundles were then placed in a box. In a different box they placed thirty tickets, each describing a township by its range and number. At the partition, a ticket was drawn from this second box and read out to the directors. Then a classification bundle was drawn and opened. The losses in class one were compensated for by section one of the township in that classification, class two by section two, and so on until the land was parceled out. The disadvantage, of course, was that a single large claimant might have his land scattered about instead of concentrated in a single piece.

With the allotments made and the deeds drawn, the Sufferers at long last were free to leave Connecticut and make their new homes on their own land in a wild wilderness. In the circumstances it is not at all surprising that the Sufferers did not rise up in mass and migrate. They were, in fact, slow in coming—as we shall see.

CHAPTER SEVEN

THE PATTERN OF SETTLEMENT

THE peculiar pattern of settlement in the Reserve was a natural result of the organization of the Connecticut Land Company and the elaborate system of partition for equalizing the shares and distributing them all at once. After the distribution each proprietor was responsible for his own lands. Inevitably the settlements were widely scattered. They did not begin solidly at the Pennsylvania line and move west as a neighborhood developed, nor did they commence along the lake and move south. Instead, each family, or each little party, fought its way through the wilderness along the township lines until it came to its assigned spot; and there, in the vast loneliness, perhaps fifteen or twenty miles from the nearest neighbor, it chopped out its own hole in the forest, erected a cabin, planted a few acres of corn or wheat, and struggled to keep alive. It was a colossal undertaking—a gamble loaded with serious hazards and, at best, with few prizes.

It is notable that only about a half-dozen men from the surveying parties of 1796 and 1797 came back to live in the Reserve. Moses Cleaveland never visited it again. Only two of those who had entered so insistently into the contract for Euclid in 1796 ever returned to fulfill it. But a few settlers did filter in during these early years. One day in 1796, when Cleaveland was making his first survey, young James Hillman was paddling his canoe down the Mahoning River. For ten years he had been trading in this region. He had served as pack-horse man for the firm of Duncan & Wilson of Pittsburgh, accompanying a caravan of ten men and ninety horses across the Indian trail from Pittsburgh through present Youngstown, Weathersfield, Milton, and Ravenna, and down the Cuyahoga to Cleveland, with goods to be shipped on to Detroit. For the last several years he had been in business for himself trading with the Indians in the Western Reserve. As he came down the Mahoning on this evening in 1796, he saw, at the present site of Youngstown, a wisp of smoke rising from a campfire. He landed to investigate. He found John Young and Mr. Wolcott who had just arrived to make a survey of the lands which Young had acquired in this southeast corner of the Reserve. Hillman rejoiced to see them. He had left of his stores for trading with the Indians a quart of whisky which he offered to the newcomers. Young, however, insisted on buying it at the standard price—one deerskin, legal tender for one dollar. He took the skin which he had spread for his bed and gave it to Hillman. Young founded the town which bears his name, and in 1798 there were ten families settled there. It had the advantage of easy access from Pittsburgh by the river ways.

Following the completion of Pease's survey, a few more families trekked into the Reserve. Alexander Harper led a small party of three families into Ashtabula County in March 1798 and founded Harpersfield. Three other families had settled deep in the woods at Burton where they nearly starved during the first winter. Joseph Burke brought his family to Euclid. Reverend Badger visited them three years later, and found them very lonely. Mrs. Burke "had been obliged to spin and weave cattle's hair, to make covering for her children's bed." Nathaniel Doan, who had been in both surveying parties, arrived in Cleveland to set up his blacksmith shop on Superior Street, though he fled four miles inland toward Euclid the following year to escape the sickness on the Cuyahoga River. The hamlet that grew up around his shop where the Newburg Road intersected Euclid was for many years known as Doan's Corners. David Abbott, who had left Yale because of ill health, came to Willoughby in 1798, where Charles Parker, one of Cleaveland's surveyors, had built a house and some huts at the mouth of the Chagrin River. When the Reserve became Trumbull County, he was appointed sheriff. He removed to Milan in 1809 when the Firelands were finally opened to settlement.

Though few came that year to settle, others came to explore and prepare the way. Turhand Kirtland of Wallingford, represented in the Connecticut Land Company by Caleb Atwater, received at the drawing as his draft of land a portion of Auburn and the township of Mecca. With Benjamin Doolittle and others he drew the townships of Poland and Burton, widely separated, we note, and some 2,000 acres in Kirtland. He had put into the company, he records, $4,750. He traveled through the Reserve to see and survey his lands during the seasons 1798-1800, and he left a record in his very interesting diaries.[1] They might have been kept by Pease or Holley. The extreme hardships were accepted in high spirit as a matter of course. After fighting his way through woods and swamps, hunting his horses and cattle which had strayed away during the night, he entered in his diary for June 12th:

. . . having travelled all day as wet as water could make us, pitched our tent, pealed bark, made a good fire, drank our brandy and made a good dish of chocolate and was as happy as if we had been keeping Election at home.

He cut a road into Chardon, and was delighted when he found a good spring and a warm place for a garden.

Sat. June 16th.—We caught a very fine fawn we judged about one month old, which made us an excellent Dinner. We thought of the good old Patriarch's Savory Meat and commended him for loving it. . . .
Monday, June 25th.—Being out of bread and flour was obliged to give up surveying this day. We went and explored the land for our farm to settle on . . . and cut the road two miles. . . .
Sun. Sept. 1, 1799—I went to Youngs Town to attend Public Worship. The Rev. Willm Wick from Washington County preached, it being the first sermon ever delivered on New Connecticut.

Young Benjamin Tappan, Jr., acting as agent for his father, came out from Connecticut to Ravenna in 1799. He made his way

---

[1] Published at Poland, Ohio, 1903.

THE CANAL NEAR 8-MILE LOCK ABOUT 1890

THE CANAL NEAR ROCKSIDE ROAD ABOUT 1893

WESTERN RESERVE COLLEGE BUILDINGS, 1830-1840

up the Cuyahoga by boat to Boston. There he stored his goods and began to clear out a road to Ravenna. His yoke of oxen were driven overland from Connecticut. While he was dragging his goods in from the Cuyahoga, one of the oxen died. Tappan had left only one dollar in money. He sent a man, with a compass to guide him, all the way back to Erie, Pennsylvania, to secure a loan from the commandant. Tappan himself went through the woods to Youngstown to get another ox. James Hillman, who had never seen him before, sold him one on credit. Tappan spent the first winter at Ravenna in a tent and a crude bark camp.

In western New York Tappan had fallen in with David Hudson of Goshen, Connecticut, who was also on his way to New Connecticut. He and Birdsey Norton had drawn the townships of Chester and Hudson. Elias Harmon and his wife were in the same party, bound for Mantua. Harmon's boat was wrecked in a storm off Ashtabula, and he proceeded overland to his lot. Hudson repaired the wrecked boat and shipped his goods by it to Cleveland. The Cuyahoga was almost dry, and they had to drag their boats over the shallows and shoals. It took Hudson six days of searching to find the line that led to his township. He spent the first night there lying without any covering in the rain under an oak tree, but he was filled with "grateful pleasure" by the sensation of being at peace on his own land. Hudson's two yoke of oxen and two cows were driven along with Tappan's, each with bags of flour and pork, two blankets, and an ax tied on its back. Hudson set his men to building a log house and clearing land for wheat.

Hudson went back in the autumn to get his family and some more settlers. On New Year's Day 1800 he was ready to return to the Reserve. He had his moment of doubt, knowing what might be in store for them. He gives us one glimpse into his troubled spirit:

. . . while my dear wife and six children, with all my men, lay soundly sleeping around me, I could not close my eyes, for the reflection that those men and women, with almost all that I held dear in life, were now to embark in an expedition in which so many chances appeared against me; and should we survive the dangers in crossing the boisterous lakes, and the distressing sickness usually attendant on new settlements, it was highly probable that we must fall before the tomahawk and scalping-knife. As I knew at that time no considerable settlement had been made but what was established in *blood,* and as I was about to place all those who lay around me on the extreme frontier, and as they would look to me for safety and protection, I almost sunk under the immense weight of responsibility resting on me. Perhaps my feelings on this occasion were a little similar to those of the patriarch, when expecting to meet his hostile brother. But after presenting my case before Israel's God, and committing all to his care, I cheerfully launched out the next morning upon the great deep.

He arrived safely and found that his colonists had survived the winter. He then gathered them all together and held a service of thanksgiving to God for His mercy in protecting them from peril and to pray His blessing upon their enterprise.

Judge Austin led a party of settlers into the northeastern corner of the Reserve in 1799 and founded Austinburg. They had their wheat ground at a little mill forty miles away through the forest on Elk Creek. Joel Thorp and his wife and three small children settled at Millsford. John Walworth of New London bought 2,000 acres in Painesville and traveled over the ice and along the lake shore with his horses and oxen in February 1800 to make his settlement. In early May 1799 Lewis Day and his son Horatio, of Granby, Connecticut, with two other men came out with a one-horse wagon. They settled at Deerfield, twenty-five miles west of Youngstown, and were the first men to take a wagon into this part of the wilderness. Caleb Atwater's township road, which he was cutting through from the west, passed through Deerfield—a town named for Deerfield, Massachusetts, in honor of Lewis Day's mother, who was born there. The neighboring town of Palmyra was first settled in the same year by David Daniels of Salisbury, Connecticut. Several other families immediately joined both of these settlements. They too were sorely pressed for provisions during the first season. According to the Judge Barr manuscripts, "they were supplied from settlements on the opposite side of the Ohio, the nearest of which was Georgetown, forty miles distant. These were conveyed on pack-horses through the wilderness." Captain Ephraim Quinby, proprietor of Warren, built his cabin there in 1799. By the end of the next year there were sixteen white settlers at Warren.

Moses Cleaveland's city at the mouth of the Cuyahoga was faring poorly during these first years. From the practical point of view, it was hardly as desirable then as other townships in the interior of the Reserve. Settlers did not hasten to buy the city lots at the price of $50 asked by the company. They even balked at $25. Turhand Kirtland, as field agent for the company, wrote to General Cleaveland from Cleveland on July 17, 1800, to report that Major Spafford, Lorenzo Carter, and David Clark were the only inhabitants of the city. Major Austin was willing to buy at $12 per acre.

You will please excuse me, for giving my opinion, but it really seems to me good policy to sell the city lots, at a less price than twenty-five dollars, (two acres) or I shall never expect to see it settled.

Mr. Carter . . . has been of essential advantage to the inhabitants here, in helping them to provisions in times of danger and scarcity, has never experienced any gratuity from the company, but complains of being hardly dealt by, in sundry instances. He has money to pay for about thirty acres, which he expected to have taken, if the price had met his expectation; but he now declares that he will leave the purchase, and never own an acre in New Connecticut. Major Spafford . . . says he has no idea of giving the present price, for sixteen or eighteen lots . . . and he is determined to remove to some other part of the purchase immediately, unless he can obtain better terms than I am authorized to give.

Kirtland then adds the encouraging note that "crops are extraordinarily good, and settlers healthy and in good spirits." But he found them plagued for want of cash, as they were to be for many years to come. He continued:

The universal scarcity of cash, in this back part of the country, renders it extremely difficult to sell for money, and the vast quantity of land in market will prevent a speedy sale of our lands. . . . Mr. Tillitson, from Lyme, wants two, one hundred acre lots, and would pay for one in hand if horses, cattle or provisions would answer, or would take them on credit, if he could have sufficient time to turn his property, but has no cash to advance.

Kirtland may have been exaggerating about the health and spirits of the settlers. Samuel Huntington of Norwich, Connecticut, later to become the second governor of Ohio, toured the Reserve this same year to find a place to settle. He spent the night of October 7 at Carter's. He noted in his diary that "there are only three families near the point, and they have the fever." Huntington selected Youngstown and moved his family to the Reserve, but he immediately decided that Cleveland offered great possibilities. He engaged Amos Spafford to build for him a fine block house near the bluff south of Superior Street and began his long career as solid citizen and servant of the new state of Ohio. Elisha Norton arrived and opened a store, and David Bryant came to build a log distillery. Up at Newburg at the Falls, Wheeler W. Williams of Norwich and Major Wyatt had built a gristmill in 1799—one of the first in the Reserve. And in 1800 they added a sawmill. Huntington visited it and reported that it was nearly complete. The colonists on the Cuyahoga were able for the first time to have bolted flour made from their own grain, and to have sawed lumber.

The population of Cleveland, however, was only fifty-seven people in 1810, twelve years after the completion of the surveys. There was no physician anywhere near. The prospect for one was not too bright. In 1809 we find Stanley Griswold writing back to a friend in Vermont:

Cleveland would be an excellent place for a young physician. . . . This is based more on what the place is expected to be, than what it is. . . . But settlements are scattered, and roads new and bad, which would make it a painful practice. Within a few weeks Cleveland has been fixed upon by a committee of the Legislature as the seat of justice for Cuyahoga county. Several respectable characters will remove to that town. The country around bids fair to increase rapidly in population. A young physician . . . will be certain to succeed, but for a short time, if without means, must keep school, for which there is a good chance in winter, till a piece of ground, bring on a few goods, (for which it is a good stand,) or do something else in connection with his practice.[2]

The region between the Cuyahoga River and the Firelands, now Lorain and Medina counties, drew almost no settlers until after the close of the War of 1812. Nathan Perry established a trading post at the mouth of the Black River in 1807, and a few families came from Waterbury to Ridgeville, Amherst, and Eaton three years later. Settlers did not arrive at Elyria until 1817.

More came into the well-publicized Firelands. Surveyor Almon Ruggles of Danbury received as a bonus for his services a tract one mile square to be located wherever he might choose along the lake shore. Having tramped over and mapped all the 500,000 acres, he chose his lot in Berlin Township, in some respects certainly the fairest location in the Firelands. As soon as the township of Milan was available in 1808, David Abbott bought 1,800 acres along both sides of the beautiful Huron River, but he did not come to the Firelands until 1809. Colonel Jared Ward purchased some of his land and made the first actual settlement in 1808. Vermilion was settled in the same year. The charming town of Milan was not laid out until 1816. John Beatty of New London bought up 40,000 acres in the Firelands, built a house five miles south of Sandusky Bay, and brought his family out in 1815. He became mayor of Sandusky nearly twenty years later.

This spot survey will indicate the pattern of settlement during the early days on the Western Reserve. We sweep our eyes over the 3,000,000 acres, across the 120-mile stretch of wilderness; we see the short rivers running down to the lake as the chief highways into the land; we see the Indian trails crossing it; and we see these few hundred families set down miles apart in little oases hacked out of the woods in the scattered townships, isolated, lonely, trying in many instances desperately to keep alive and advance the station of themselves and their children.

---

[2] Whittlesey, p. 427.

They remained in their loneliness for many years. For the stream of immigration, as we have just seen, flowed slowly during the first two decades after Moses Cleaveland's expedition in 1796. Another war had to be fought before the young nation had recovered from the Revolution. Perry had built his ships on Lake Erie at Erie, Pennsylvania. He had rendezvoused his fleet among the Wine Islands off Sandusky Bay at the western limit of the Reserve. And he had gained his great victory on the lake within sight of his present monument that gleams in the sun on South Bass, also a portion of the Reserve. The news of these epoch-making deeds and the reports of soldiers and sailors whose war experience had taken them into the region came along in 1815 and 1816 to revive and reinforce the legend that had followed the Revolution. New England, and especially Connecticut, was again impoverished and much of it in ruins. The British had raided, sacked, and burned the towns on the coast along the Sound. Their overwhelming fleet had held American ships in harbor where they were bottled up and rotting. Foreign trade was ruined and New England traders were bankrupt. The country had won another war, but the victory had been costly.

And before recovery was well under way, another blow fell. This time it was the heavy hand of winter. The summer of 1816 in New England was the coldest within the memory of the oldest citizen. Winter had held on well into spring. Farmers plowed and planted between freezes. There were severe frosts in June, in July, and in August. Not a single month escaped. The corn crop was almost completely destroyed, and the oats and potatoes were half ruined and of poor quality. The winter following was exceptionally severe. People suffered. Men walked forty miles to buy a half bushel of corn for their families and paid two dollars for it. Cattle died for want of food. Following as it did so closely on the devastation of war, this added and gratuitous calamity plunged the people into despair. New England seemed to many to be worn out and done for, and the glacial age was returning to claim it again.

These were harsh disciplines, indeed. That generation had known privation and sacrifice, and it had learned dogged endurance. Many had suffered financial ruin in the cause of freedom. In the long campaigns they had become inured to physical hardship of the most grueling nature. A ration of baked potato and the bloodstains from bare feet in the winter snow were the symbols of this discipline. Compared to these exactions no hardships on the Ohio frontier seemed insupportable. Impoverished by war, with little left except faith in their newly liberated country, their own great physical strength, their courage and ambition, and their Yankee ingenuity, the thought of security on the land—their own land, bought and paid for by their own toil, and developed by the sweat of their own brows—was in itself a motive powerful enough to drive them on across the mountains into the wilderness.

And such land! According to the advertisements and the rumors that spread from village to farmhouse across Connecticut, this new land in the west was not a grim wilderness but Eden itself. It was freely referred to as "the *fabled region* of the West," "the *garden* of America," "an *earthly Paradise,* where every thing which is considered a luxury, might be had almost without care, labour or exertion." It is not surprising that Connecticut men, looking out on their thin soil with the glacial boulders piled thick upon it, and the snows of the long winters drifting up to the roofs of their cabins, should jump lightly in imagination to the fertile, level ground of the Reserve with its reputed fat loam and its salubrious climate. There, it was said, the livestock could winter outdoors in the woods of black walnut, hickory, chestnut, and sugar maples. There the snows were light and spring came early. There, indeed, the poor man of Connecticut could become a man of property, a landed gentleman secure and at ease on his own acres.

It was the moment of golden opportunity. A few days, a few weeks, maybe a month or two of hard travel lay between the old and the new. A few years of loneliness and hardship must, of course, be endured. But New England men were schooled in the doctrine that the pleasures of today must be sacrificed for the rewards of tomorrow; even, perhaps, delayed until the triumphant entrance into the Blessed Kingdom itself. The American habit of thinking, even then, always of "progress" led them to gloss too lightly over the deprivations that lay between them and the fulfillment of their hopes. Surely this land flowed with milk and honey, it had been given to the men of Connecticut, and they had only to move in and possess it. A stampede toward the Reserve hit Connecticut. By the summer of 1817 the tide of immigration was flowing full. Hardly a family seemed untouched by it— younger sons determined to go west, daughters boldly marrying and setting out for the new land, neighbors loading their goods and youngest children into carts and wagons, fathers going alone to prepare a place for their families—it was one of the largest and most homogeneous mass migrations in American history.

Two routes led into the Reserve and both were crowded with the travelers. Some went up to the Mohawk Valley, crossed New York to Buffalo, and entered Ohio by boat or made their way over the rough trail through Erie to Conneaut and down the town lines to their chosen place of settlement. Others crossed Pennsylvania, climbed the mountains, came down to Pittsburgh, followed the pack-train trails across to Youngstown and so into the Reserve from the southeast. The distance in travel time was just about the same. In fact, two young men left Litchfield, Connecticut, on the same day. One of them, Uriah Holmes, took the New York route by way of Buffalo, and the other, Titus Hayes, went across the Pennsylvania mountains. They both arrived at Youngstown on the same day.

Those who could afford a horse and covered wagon loaded all their effects and traveled in luxury. Often it was a father, mother, and six, eight, ten, or a dozen children setting out. They stowed under the cover of the wagon a bed, perhaps a blanket chest or a stand, a churn and crocks, a few dishes, the family gridirons, some quilts and feather beds, and a trunk full of old clothing. Some carried the family Bible, Watts's *Psalms and Hymns*, and Webster's *Spelling-book*. Pots and kettles swung from the rear on the ridgepole and the side braces of the cover on the wagon. The cat dozed in the wagon among the blankets, and the dogs trotted along beside the horse and between the wagon wheels. The father, with a long walking stick in his hand, and a big hat with a flopping brim on his head, strode forward on foot beside the horse, the older children trudging alongside or behind the wagon, ten miles a day, and the mother, with her youngest at her breast and the smaller ones sprawled among the goods, bumped and rocked along in silence on a hard seat in the front of the creaking wagon.

Others traveled by oxcarts, walking all the way through the deep wagon ruts and mudholes, up the steep mountainsides and down the rough slopes. Samuel Goodrich, better known by his pen name of Peter Parley, who saw the trek of 1817, wrote:

In several instances I saw families on foot—the father and boys taking turns in dragging along an improvised hand-wagon, loaded with the wreck of the household goods—occasionally giving the mother and baby a ride. Many of these persons were in a state of poverty, and begged their way as they went. Some died before they reached the expected Canaan; many perished after their arrival, from fatigue and privation; and others, from the fever and ague, which was then certain to attack the new settlers.[3]

Doctor Hand, a young physician of Berlin, supplemented this report. After visiting the region, he described the grim picture as he saw it on the road back:

The roads over the Alleghanies, between Philadelphia and Pittsburg, were then rude, steep, and dangerous, and some of the more precipitous slopes were consequently strewn with the carcases of wagons, carts, horses, oxen, which had made shipwreck in their perilous descents. The scenes on the road—of families gathered at night in miserable sheds, called taverns—mothers frying, children crying, fathers swearing—were a mingled comedy and tragedy of errors. Even when they arrived in their new homes frequently the whole family—father, mother, children—speedily exchanged the fresh complexion and elastic step of their first abodes, for the sunken cheek and languid movement, which marks the victim of intermittent fever.[4]

They were going into a great loneliness. In our day of crowded populations it is hard even to imagine what it was like on the

---

[3] Peter Parley's *Recollections of a Lifetime*, etc., New York, 1856, p. 542.
[4] *Ibid.*, pp. 542-543.

Ohio frontier in those early years, especially for the women. Mrs. Terrell Tillotson, who had come out to Lorain County in 1810 with her husband and three children, went out to the spring near their cabin to get water. She decided to go on a few paces to find her husband who was building a cabin in the woods. She got lost in the dense forest. Panic-stricken, she wandered all day long through the woods. Finally near nightfall she stumbled on the Indian trail which led down to the mouth of the Black River. With the trail as a guide she finally found her way back to her husband and children. David Beebe, a neighbor of the Tillotsons, went into the woods to find his strayed horses. He got lost and wandered four days and four nights, sleeping in hollow trees and living on hickory nuts, before he reached the lake shore and the trail that led him back to Ridgeville. When the Beebe family arrived in the Reserve to become "neighbors" of the Tillotsons, Mrs. Tillotson went to call on Mrs. Beebe. She had not seen another woman in three months. They were so overcome by their emotions that for some minutes neither could speak.

Peter Parley recorded a touching episode related by Doctor Hand when he was visiting the isolated cabins. Riding in the woods one day, far from any settlement, he met an eighteen-year-old boy in a hunting jacket and carrying a rifle. The young man stared at the traveler on horseback.

"Where are you from?" said the youth, at last.
"From Connecticut," was the reply.
"That is near the old Bay State?"
"Yes."
"And have you been there?"
"To Massachusetts! Yes, many a time."
"Let me take your hand, stranger. My mother was from the Bay State, and brought me here when I was an infant. I have heard her speak of it. Oh, it must be a lovely land! I wish I could see a meeting-house and a school-house, for she is always talking about them. And the sea—the sea—oh, if I could see that! Did you ever see it, stranger?"
"Yes, often."
"What, the real salt sea—the ocean—with the ships upon it?"

"Yes."

"Well," said the youth, scarcely able to suppress his emotion—
"if I could see the old Bay State and the ocean, I should be willing then to die!"

Reports of this kind tell us more about the early conditions on
the Reserve than a whole chapter of historical analysis could con-
vey. It was a stern and rugged adventure which these men and
their families undertook. They were, indeed, coming into a potentially rich land, but few of these eager immigrants could envisage
the long and sacrificial period of development which lay ahead
of them before their dreams would materialize.

CHAPTER EIGHT

STRUGGLE OF THREE DECADES

THE settlers had to endure three decades of this relative isolation and slow development. They were abused by want and by ill health, and they languished for lack of trade routes, markets, and cash. There was no consuming public in the Reserve to absorb the local products, and there could be little exchange because everybody produced the same things—chiefly grain, pork, and cheese. All the travelers to the Reserve in these early years commented on the plight of the settlers. Almost everybody in those days kept a journal. Many of them have been published. Let us now conclude this portion of our story by calling upon the eyewitness accounts of three notable observers who spent time in the Reserve exactly a decade apart. The first of them, made by Reverend Joseph Badger (1757-1846), was published at Hudson, Ohio, in 1851. It contained his autobiography and selections from his private journals and correspondence. This devoted man had served his country with distinction during the Revolutionary War. In the year 1800 the Missionary Society of Connecticut sent him to the west to survey the situation in the Reserve and to minister to the Indians between the Cuyahoga River and Detroit. He rode horseback over the mountains through the November and December snow to Pittsburgh. In some places the snow drifts were so deep that he had to clear a way for his horse. He forded icy streams, getting wet to his waist and risking the life of his horse and his own neck. Why he did not perish is one of God's miracles. When he finally arrived among the little group of settlers at Youngstown inside the Reserve, he called them together and "preached a lecture" for their edification.

Badger then made a systematic visitation of the settlements

scattered through the Reserve. He noted the conditions of life in 1800-1801, and listed the number of families in each community. His list helps us to see how widely scattered the pattern of settlement was, in contrast with the tendency of communities like Marietta, Gallipolis, Manchester, Chillicothe, and Cincinnati to concentrate in larger groups. He found in Vienna only one family, in Hartford three, Vernon five, Warren and Canfield eleven each, one at the Salt Works, five each at Deerfield, Boardman, and Poland, seven at Mesopotamia, three at Windsor, one at Nelson, and two or three at Mantua (with several young men opening up places). He does not say how many were at Hudson, but on the Fourth of July thirty people gathered at Hudson's cabin to hear Benjamin Tappan of Ravenna give the oration. Badger disapproved of his address because it was "interlarded with many grossly illiberal remarks against Christians and Christianity." As he rode north, he found five families at Newburg, two at Cleveland, one each at Euclid and Chagrin, four at Mentor, two at Painesville, an unspecified number at Burton and Aurora, and two each at Austinburg and Harpersfield.

After visiting these settlements, preaching to each group in turn, he went on to the west to minister to the Indians. He was ill with fever and medicated himself with calomel and jalap. He returned to the Reserve by way of Hudson to Austinburg. He was at times so far from settlements of any kind that for two days he lived on chestnuts in the woods as he rode through in solitude. He was rewarded at Austinburg to find that the Christians there wanted to found a church. Badger records, "A meeting was accordingly appointed on Thursday, the 24th of October, and a church formed, consisting of ten male and six female members. This was the first church organized on the Connecticut Western Reserve."

He returned to Connecticut to report. The Missionary Society promptly asked him to go back to the field with his family to work among the settlers at a salary of seven dollars a week. His journal gives us a brief but illuminating glimpse into his heart as he made the sacrificial decision to go. Here are his own words:

The subject of removal to a distance of six hundred miles, began
now to fill our minds with very serious reflections. We could carry
no furniture excepting a few light articles such as brass utensils
for cooking, clothes and bedding, with a small supply of table
furniture. Our family of six children must now be taken from
school, to grow up in the woods without any advantage of even a
common school, for years; and in circumstances extremely difficult to make them or ourselves comfortable with clothing. But
we concluded to submit our cause to Him who feeds and clothes the
lilies of the field.

Badger traded his lot in Blandford for land in the Reserve,
loaded his few effects on a wagon and began the tortuous three
months' journey westward through New York in the early winter
of 1802. He fought through snowdrifts and stopped where he
could when night fell. The wagon broke down at intervals on the
rough trail. He removed the wheels, fashioned crude sled runners
and attached them to the bed to form a sleigh. In several places
he had to hack a road through the forest. Between Buffalo and the
Pennsylvania line he found not a single house or cabin on the
route.

At the south end of Austinburg he erected a coarse cabin of
round logs. It was only half floored with "split stuff," and partly
roofed with boards from Austin's mill. It had no chimney. Food
was scarce and dear. He bought for twenty dollars at Painesville,
thirty miles away, 170 pounds of pork. "It was the whole hog,
feet, head, snout, and ears." This must have been a grim habitation for Mrs. Badger and the six children when Reverend Badger
committed them in this state "to the care of our heavenly Father,"
and set out on his mission to the settlements.

The task of ministering to the people on the Reserve in those
first years tried the soul and taxed the charity of this devoted man.
The professing Christians were mourning the loss of their former
privileges and wondering why they had come. Badger encouraged
them with visions of a bright future. Others were openly cynical
and irreligious, like Benjamin Tappan. Badger was deeply discouraged over the fruitless results of preaching to stupid or listless

groups who gathered at a neighbor's cabin to hear his sermons. He castigated the five families at Newburg: "They seemed to glory in their infidelity. . . . Infidelity and profaning the Sabbath are general in this place; they bid fair to grow into a hardened, corrupt society."

Other settlements were, of course, more responsive and many congregations were established. And even though his salary was reduced to six dollars a week and he was required to distribute great loads of religious books to his extensive parish, he continued to trust Him who clothed the lilies and whose ravens brought sustenance in time of need.

This tall, slim and erect man, with blue eyes and brown hair, impulsive but considerate and godly, was laboring in this still barren vineyard when another visitor rode through the Reserve on an inspection trip in October 1811. He was the canny-eyed Scotsman, John Melish. Melish had systematically listed a dozen inquiries to be made during his journey to the west: he would discover the nature of the soil; the lakes, streams, and swamps; the variety of plants and animal life; the climate and seasons; the dates of the settlements; the health, customs, occupations, and state of mind of the inhabitants; the number and style of the buildings; the condition of the roads and bridges; the price structure, and the value of land, labor, and provisions; the classes of settlers most adaptable to the country; and the possibilities for manufacturing.

He approached the Reserve on horseback from Canton. On the outskirts he saw a tent pitched in the woods a little off the road. He turned aside to make inquiry. He found an emigrant living in the tent with his wife and two children. Their means had carried them only this far in quest of a settlement and they could go no farther. He states:

They were obliged to stop short at this place, where they meant to *sit down* and clear and cultivate a piece of land. In the language of the country, they were *squatters*. The only visible substance they had, was a tent, a waggon, a horse, a cow, and some bedding.

The tent and bedding had been drenched by the rain, but they had a large fire before the door, at which the bedding was hung up to dry, and they sat round it apparently very contented.

Melish did not see them as objects of pity. In the spirit of Rousseau, he commented that their life was, perhaps,

most to be envied; they are free from all care except that of providing for their families, and the *real* wants of a family are easily supplied; they have no credit *to support* nor bills *to pay;* and they can train up their children in the paths of virtue and of industry, far removed from the evil example of the wicked. . . . They can work their daily task, confident of a reward; and, blessing the God of mercies, they can repose their heads on the pillow, and enjoy a sweet sleep, the reward of rational labour, and a good conscience.

Melish, of course, traveled on back to the region of "the evil example of the wicked," leaving the man and his family standing before their water-soaked bedding in the uncleared wilderness. Within the Reserve he found the roads all but impassable even on horseback. He was warned against trying to ride from Stow to Hudson, "an old and thriving settlement . . . where I was told there were a number of handsome *frame houses,*" because the road was so bad he could not get there. Even on the road taken along the Cuyahoga to Boston and Cleveland his horse sank in the mud swamps up to his knees and tired rapidly in the struggle. Melish described the eight miles in Boston township as "the worst road I had yet seen in America." A wagoner was attempting to haul salt from Cleveland to the portage at present Akron, forty-two miles over this road. He had been drenched by cold rain, had spent the night without shelter, and had no means of making a fire. A few crude wooden bridges spanned some of the creeks; the others had to be forded. Everywhere, except in a few favored high spots of land, the scattered settlers were sickly from fever and ague, unusually severe in 1811, and from which all suffered. Some families were moving on to the Firelands to escape the infection. The soil was good for land "of third rate." It grew enormous pumpkins. "The people," Melish recorded, "live a good deal upon pumpkin pies." Most of them liked the new country, especially the mild winters, "mighty well."

Since he could not get to Hudson, he saw nothing but the most primitive log houses. He lodged the night in a house where the only food was a few slices of bad potatoes stewed with pork and served up "swimming in butter"; the family had no bread, no beef, and no sugar. He was bedded in a cold, dark room, in the bitter chill of an October night without a fire. He "shoved an empty bag" into the window where a pane was missing. In the morning light, shivering with cold, he discovered that "the house was literally like a riddle, and there was an opening almost close by my bed-side, that would have let in a horse. . . . I could not but laugh at my precaution of last night, in stuffing up the broken window; where, however, I allowed the bag to remain, as an admonition to the people to repair the house before winter."

Nearer Cleveland he noted some mills, "but they were idle, and appeared to be going to decay." The country was dull, "without a single object to exhilarate the imagination, or cheer the spirits; and latterly the people looked pale and sickly." The Cuyahoga Flats were "extensive and fertile," but the river, clogged with sand at its mouth, was stagnant, foul with decomposing vegetable matter, and gave off a putrid smell "almost insufferable." The magnificent view of serene Lake Erie "was really sublime," and he was delighted with it; but the "paltry *village*, containing a few houses only," and the pale and dejected people trying to live there, depressed him. "O!" he exclaimed, "what a contrast was there!"

Like other men of vision who had traveled across the state, he observed that the rivers drained from the narrow divide along the 41st parallel into Lake Erie to the north and the Ohio River to the south, with only a short portage separating them at their headwaters. He predicted that the deepening of the harbor at Cleveland would relieve the putrefaction of the Cuyahoga, and that a canal, linking this harbor with the Ohio River, would "confer a lasting advantage on the state of Ohio" and enormous benefit upon residents "in the Connecticut reservation." He was right on both counts.

In the absence of rudimentary improvements in the harbor, Cleveland was languishing in 1811. There were "only 16 dwellings, 2 taverns, 2 stores, and 1 school." The trade, limited to salt, sometimes a little flour, pork, and whisky, was trifling. Emigrants consumed all provisions that could be spared.

Wheat was 1 dollar per bushel, rye 75 cents, oats 37½, potatoes 50, flour 7 dollars per barrel, beef 3 dollars 50 cents per cwt., mutton and veal 5 to 6 cents per lb., pork, 5 dollars per cwt., cheese (good Hudson) 10 cents per lb., butter 12½, whisky 50 cents per gallon, cyder 7 dollars per barrel, salt 1 dollar 20 cents per cwt.

Whitefish from Lake Erie were put up in barrels at $10 a barrel. Horses sold for from $50 to $100, cows from $20 to $25, and sheep at $2.50. Board at the tavern was $3.00 a week. Such, according to Melish, was the price structure at Cleveland in October 1811.

Melish found no settlements between Cleveland and Rocky River. He saw emigrants on their way to Sandusky Bay which was then attracting many new settlers. Among them was a number of mechanics, which Melish thought was a good sign.

Melish returned to Cleveland and took his way eastward along the lake. He had breakfast at Judge Don's house, seven miles out, in the midst of pretty good soil, "though all third rate. . . . Judge Don's family were busy manufacturing homespun, and appeared to be quite healthy." At Chagrin River he found "a fine farm, and an orchard well stocked with fruit trees. In the house the females were busy carding and spinning wool." At the Grand River he saw a really handsome house, "the seat of governor Huntingdon." Here he fell in with a Mr. Baird who was taking a drove of cattle to Buffalo. They used the sands of Lake Erie for a highway, but on the second day a northwest wind rolled the waves right up to the high shore and they had to ride through water and dead fish blown ashore in the gale. At the Ashtabula River, Baird, knowing the route, drove his cattle a hundred yards out into the lake and crossed on the sand bar. They spent the night at the house of Squire Leet. It was township court day and a number of men with their wives and daughters had come to the squire's house. They too spent the night with him. They all sat up "till a pretty late hour" singing songs and telling stories.

As he left the Connecticut reservation east of Conneaut, Melish summarized his impressions of this publicized region. He thought it "a pity that the Connecticut reserve was made the subject of individual speculation at all." The proprietors had kept the lake shore *"on speculation,* expecting a very high price for it after the other parts of the country are settled." This was, Melish thought, a grave mistake. Settlers struggling through the mud in a region without settlements got a bad impression of the country "which has considerably retarded the settlement of the interior of the district." Everybody would have profited more, he thought, if Connecticut had held the land, improved it with roads and bridges and harbors, and had then sold it as there was a real and not a speculative demand.

If the banks [of Lake Erie] had been laid out in farms having a quarter of a mile in front, and one mile deep, they would have amounted to 600; and, allowing 10 persons to each, the lake shore alone would have contained 6000 inhabitants, being nearly equal to all the inhabitants in the district, with the exception of Trumbull county,[1] no part of which is on the Lake.

Melish was also impressed by the high quality of the New England people who were coming west. They were frugal and industrious, civil in manner, and moral in deportment. They generally had received "a virtuous education," were handsome and hardy, independent in spirit, and "the very flower of them" had migrated. In view of the fact, however, that the Ohio population of 228,861 contained 125,803 children under 16, only 20,682 persons over 45, and 3,500 more men between 16 and 45 than women, Melish concluded with this recommendation:

I will only suggest to the males to take a greater portion of the "blooming Yankee girls" along with them, and not suffer nearly

---

[1] Trumbull County had 8,671; the rest of the Reserve 7,371.

17,000 of them to pine away as *old maids* in their own country, when it is seen they are so much wanted in this.

Melish's report does not lead us to believe that conditions had improved markedly during the first decade of settlement. What about the next ten years? We turn to the record carefully compiled by Dr. Zerah Hawley who came to practice medicine in the Reserve from September 1820 to late August 1821. His observations, made in the spirit of an objective scientist, were published in New Haven in 1822 under the title, "A journal of a tour through Connecticut, Massachusetts, New York, the north part of Pennsylvania and Ohio, including a year's residence in that part of the state of Ohio, styled New Connecticut, or Western Reserve." He frankly acknowledged that his primary motive for publishing his book was "to undeceive the community, respecting a portion of the Western Country, which has been represented as an *earthly Paradise*." People will think, he forewarned, that he has represented suffering and deprivation in too strong a light. He regrets the conditions, but he saw them with his own eyes. "I am ready to answer to the facts," he wrote.

The facts were stark. Hawley was disappointed to find how thinly settled the Reserve was after a quarter of a century of emigration, and how severe were the poverty and distress. He visited a sick woman in Harpersfield. He rode through mud, his horse stumbling over roots and stumps. "I entered," he said, "for the first time in my life into a log house with one room without any fire-place, the log being laid against the logs of the house and the fire built in front." There was no chimney; the smoke escaped through a hole in the roof. This primitive arrangement was so common that the inhabitants had a saying, "It is against the law to have any chimney until three of the logs of the house are burnt in two." Two stones served as andirons, a wooden poker for shovel and tongs. No clay filled in the chinks, and the roof leaked. The furniture was a few indifferent chairs, a bedstead of saplings, a chest or two, and shelves for the hollow ware.

This standard of living was not exceptional, Hawley swears, but typical. He tells of visiting a child sick from "mercurial cathartic." The parents and two children were living in a shanty eight by ten feet. Rain dripped through the holes in the shed roof and there was no dry spot where the sick child could be laid. Even the "titled men," as Hawley calls the judges, representatives, senators, and colonels, lived in one-room cabins "in which all the family, with their guests, eat, sleep, and perform all domestic operations." Beds stood in two corners of the room, a cupboard in a third, and a swill barrel in the fourth. A two-room house was two such cabins connected by a hall, with the swill barrel, tubs, pots, and kettles stowed in it. The hogs would gather there and "dance a hornpipe to a swinish tune" all night long. Wrightsbury had the best finished dwelling Hawley saw during his year's residence. It was painted white outside, and all the rooms were nicely plastered and painted. It belonged to "B.S., Esq."

The isolation and lack of markets had depressed the standards of living. Even when the families brought nice things with them, the moving, the wear and tear of daily use, and the inability to replace broken articles steadily reduced their appointments. Glasses, cups, and hollow ware disappeared, iron pots were borrowed and broken. Hawley was entertained by a family who had been in the Reserve for seventeen years. They had one knife and one fork which they gave to the guest. The others ate with improvised implements—a shoe knife or an old razor blade with a wooden handle. There were no glasses. The teapots were chipped, the spouts and handles broken. The food was served in a single large dish in the middle of the table.

Hawley felt that Melish's rhapsody on the moral grandeur of the wilderness was unrealistic. He observed that these conditions did not elevate the inhabitants, but caused degeneration. The people grew indifferent and lazy. He noted a marked contrast between grandparents, parents, and children. The older generation was cultivated, their children less so, and their grandchildren, who had spent their days in the Reserve, were crude and ignorant of the world. Few could read or write adequately. Hawley wrote a long essay on the evil effect of large families living in a single room. "Of its immoral effects, I could mention some instances, if it were advisable."

The schools were makeshifts. Some were conducted during the summer for only eight weeks, a few for only six, and exceptional ones for three months. A female would instruct the children in reading, writing, and plain sewing. Some winter terms were taught by men, with the same curriculum except that arithmetic was substituted for sewing. Two elder brothers of the famous Senator Ben Wade of Jefferson taught such schools at Madison and Monroe in 1821. The salary of one was six barrels of whisky; of the other, five barrels. Few books were available. The opportunities and the results were notably inferior to those enjoyed by the parents in the East. We do note with some pride, however, that in 1820 Seabury Ford and D. Witter walked east through the wilderness all the way to New Haven to attend Yale College. They were among the first of the Reserve's young men to go there, and they became successful men.

We also do not overlook the fact that about the time Hawley was making his observations young Joshua R. Giddings of Jefferson was tramping forty miles through the wilderness to reach Canfield to study law with Elisha Whittlesey. Whittlesey had come to the Reserve very poor in 1807. He became a great lawyer, statesman and national figure as a founder of the Whig Party and first Comptroller of the U.S. Treasury. His interesting old home on the higher ground west of the long oval village green at Canfield and the little brick office where he practiced are both still standing. He received Giddings into his office as a student, helped the poor boy in his struggle for an education, and had the satisfaction of seeing him a successful member of the bar and the author of the Republican Party's first platform (1856). Giddings' law office, built in 1823, is also still preserved at Jefferson.

Hawley, of course, did not know the hard-working, ambitious young fellow from Jefferson. He did know that the citizens of the Reserve had no money and no way of getting any. Shoes could not be had. Both the children and the adults went barefoot. Their wardrobe was "miserably deficient. . . . Some wear a semi-leathern apron ending in half legs, covering the forepart of the legs, and fastened behind by leathern straps and buttons." There was a shortage of bedding and blankets. The older women, sixty or more years of age, dressed severely and plaited their gray hair. Young females who owned brass combs twisted their hair on top of their heads; others, says Hawley, "dock the hair square behind, leaving it about six inches long, which gives them a very uncouth and forbidding appearance."

Hawley's description of the manners of the period is much the same as reported by Charles Dickens two decades later. Men and boys entered the house with their hats on. Women and girls eased in through the door, carefully inspecting every article of furniture. All remained generally silent for the first half hour or so. Then curiosity would compel them to utter a few monosyllables: "What's that?" "Where you been?" In Hawley's opinion the Sunday services did not advance the cultural level of the Reserve. He criticized the Methodist preachers as "uninformed and fanatical. . . . Their sermons are without plan or system, beginning with *ignorance,* and ending in *nonsense,* interlarded with something nearly approaching to blasphemy in many cases."[2]

In addition to these observations on the life and character of the people, he wrote many pages on the violent changes in the weather along Lake Erie. He would enter the house of a patient on a warm and balmy day, and leave it an hour or two later in a snowstorm. Settlers who expected to escape New England's severe winters, and turn their livestock into the woods to thrive, were saddened to find that neither was possible. Sheep and cattle were still scarce. Lack of roads, markets, and money warped and strangled the economy. Quite naturally the grain was reduced to the more concentrated and more easily handled by-product of whisky. In Hawley's day Ashtabula, with a population of 700–800, operated three "very large distilleries, a number of smaller ones, one brewery, three stores and three or four taverns, but no church of any denomination."

---

[2] Hawley footnoted this statement, saying he was aware of its severity, and he wished that it was not true.

These reports of the Reserve in 1800, 1810, and 1820 are not very heartening. The pictures painted by our three travelers may have been warped by their own personal experiences. But even when we correct for bias, the inescapable fact seems to be that conditions were wretched during the first quarter of a century, and that no improvement was likely to come without a transportation system and a supply of cash.

CHAPTER NINE

JAMES HILLHOUSE

THE settlers in the Reserve, more specifically the children of these settlers, finally brought the region to such prosperity that we tend to forget what the first generation experienced during the first twenty-five or thirty years of their venture. The handicaps which we have just seen threatened for a time to imperil the whole speculation. It was ultimately profitable only for those who had the resources to hold on against heavy expense over a fairly long period of time and turn their property over to their children. People in the Excess Company lost their money. The six townships reserved by the company for sale to meet expenses did not attract buyers. The city lots would not sell for the prices asked and had to be cut in half, or more. The surveys had taken longer and cost more than expected. Instead of finding their purses getting fuller, members of the company had to put in more cash under levies and assessments to meet these demands. And while the lands went unsold, or sold for promises and mortgages instead of cash, taxes fell due and interest charges mounted. The frontier enterprise had to face the stern laws of economics, and many people suffered.

Let us see it now through the character and the heroic activities of one man who did more than any other single individual to rescue the venture from ruin. He was a most unusual person, but his name is, oddly enough, seldom even mentioned in existing literature on the Western Reserve. He was James Hillhouse, of New Haven, Connecticut, a name held in honor there and perpetuated by stately Hillhouse Avenue, and the mansion and grounds which are now a feature of Yale University. His portrait reveals an irregular face, rather tense, with firm mouth, long nose, high forehead, and fine, perceptive eyes that have a surprising air of repose. Those who knew him said that "his face and person were such that no stranger could look upon him for a moment without looking again and saying to himself, 'That is no ordinary man.' Tall, long-limbed, with high cheek-bones, swarthy, lithe in motion, lightness in his step, and strength and freedom in his stride, he seemed a little like some Indian Chief of poetry or romance . . . so much so that with a kind of affectionate respect he was sometimes called 'the Sachem.' "[1]

Hillhouse attended Yale from 1769 to 1773 when the faculty consisted of Acting President Daggett, Professor of Divinity, and Nehemiah Strong, Professor of Mathematics and Natural Philosophy, aided by three tutors. He then studied law and was admitted to the bar. He took over part of the big, profitable practice of his uncle James Abraham Hillhouse, who had adopted him. He became an ardent patriot during the Revolution. He was captain of twenty or thirty young men who marched out of New Haven to meet the invasion of the British on July 5, 1779. He became treasurer of Yale in 1782 and continued in that office for fifty years—until his death in 1832. The people of Connecticut drafted him early for public service; they elected him to the Second Congress when he was only twenty-six, and re-elected him to the Third and Fourth. Then in 1796 he was appointed Senator. He was re-elected to the Senate in 1797, 1803, and 1809. This service had taken him through the Presidencies of Washington, Adams, Jefferson, and into that of Madison. He fought a hard but losing battle to limit the powers of the President, to prevent centralization of government, and to develop a sturdy, independent strength in the states.

When he returned to New Haven from the session that closed in May 1810, he was waited on by a delegation of Connecticut citizens who urged on him an appointment as Commissioner of the

---

[1] Leonard Bacon, *Sketch of the Life and Public Services of Hon. James Hillhouse of New Haven,* New Haven, 1860, p. 42.

School Fund. He considered this onerous and herculean task so important to the general welfare that he resigned from the Senate and accepted the responsibility. His stipend was only $1,000 a year.[2] The fund, inextricably tied in with the development of the Reserve, was in such a desperate state that it was threatened with complete disaster.

As we have already seen in some detail, the state had sold its land to the company for $1,200,000 in 1795. The General Assembly had argued and debated for years what to do with the money it would get from the sale. The town meetings had spent months discussing the question, and ministers had preached sermons about it from the pulpits of Connecticut. Then in May 1795 the General Assembly reached a final decision. It passed an act specifying

that the principal sum which shall be received on the sale of the lands belonging to this State, lying west of Pennsylvania, shall be and remain a *perpetual fund* . . . and the interest arising therefrom shall be, and hereby is, appropriated to the support of schools in the several societies constituted . . . within this State.

It was a notable and typical gesture of the New England interest in education, and to this day Connecticut draws from this fund a portion of the expenses of its school system.

The Land Company to which it sold its property, however, paid very little cash down. It merely secured the debt with mortgages and personal securities pending resale of land in the Reserve. Interest at six percent was to begin at the end of the first two years, i.e., in 1797. When the first $72,000 became due, the debtors were still paying out money for surveys. They had not resold and were in no position to pay the state. They fell into arrears. In fact, during the first thirteen years, only about half or less of the amount due was actually paid. The business was directed by a board of five "Managers of the funds arising on the sales of the Western Reserve." The managers reported to the legislature in 1809 that

---

[2] It was raised to $1,500 for a time, and then reduced again to $1,000.

the arrears in interest were critical, in some cases equaling the principal, and that the capital itself was in grave danger of being lost. The debtors had scattered with the years over the various states, many of them had become insolvent, and their securities worthless. The original thirty-six bonds given by the company for the $1,200,000 had been divided, broken up, and dispersed through reinvestments until they had become 500 in number. And the land which was to secure them was being developed so slowly that the settlers themselves faced bankruptcy. The affairs of the Reserve had come to a desperate pass. It was James Hillhouse's complicated task to straighten out these moribund finances in the interest of all concerned—state, schools, company, and settlers.

The Board of Managers was honorably discharged. The entire authority and responsibility for managing the fund were vested in the wisdom and integrity of one man. He was given the title Commissioner of the School Fund. In the days when Hillhouse was arguing against the vast powers of the President of the United States, he used to say that this office was made only for George Washington. His friends in Connecticut said likewise that the office of commissioner was made for a single individual, the Honorable James Hillhouse. His zeal and industry, and his selfless devotion to this assignment at great personal sacrifice, were unique even in that age of high-minded public service.

Hillhouse immediately made himself familiar with every single debtor and the state of his property. Many of them represented extreme hardship cases. Some of them were widows and orphans who inherited only bankruptcy or the heavy burden of mortgages overdue, interest unpaid, and financial desperation. Hillhouse took a wise, friendly, and even paternal course in dealing with them. He called on them in the spirit of their own personal attorney rather than as the representative of a prosecuting creditor. He went over their affairs and problems with them and advised them as a skilled lawyer in ways to improve their condition. Instead of throwing them into court, he helped them to save themselves. During his fifteen years of active service he avoided litigation entirely and paid out not a single dollar for counsel. People might easily have come to hate him as the symbol of their misfortune, or fear him because of the power and the authority which he held over them. For in those days, and for a long time thereafter, in the United States of America men could still be imprisoned for debt—and sometimes were. Instead they loved him, trusted him, and admired him for his help and counsel. He imprisoned no one.

It became Hillhouse's duty to deal with the family and the estate of Oliver Phelps and Gideon Granger. We remember that Phelps was one of the Committee of Eight appointed to sell the state lands in the Reserve, and that he himself was by far the heaviest investor in the Reserve, with $168,185 of his own capital and $80,000 in association with Granger. The Reserve did not develop rapidly enough to save Oliver Phelps. He could not convert his vast landholdings into cash. His creditors closed in upon him, put him into prison, and he died there in debt. With the accumulation of unpaid interest, he owed on his Western Reserve lands almost $300,000, and that was twenty-five years after the sale. His family was impoverished, and his estate in such a tangle that it seemed absolutely hopeless.

James Hillhouse saw how fruitless it was to throw people into jail because they were in debt and could not pay; that archaic procedure was a loss to everyone and broke the heart of the debtor. He went personally to the Reserve to see Phelps's property and to try to restore it to order. Patiently he worked on it night and day. He skillfully negotiated sales, payments, and settlements. He slowly threaded his way through the labyrinth of investments, sales, and mortgages. He managed to clear up every title, to settle the accumulated debts which had sent Phelps to prison, and to pay in full the claim of the School Fund. Judge Sherman, in reviewing Hillhouse's success in these difficult transactions, wrote:

So much were the family of Mr. Phelps benefited by the services which he rendered them, beyond what the interests of this State required, that besides paying all the expenses incident to the operation in searching records, foreclosing mortgages, defraying taxes, paying agents, &c., they allowed compound interest on the School

Fund debt, which exceeded more than $14,500, the amount which could have been recovered by law.[3]

The grateful family, rescued from poverty and restored to affluence, gave Hillhouse $6,000 for his personal service rendered over and above anything required by his office as commissioner. Hillhouse accepted the gift. We must quote the fine and revealing sentences of comment by Leonard Bacon, written in 1860:

Yet strange as it may seem, and hardly credible in these days of plunder and official venality, he "declined retaining a donation from those with whom he dealt as a public agent, and paid the $6,000 into the treasury of the School Fund." This "Delicate sense of honor" was actually extant less than thirty years ago, in a man who had been almost twenty years a member of Congress, and who came directly from Washington to the management of a great pecuniary trust for the public.[4]

Hillhouse followed the same scrupulous procedure with the $2,500 given him by Gideon Granger, and by other grateful men who tried to show their appreciation of his remarkable service to them.

The unbounded tribute paid him by his contemporaries was merited. He set a high example in public spirit in sacrificing his personal interest and convenience to a cause in which he believed with his whole heart—the development of the Reserve and, as a corollary, the health and security of the School Fund. He could have had a life of wealth and ease in New Haven; he chose instead the hardships of administering the finances of the frontier. Leonard Bacon writes of the sheer physical exertion required of him:

No young immigrant making his way into the wilderness to lay there the foundations of future wealth, ever encountered hardships, fatigue and peril, more patiently or cheerfully than he. Unattended, he made long journeys westward, year after year, at all seasons, and with all sorts of hazards, in his sulky, at the heels of the fleet and hardy little mare that was his chief locomotive power

---

[3] Bacon, p. 33.
[4] Bacon, pp. 34-35.

for the first six or eight years of his commissionership. Once he
came near death by freezing in a winter drive; twice by fever,
caught in miasmatic regions which his duty required him to explore. But it is safe to say, that whether using the utmost speed
of his mare to leave at a safe distance behind him some dogging
ruffians who had attempted to rob him, or making his way slowly
through the woods with an armed Indian silently and wistfully
trotting at his side, or arrested as a criminal at the instigation of
a malicious debtor (which was once the case), he never lost for
an hour his courage or cheerful good humor. No difficulties of the
way could turn him back. The story is told that "after half a day's
solitary traveling, he once came to a stream, apparently swollen
with rain to an unusual depth. It was necessary to cross it, or be
frustrated of his object, besides measuring back a weary way. He
undressed himself, strapped his trunk of clothes, papers, &c., on
the top of his sulky, and reached the opposite bank with no other
inconvenience than an unseasonable bath."[5]

From 1810, when Melish made his disheartening inspection trip
through the Reserve, to 1825, when Ohio decided at last to dig a
canal across the state, Hillhouse labored at his task of helping
people to manage their property and pay off their mortgages. He
rescued many from discouragement and ruin, and showed them
how to hold on until the chartering of banks and the improvement
of transportation could give them permanent relief. Of course, he
was interested, first of all, in the School Fund. But the experiences
of the fifteen years before he became commissioner had shown
that the fund was only a worthless legislative act unless the people
who were buying and moving onto this land could prosper.

When Hillhouse retired as commissioner in his seventy-first
year, his success in this most difficult undertaking had surpassed
even the expectations of his friends. He had completely reorganized the School Fund and created for it a pattern of administration. He not only restored it to health and brought it from
collapse back to the original sum of its supposed capital, but he
added another half-million dollars to it. And he lived to see the
construction of the canal across the Reserve which linked it with

---

[5] Bacon, pp. 34-35.

the markets of the world, and the children of the pioneers begin their march toward prosperity.

In the long seventy-eight years of his life, from the Revolutionary War to the canal era, the old gentleman had become somewhat archaic in his speech and dress; like Milton he said "cowcumber," "much obleeged," and "yaller"; he wore knee buckles and powdered hair in his young days; and he wore his great dignity to the end of his life.

He was as dignified with his coat off and with a scythe in his hands, leading the mowers across the field, and cutting the widest swath of all, as when he stood conspicuous and honored in the Senate, or on a Sabbath morning walked to the house of prayer with patriarchal grace, beneath the stately elms which his own hands had planted. . . . His dignity was not put on, and could not be put off. It was nothing else than his transparent simplicity, continually revealing an unaffected nobleness of soul.[6]

He continued as treasurer of Yale until his death on December 29, 1832. After a day of college business, he went to his room to read his mail. He died there quietly a few minutes later in the midst of his work.

---

6 Bacon, p. 45.

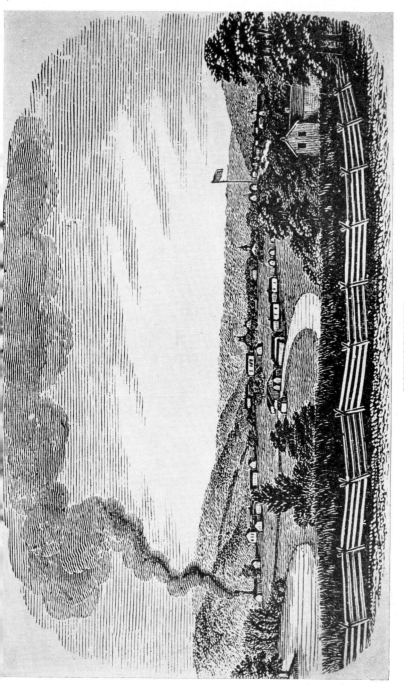

YOUNGSTOWN

Drawn by Henry Howe in 1846

DOWNTOWN YOUNGSTOWN FROM THE AIR

CHAPTER TEN

$C A N A L S$

Travel is now so easy and fast in the Western Reserve that it is accepted as a commonplace. People living in Burton, Chardon, Hudson, Oberlin, and other communities work in Cleveland. The intricate pattern of roads ties all the towns and villages together and links them by arterial highways with the larger cities. Railroads radiate from Cleveland and cross the Reserve in all directions. Distance has been abolished. Akron is only a few minutes' drive from Cleveland over Route 8 or U.S. 21. It is hard to recollect the day when Melish could not even ride horseback from Portage Summit to Hudson because of the mud and the stumps. People now living in Canfield can be in Cleveland to shop in less time than it took Melish to ride halfway across the muck in the township of Boston. Because of this present ease of communication it is somewhat hard to reconstruct the era which it rendered obsolete.

Lying in the Cuyahoga Valley between Route 8 and U.S. 21 is a fine old relic which stimulates our imagination. It is the well-preserved remnant of the Ohio–Erie Canal. The Cuyahoga River rises in Geauga County, only about fifteen miles from the Lake Erie shore, and flows southward toward Akron. There it runs into the rock obstruction of the divide, bends round through the gorge, reverses its direction and flows northward to Cleveland. After it spills over the falls and cuts through the canyon which lends grace to the Akron suburban terrain, it is contained as a gentle stream in the narrow valley marked by steep side slopes with parallel contours all the way down to Cleveland. The engineers chose this natural route for the Ohio canal.

The canal is still intact. The banks are kept up, the towpath is clear, the aqueducts over the streams are tight and drip very little, and the channel is full of water. The locks are as sturdy in appearance as when the stonemasons first laid them a century and a quarter ago. It is a pleasant experience to drive up the valley alongside this old canal. You pass by the crowded Flats, overflowing with busy industries; you leave the teeming arterial highway at the 71st Street Bridge and descend to the intimate and quiet Canal Road on the valley floor. You are instantly in another world. The canal is dreamy and somnolent. You half expect to hear the cry of bargemen at the locks, and to see a gray horse rounding the bend drawing a boatload of wool or cheese or grain. The only discordant note is the conspicuous signs warning you not to fish or trespass on this property.

The canal is narrow and shallow, and yet this trickle of water, conducted through the valley between its low, man-made banks, first connected the interior of the Western Reserve with New York, New Orleans, the interior of Europe, and the markets of the world. It expressed the vision and the hopes of our forefathers. It was for them a huge and daring venture, the expression of their faith in the future of their country and their magnificent gamble with their destiny. They likened their undertaking to "the Revolution achieved by our fathers." On its four feet of water floated the products of their toil. It made all the difference between a stagnant and isolated western frontier and a thriving, prosperous and growing region linked up with the rest of the world.

Transportation by water is the most economical yet devised by man. It was also the only practicable means for heavy hauling over the sparsely settled Ohio frontier. Early travelers who explored the terrain between the Ohio River and Lake Erie saw immediately the natural routes over which canals might easily be projected to connect the two great waterways. George Washington himself in 1784 had pointed out the desirability of such a system, and Thomas Jefferson had concurred. The Indians in their regular seasonal journeys from river to lake had already provided the first reconnaissance engineering. They had their own waterway system across the compact state. Three of their natural journey routes lay across the Reserve. One followed the Grand River and Mahoning Valley to the Ohio at Beaver, Pennsylvania. Another went by way of the Cuyahoga, over the short portage at Akron, and down the Muskingum. A third followed the Black River into the Killbuck branch of the Muskingum. And we might add a fourth, lying just west of the Firelands, which ran up the Sandusky and crossed into the Scioto a little northwest of Marion. The land south of the divide, however, was so generally interveined with tributary streams that the canal engineers had a choice of several combinations of these routes.

The feasibility of a canal across Ohio, therefore, was never in serious question even before the actual surveys were made. The cost would certainly be less in Ohio than in New York and Pennsylvania where canals were being dug. But how could a raw young state, whose total real estate in 1826 was valued at only $15,946,840, and whose revenues for the fiscal year ending November 15, 1825, were only $131,738, undertake to spend upward of $3,000,000 for a canal? If they were so foolhardy, should they seek private-venture capital, or try to borrow against the credit of the state? Would it make or lose money? Could water be supplied at the high points on the summit to keep the canal full? What routes should be followed in the face of the pressures of interested groups who would want the canal to pass through their locality?

The idea was so stupendous that it seemed to frustrate the citizens at the same time that it intrigued them. It took the best leadership in the state almost two decades to bring the legislature to the test of action. Steady progress in New York encouraged them. The Erie Canal Commission, headed by the energetic DeWitt Clinton, was set up in 1810. Soon they were pushing that strategic ditch westward up the Mohawk Valley toward Buffalo on the lake. It would link the Ohio shore with the Hudson River and the port of New York. This spirited determination of the New Yorkers to get forward with their expensive project, and the relentless pressure of actual need in Ohio, finally persuaded the legislature to action. The Ohio country must find outlet or perish from stagnation.

Micajah T. Williams, a member of the House of Representatives, headed a committee to study the proposals and make a report. The committee attacked their job with diligence and were ready with their recommendations in January 1822. They supported them with overwhelming data. They pointed out that flour was selling in Cincinnati at $3.50 a barrel. In New York it would bring $8.00 and the demand was heavy. Shipping by canal to New York would amount to $1.70 a barrel. The profit, therefore, would be $2.80 a barrel. The distance would be much shorter than to New Orleans where the markets were often glutted, and where farmers and merchants, after making the long, hard journey down the rivers, might be forced to sell at ruinous and heartbreaking losses. Overland transportation to New York was out of the question. It cost $25 a ton to move goods from Ohio to New York by land; it would cost only $3.00 to move it by boat. If the canal were built, Ohio goods could be taken to market cheaply enough to compete with produce from other sections of the country, and needed articles could be purchased and shipped back to the state. If the first estimates of the cost—$2,500,000—were approximately correct, the state would recover its investment with interest within six years. Besides this direct monetary return, the increased value of Ohio lands and enterprise would be immense and beneficial.

The legislature was convinced. With pork selling at two cents a pound, beef at three, eggs at four cents a dozen, and chickens for a nickel, they were ready, at least, to take the next step. Four weeks after the Williams report was presented, the legislature appropriated $6,000 and authorized the governor to employ an engineer and appoint seven commissioners to survey the routes and make estimates.

One of the best engineers of his day, Mr. James Geddes, was engaged to explore the routes.[1] He had been employed by New York and had had wide experience on the Erie Canal. Under his

---

[1] The O. S. A. & H. Society preserves Governor Trimble's letter to Kelley announcing Geddes' employment at $1,500 per year, with time and expenses from New York.

able and vigorous direction a total of over nine hundred miles of possible routes was surveyed in the next eight months and levels run over about eight hundred miles. He was able to report to the legislature in 1823 that all of the five possible routes were practicable. The surveys and studies were continued through the next two years. The unselfish zeal of the commissioners was inspiring. Alfred Kelley, the ablest and most determined of them, left his lucrative law practice in Cleveland, and threw himself into the project. He made a special trip to New York to inspect the work going on there. The Erie Canal was a laboratory showing every stage of construction from ground-clearing and breaking to letting in the water and closing the locks. Kelley talked with all the officials in charge and was able to bring back invaluable technical information.

Locating the canal across Ohio was rigorous and dangerous work. Much of the route was uninhabited wilderness. The men had to fight their way through miles of forest, through low swampy ground and along damp riverbanks. Their sufferings duplicated those of Moses Cleaveland's first surveying party. Few of them were able to keep healthy for more than a week at a time. Some had to give up, and one engineer died. But they did their work well, and when the legislature met in 1825, it paid its tribute to them by taking definite action on their recommendations. On February 4 it passed the now famous act "to provide for the internal improvement of the state of Ohio, by navigable canals," and authorized the commissioners to fix the location from Portsmouth to the lake by way of the Scioto River, Licking Summit (near Newark), and the Muskingum River.

They lost no more time. They promptly invited DeWitt Clinton, and other New Yorkers prominent in canal promotion, to come out to Ohio for the grand opening on Independence Day 1825. Clinton accepted. He announced that he would arrive in Cleveland on June 30. He failed to say whether he would come by stagecoach or by ship. Cleveland prepared an impressive reception whether by lake or by land. The citizens met the stage when it jolted in, but Clinton was not on it. He arrived a few hours later aboard the *Superior*, Captain Fish in charge. All Cleveland gathered on the Cuyahoga bluff to watch the approach of the ship. It was a hot summer day, the sky was clear, no wind was blowing, and the lake was calm and glistening. The ship, dressed in all her flags, steamed proudly past Water Street and dropped anchor in a good draft a mile offshore opposite the mouth of the Cuyahoga. The captain fired the signal gun, and the crowds cheered. The ship's ladder was lowered, a yawl drew alongside, and the captain took Clinton by the hand and helped him into the stern seat. Clinton was followed by his aides, Colonels Jones, Read, and Van Rensselaer, and other very important people from New York. Among them were Rathbone and Lord, financiers, who had lent money for the canal.

With the American flag flying, the yawl came up the river past the cheering crowds to the foot of Superior Street where the reception committee and carriages were awaiting the distinguished visitors. Clinton was a large, robust man, commanding in appearance. His high and broad forehead, black curly hair, and brilliant black eyes now dignify every package of American cigarettes. He greeted the Clevelanders and proceeded to the Mansion House. Judge Samuel Cowles made an address of welcome. Clinton replied by reassuring Ohio that even if the canal should cost $5,000,000, it would be worth three times the cost through increased prices for Ohio goods, through money saved on transportation, and through the income from the tolls. He then proceeded down to Newark and over to Licking Summit to turn the first spade of earth at the approximate halfway point on the canal.

Intense rivalries had developed between villages competing for the canal in their locality. Since the population in 1825 was largely concentrated in the northeast, south, and southwest, engineering problems were not the sole consideration; the commissioners quite properly wished to serve as wide an area of the state as possible. Many ambitious villages were disappointed when the canal passed them by. Both Lorain and Sandusky hoped to be canal ports on Lake Erie. From the moment when the choice went to Cleveland, these villages languished and the port on the Cuyahoga began to forge ahead. On the whole, however, the selection of the route was reasonable, and the disappointed citizens whose villages were left behind accepted it. The 500 people then living in Cleveland were jubilant. They gave over $5,000 toward the project. Other public-spirited citizens along the route donated land and money. With Cleveland determined on as the lake terminal, the Cuyahoga Valley became the inevitable location for the canal across the Reserve. This particular strip, from Akron to the lake, was given top priority. It was placed immediately under contract and the digging began.

By Thanksgiving Day 1825 about two thousand men were swarming in the Cuyahoga Valley. They looked like a colonial army assembled along a thirty-eight-mile front to throw up breastworks for an impending engagement. It was indeed a struggle for survival. Men and animals worked from sunup to sundown. All along the valley they cleared out the trees, brush, roots, grass, and herbage so that the canal banks, as the contracts specified, might "unite securely with the solid earth beneath." They dug the ditch at least six feet deep. The specifications called for a minimum of four feet of water at all points on the canal, and the banks had to be not less than two feet and not more than five feet above the water level. They dug it twenty-six feet wide at the bottom, and they sloped the banks so that it would be at least forty feet wide at the water level. On one bank they fashioned a towpath that was ten feet wide at the surface and so level that it never rose or fell more than one foot in sixty-six feet. It had a six-inch side slope away from the canal for drainage.

The terrain was uneven, and this portion of canal proved to be one of the most expensive and difficult in the entire state—though no other canal in America cost less per mile as a whole to build than the Ohio-Erie. On the level stretches it was largely a matter of digging a ditch and piling up dirt for the banks. But in some places a way had to be blasted through rock, and in other places the excavation was in muck and through water-covered land. Loose banks had to be puddled and the slopes protected from washing away.

At forty-one spots along the route other men were digging special pits, hauling in stone, chiseling it into blocks, and laying it to form the walls of the locks. Through these locks the canalboats would drop down over the 400-feet difference in elevation between Akron and Cleveland. The chamber wall of each was ninety feet long, and the lock was fifteen feet wide "in the clear." You may still examine their construction at your leisure at several points along the canal.

Still other workmen were hewing out timber and constructing the aqueducts which carried the canal over the three tributary streams which flow into the Cuyahoga from the east.

It all sounds quite simple. Actually it was painful, backbreaking, dangerous work. Most of the workers were the men and boys of the Reserve. Contracts were let in small sections, and the contractors engaged local help. Their number and strength were augmented by Irish and German immigrant labor. Many of them had worked on the Erie Canal, and had moved on west when it was completed. Working conditions were not ideal. At the beginning wages were thirty cents a day plus board, a bunk in a dirty shanty, and a jigger of whisky a day per man. The wage scale rose, however, as the work progressed, from eight dollars to twelve and then to fifteen per month. In fact, the general rise of the price level accounted for a large portion of the excess of the canal costs over the original estimates.

Men waded about in the muck and got filthy in the ditches. Mosquitoes swarmed in season and spread malaria among the workers. Canal fever smote them, and many died. The hazards were so great that, according to the official report for 1826, the work was suspended from July to September to protect the health of the laborers. We think in contrast of the 120,000 slaves who died miserably while digging an ancient Suez canal in 600 B.C.

The contracts were let in small segments along the route. Some of the contractors were dishonest men. When they thought they would not get caught, they would pile dirt over logs and brush along the banks. Later, of course, the banks would break at these points. Alfred Kelley would go personally along the fills with a long iron stick and prod into any suspicious place to expose fraud.

A few of the contractors failed to pay their men. They had to be disciplined and coerced by the commissioners. In some cases the commissioners paid wages to the men directly and withheld from the contractors. Some of the contractors were simply improvident or incapable. They failed, and the contracts had to be relet in a hurry to keep the job going—incidentally running up the cost. But a fair percentage of the contractors were honest, patriotic citizens who, though they didn't mind making some profit, were genuinely interested in giving Ohio a fine canal as quickly as possible.

We have mentioned the fact that the Ohio terrain seemed especially designed to accommodate canals. Its natural favors extended to the water supply. Summit County has many lakes. The Indian portage path from the Cuyahoga across the Akron summit into the Muskingum was only a half-dozen miles long. The immediate area embraces a watershed of forty-two square miles. The elevations are such that, with a little engineering and considerable hard labor, the watershed could become a system of lakes and reservoirs. Storage capacity was later enlarged by damming the outlets to the West Reservoir and Turkey Foot Lake and by turning the Tuscarawas River into them through the Tuscarawas feeder. The worried speculations of the citizens on the problem of getting water to the summit of the canal were thus rather easily put to rest. Even to this day the improved remains of this system supply on a rental basis much of the water for the industry of Akron.

This Western Reserve portion of the canal was ready for the formal opening in July 1827. In keeping with the traditions of our forefathers, they chose Independence Day for the festivities. Their spirit was eloquently expressed by the celebration which attended the opening. It was fully and glowingly reported in the *Cleveland Herald* for Friday, July 6, 1827. Preceding issues had announced the forthcoming festivities and built up enthusiasm in the Reserve. A beautiful new boat had been fashioned in the boat yard at Lock No. 1 just south of Exchange Street in the village of Akron. In honor of the occasion it was ceremoniously christened

the *State of Ohio*. On the third of July the official party, consisting
of Governor Trimble, the Commissioners of the Canal Fund, the
Canal Commissioners, the Secretary of State, the Commissioner
of the School Fund of Connecticut, and other distinguished citizens, boarded this boat for the thirty-eight-mile journey down to
Cleveland. The 250 citizens of Akron cheered and drank toasts
as the boat moved away drawn by Job Harrington's sleek black
horses. The pace of the horses' hoofs on the towpath was stately
and the movement slow. The water had been turned into the new
channel a few days before to test the fresh banks. Only one breach
occurred which delayed the party for a few hours. People gathered
at each of the locks to see the boat drop down from one level to
the next.

At Boston the official party was joined by the *Allen Trimble*,
likewise crowded with rejoicing and excited passengers.

Down at Cleveland the great day dawned gray and wet. It was
greeted with salutes from the cannon on the riverbank. At eight
o'clock under gloomy skies a capacity load of passengers crowded
aboard the *Pioneer*. It was lying in the basin in the Flats above
the foot of Superior Street, decked with flags and carrying a cannon to fire salutes. Noble H. Merwin had bought this boat at
Buffalo, towed it out to Cleveland, and hauled it with teams out of
the Cuyahoga and over the riverbank into the canal in order to
have it ready for the opening. His gay party now moved up the
canal to meet the official party coming down. When they got up
by the present Jefferson Avenue Bridge, the sun suddenly burst
forth and inspired them to believe that this was an omen of the
bright future.

Six miles up the canal the *Pioneer* met the governor's party
coming down. They exchanged cannon salutes, grouped in procession, and amid prolonged cheers proceeded down the valley to
Cleveland. The *Herald* reported that the scene at this village "was
truly exhilarating." And then in a crowded sentence, it added:

The banks of the canal and the neighboring eminences were
lined with spectators—the boats with their flags and decorations

presented an imposing appearance—the flags with appropriate inscriptions and the standards of the State and Union, displayed from Belden's Tavern and the Franklin House, the alternate discharges of cannon in quick succession from the shore and the boats, mingling their thunders with the lofty strains of the band and the merry windings of the horn and bugle, all these circumstances combined with the idea that these were the effects and evidences of the enterprise and spirit of "Young Ohio," which but a quarter of a century since, was to all intents and purposes *terra incognita* to the rest of the world, produced an impression on the mind not to be soon obliterated.

H. H. Sizer was Marshal of the Day. He led the guests from the boats up the bluff and along Superior Street to an arbor on the Public Square. There the Reverend Mr. Bradstreet offered the prayer, John M. Sterling read the Declaration of Independence, and Reuben Wood delivered the oration, "eloquent and impressive" and "highly creditable to the author and gratifying to his audience."

The company then marched over to Belden's Tavern for a "sumptuous dinner" which began at three o'clock and continued through the rest of the day. The *Herald* declared: "The 'feast of reason and the flow of soul' rolled in full tides. . . . The rising sun had been hailed by the discharge of a National Salute and as he sunk at evening into the bosom of the lake, his departure was announced by the same formality."

The party gathered again in the Assembly Room for the inaugural ball at two dollars a person. At each end of the room was a transparency, one spelling out in large letters "Erie Canal," and the other "Ohio Canal." The guests drank fifteen regular toasts to the accompaniment of music and the firing of cannon. The toasts indicate the temper of the celebration. They paid respects to "The Day we celebrate"; "The President of the United States"; "Our National Independence"; "Gen. George Washington" (drunk standing); "The Present Administration"; "Domestic Manufacturing"; "The arrival of the first boat on the Ohio Canal"; "Bunker Hill—Rather small, but rugged and steep, it cost the British sweat to climb it"; "Canals and Roads—The favorite policy of Ohio—May their construction progress, until boats may glide and wheels roll, unobstructed to every part of the American Continent"; "The Heroes of the Revolution"; "The Fourth of July, 1826—The day that bore witness to the mortality and immortality of Adams and Jefferson"; "Greece—May the Laurels, now watered by the tears of her widows and orphans, e'er long crown her victorious Heroes"; "The Governor of the State of Ohio."

Governor Allen Trimble then spoke briefly and offered a toast to "Education, Internal Improvement, and domestic Manufactures." Alfred Kelley paid tribute to the people of Ohio for their accomplishments despite their youth, poverty, diversity and sectional jealousies, and proposed his toast to "The PEOPLE of the State of Ohio." Then there were eight volunteer toasts to complete a jovial evening.

The opening of the canal was an occasion of such transcendent importance that one celebration was not enough. While the officials were enjoying the festivities just described, the Mechanics and Farmers were conducting their own ceremonies. Their secretary, Ahimaz Sherwin, Jr., had issued a call through the *Herald* for their group to assemble at eleven o'clock in front of the Franklin House. Led by their Marshal of the Day, Colonel Williams, and preceded by the Euclid Rifle Company in full uniform and a "large and well-selected band of musicians," they marched through Superior Street to the Square, then up Ontario to a bower erected on the high bank of the river, overlooking the basin of the canal and the Cuyahoga Valley. The band played, Reverend Mr. Sizer of the Methodist Church offered the prayer, Ahimaz Sherwin, a survivor of the battle of Bunker Hill, read the Declaration of Independence, Samuel Starkweather gave the oration before the "largest audience so far assembled in these parts," the band struck up "Hail, Columbia!" and the crowd marched through Bank, St. Clair, Water, and Superior streets back to the Franklin House for the Mechanics and Farmers dinner and ball.

Their festivities followed the pattern of the governor's party over at the Belden. They had music, cheers, and "salvos of artil-

lery." Their list of toasts was much the same, but they added one
to "The Farmers and Mechanics—The mainspring and support
of our happy republic, (three cheers)"; and they closed with one
to "The Ohio Canal—Serpentine in its course, embracing within
its coils, the most productive regions of Hog and Hominy, (four
cheers)." After these toasts, "and at a seasonable hour," many
of the company, with wives, daughters, and sweethearts, embarked
on the *Sun of Cleaveland* for an evening ride on the canal.

Goods of all kinds began immediately to flow in and out of Ohio.
During the rest of this first season, the tolls amounted to $1,500.
In 1828, the first full season, they reached $4,000. The next year
they mounted to $27,000. By 1833, when the full 333 miles of
the Ohio and Erie Canal were open from Cleveland to Portsmouth,
they swelled to $136,555.70. The tolls were moderate: seven and
a half mills per thousand pounds per mile for most articles; one
cent for certain selected items such as feathers, brooms, writing
paper, and ginseng.

The toll list itself tells a fascinating story about the wants and
the products of our ancestors. The rate sheet lists over a hundred
items transported on the canal. Wheat, stone, coal, wool, and
homespun head the list in volume, but they are followed closely
by pig iron, lumber, ashes, flour, butter, lard, pork, cheese, tobacco, and whisky. Farther along we observe with interest the
canalboats were hauling horns and horntips, "cattle's tails," tombstones, clocks, pot and pearl ashes, and oysters.

The report of 1825 had estimated the cost for the Ohio-Erie at
$3,081,880.83. The actual initial cost was $4,224,539.64. It was
a remarkable achievement. No precise surveys had been made to
estimate the exact amount of excavations, cuts, and fills. Prices
rose steadily from 1825 through 1833. And nearly three quarters
of a million dollars of the excess went for new branches and feed-
ers, for modifications of plans and changes of location "to sustain
local interest," for additional embankments, for filling and secur-
ing the canal after it was accepted from the contractors, and for
repairs.

Tribute for this accomplishment goes to many men, but to no

one man in greater measure than to Alfred Kelley. He gave up his law practice to work for a mere three dollars per day to oversee the work. He impaired his health by continual exposure and overexertion for seven or eight successive years to achieve this dream of a transportation system which would bring greatness to Ohio. In his letter of resignation, dated at Columbus, January 24, 1834, he wrote:

As the canals are now so nearly finished, and as the successful execution of the public works in which we have been engaged, their widely extended benefits and increasing profits, have settled public opinion in their favor, I can now retire from active service without discredit to my motives, or injury to the public.

The optimism inspired by the opening was turned to discouragement and despair for a few weeks in July and August 1827. One of the worst epidemics of typhoid fever in Cleveland's history scourged the intrepid citizens just at the moment when they thought they saw a bright future opening before them. Nearly everybody was sick. Seventeen died in two months. Business was halted. Many thought of leaving the unhealthy location. They were sure that the canal basin bred the epidemic. "The whole corporation," said Asa Sprague, "could have been bought for what one lot would now cost." Sprague himself closed up his shop for two months and went about from home to home to care for the sick and their languishing business.

Their trouble, of course, was not the new canal basin but the stagnant Cuyahoga River mouth in the Flats and the contaminated water supply. The citizens got their drinking water from their own wells in their back yards. They bought water for washing at twenty-five cents for two barrels from Benhu Johnson, a wounded war veteran who hauled it up from the river. Cleveland had been from the beginning a sickly place. Melish had been downhearted about it as he turned his gaze from the clean, cool beauty of the open lake to the foul river below the settlement. He wrote in his journal that the mouth of the river is choked up by a sand-bar which dams up the water, and prevents it from having a free passage. It stands in a deep pool, two or three miles long; and the water being stagnant, and contaminated by decaying vegetables, afflicts the inhabitants on its margin with fever and ague. . . . The smell was almost insufferable.

Ships could not come in from the lake. Clinton had to be rowed in from the *Superior* in a yawl. Isham A. Morgan, an early settler, remembered that the outlet was at times "completely barred across with sand by storms, so that men having on low shoes have walked across without wetting their feet."

The opening of the canal made it imperative that the channel be cleared so that commerce could flow freely in and out of the Cuyahoga.

The river makes a series of *S* curves as it nears the lake at Cleveland. Early maps show it making a final right-angle turn to the west a few yards before it reaches Lake Erie. This old river bed is still clearly defined. Even without the barrier of the sand bar, ships would have encountered trouble entering the Cuyahoga through this channel because of its tortuous windings. What was needed was a channel straight into the lake on a tangent with the last curve. With Congressional aid of $5,000 in 1825, and another $10,000 grant in 1827, Cleveland built a 600-foot pier out into the lake and cut a channel across the narrow neck of land at the bend.

The procedure was imaginative. Under the supervision of Major T. W. Maurice of the U.S. Engineering Corps, workmen dammed up the river at the bend during the dry season, and outlined a straight new passage into the lake. Then the rains came. As the water rose and gathered pressure, it was diverted by the dam and assaulted the neck of the isthmus. It tore through it with great force and quickly washed away a fair channel. Ahaz Merchant's map of Cleveland, 1835, shows the discarded old river bed and the new ten-foot deep channel going out past the breakwater pier and beacon light into deep water in the lake. The effect of these improvements was immediate. The sickness rate declined. Traffic began to flow in and out of the Reserve through its capital port.

Soon the lake vessels were making as many as 2,000 calls each year into the mouth of the Cuyahoga River at the terminal basin of the canal. The curve of prosperity began to climb. That curve is jagged with temporary panics and setbacks, but its movement has been steadily upward since Cleveland finished its sad task of burying its dead in the summer of 1827.

The curve was given another boost by the construction of the feeder canal across the Reserve from Youngstown, Niles, and Warren to Akron. It was officially known as the Pennsylvania and Ohio Canal, though it was more commonly called the Cross-Cut or the Beaver Canal. We observe that the Ohio canals ran north and south to connect the lake and the river. This purpose was natural and right for the times, but we observe also that the development of the country was not on a north-south but an east-west axis. In order to serve its full purpose, therefore, the canal system would have to tap adequately the interior of the Reserve.

Agitation began early for a canal to link Akron with the Warren-Youngstown area. This area exceeded Cleveland in prosperity and expectation prior to the canal era. The testimony is universal. Judge Rufus P. Spalding made a two-day journey from Warren to Cleveland by horseback in 1823. He wrote:

At that time, the village of Warren, where I lived, was considered as altogether ahead of Cleveland in importance; indeed, there was very little of Cleveland, at that day, east and southeast of the Public Square. The population was estimated at four hundred souls.

The first bank in the Reserve, and one of the first in Ohio, was located in Warren—the Western Reserve Bank, 1812. Cleveland got its first bank—the Commercial Bank of Lake Erie—in 1816. The secret of this early prosperity was, of course, the easy proximity by water to Pittsburgh, and the Ohio River traffic.

The surveys showed that this thriving Mahoning Valley could be readily joined to the Ohio-Erie Canal by digging a canal from the Akron summit through Cuyahoga Falls and Kent, across the Ravenna summit, past Cyclone, Newton Falls, Leavittsburg to

Warren, and then down the river to Niles and Youngstown and on to Beaver and Pittsburgh. The enterprise was begun in 1836 as a private business venture, but with the credit backing of the State of Ohio. Following its policy of stimulating internal improvements, the state advanced credit to this project of approximately $450,000. The canal was ninety-three miles long and it was ready for service in 1840. Though it carried the usual articles in demand in the Reserve or produced by its citizens, its unique and far-reaching effect on the nation's economy was the introduction of coal to households, blacksmith shops, and factories, steamers, and railroad trains.

In 1828, the year after the canal began to operate across the Reserve, Henry Newberry shipped a load of coal down to Cleveland. He drove it around the town all day in a wagon trying without success to persuade the citizens to buy it for their stoves. The only person who would try it was Philo Scovill, manager of the Franklin House, who burned it in his barroom stove. Perhaps that was a favorable place to demonstrate its usefulness. At any rate the demand increased steadily after Scovill laid his first fire with it. The reports show that 49,131 bushels of coal came down the canal to Cleveland in 1833, the year the canal was opened to the Ohio River. Then a few of the lake vessels began to use it, Buffalo sent in orders for it, and housewives decided to burn it. With the opening of the Pennsylvania-Ohio Canal the demand for coal rose as cheap transportation became possible. Over half a million bushels came in to Cleveland in 1844, and, with the opening of the Brierhill Mine, owned by Governor David Tod and others, near Youngstown in 1845, the receipts at Cleveland immediately jumped to a million bushels. James A. Garfield's much-publicized experience as a "bower"—making the locks ready, getting the boats through, trimming the lamps, etc.—was on this canal. He worked for two months during the summer of 1848 at fourteen dollars a month. He said that he hauled "240 tons of stone coal and forty tons of iron to Cleveland and 52 tons of copper ore, 150 barrels of salt, 10 thousand laths and 1000 feet of lumber from Cleveland to different places along the canal." Much of the coal came from the governor's mine. The first trip to Pittsburgh took eleven days.

In addition to opening up the commerce lanes for farm produce, therefore, the canals made possible the flow of coal to the lake just at the moment when manufacturing was beginning and when William A. Otis was founding the first ironworks (1840) in Cleveland —portent of the meeting of coal and iron which was to lift this port to its position of eminence. For another fifteen years the canals hauled the freight in and out of the Reserve in ever-increasing quantities. By that time the developing railroad system was in a position to divert traffic to the cars, and, by its growing network, to serve a wider area. Rates on the canal were reduced to meet this competition. They fell lower and lower until they were exceeded by the operating and upkeep costs. Canal traffic was slow as a walking horse; railroads were gaining speed year by year. The country was in a hurry, and in that race the rails won out. The state began to abandon portions of its canals in 1863. In 1872 it gave to Cleveland a strip of three miles of the Ohio canal in the Flats. The grant included the terminal. It was promptly turned over to a railroad. Canalboats had to be towed for two miles on the Cuyahoga River by tugs to get into the city to load and unload. The Mahoning Railroad acquired the crosscut canal, killed off its traffic, and let out the water. In their enthusiasm for the steam roads, the people of the state were quite willing to treat the canals, which they had built with such enthusiasm, as expendable on the upward curve of American prosperity.

Today you would have to search carefully to find the traces of the Pennsylvania and Ohio Canal. But the section of the Ohio-Erie across the Reserve is, as we have noted, still intact as a museum piece to remind the present generation of the prodigious labors of their forefathers. It is not a part of our story to tell how the state lands along the canals were usurped, and even sold by the usurpers to other private individuals; how the railroads encroached upon them; and how the state, through an able commission, adjudicated the claims and brought order into a tangled

mess. It saved a few strips which it placed under the jurisdiction
of the Board of Public Works. The Board leased the section in the
Reserve for industrial use. The canal is now more valuable for
the water it supplies to Akron and Cleveland industry than it
would be for hauling their products in an age of fast trains and
trucks.

It is a rewarding experience in re-creating the history of the
Reserve to follow the old canal down into the Flats to the point
above the Central Viaduct where it now disappears. But if you will
tramp on through the underbrush and climb over the refuse dumps
under the bridge on the east side of the river, you can trace its
filled-in channel and the humps of its banks right down to its final
and complete disappearance among the railroad tracks and the
roaring industry of modern Cleveland. You look up to the graceful Terminal Tower on the Public Square, where the trains come
in from all points east, south, and west; you glance down the river
to the great lake freighters from the north moored to the Cuyahoga
wharves; you watch the endless stream of automobile traffic whiz-
zing east and west over the big bridges—all carrying people and
produce in and out of the Reserve. And then you contemplate
once more the narrow, shallow trickle of canal waterway constructed with such vision and effort by Alfred Kelley and his
contemporaries—and at that point your reflections are your own.

CHAPTER ELEVEN

BUSINESS AND BANKS

W<small>E HAVE</small> been following the young men from New England with their wives and families as they moved hopefully into the Reserve. Their settlements are still sparse and widely scattered; miles of forest lie between them, and they are more separated than connected by the morass of stump-strewed tunnels through the trees which passed for roads. These fine, ambitious, hard-working people had followed their dream to the great west. They had cleared their piece of land, planted it with seed, and built their cabins. They had done what they knew how to do, and what they thought was required of them. But it was not enough. They looked for their rewards, but the rewards did not come, or came too frugally. They could not get ahead. Few of them had any cash, any hard money, any negotiable credit. They seldom saw any money from one year's end to the next. They were lucky if they raised enough to pay their taxes. The mortgage structure was burdensome. Transportation was urgently important, but it was only one step in the series necessary for prosperity. They needed banks as much as they needed canals and roads. They had to develop a sound medium of exchange, one that would expand rapidly enough to serve the expanding population. There were 230,760 people in Ohio in 1810. There were 581,434 in 1820. That is an increase of over 150%. The Reserve itself grew proportionally. In that decade the nation as a whole increased only 33⅓%.

With the population booming, as it did before 1820, speculation in land was general. Some people thought they could turn an easy penny by buying up land on notes and mortgages, holding it on

liberal credit terms until it had doubled in value, and then unloading at the top of the boom market. But the economy of the
nation, and of Ohio, was too unstable and too poorly supported by
cash reserves for these operations, and the boom-bust cycle re-
volved giddily. It was called a panic in those days. In 1816 wheat
was selling for $1.50 per bushel. In 1817 it fell to 75 cents. And
in 1820 and 1821 it dropped to 20 cents. In 1819, after the U.S.
Bank had withdrawn its specie from the Ohio banks, prices fell so
low that they failed to pay transportation costs. Land was for a
time unsalable. Flour was offered at $1.00 a barrel, whisky at 15
cents a gallon, and sheep and calves at $1.00 per head. A bushel
and a half of wheat would buy 1 pound of coffee, a barrel of flour
would buy 1 pound of tea, and 12½ barrels of flour would buy "a
yard of superfine broadcloth . . . if the farmer will sell his flour,
bacon, and whiskey to somebody else and get the cash, but the
merchant will not take produce in payment." Those people who
were unlucky enough to be sold out at marshals' and sheriffs' sales
had to see their possessions all but given away. The newspapers of
the time reported heartbreaking news. At one sale "a handsome
gig and very valuable horse" were sold for $4.00, "an elegant side-
board" for $3.00, and "a fine Brussels carpet and two Scotch
carpets" for $3.00.

This was a rough period for the new settlers in Ohio and in the
Reserve. Lacking adequate transportation and cash as they did,
they had to supply their minimum wants somewhat crudely from
local resources. Their necessity fostered invention. One of the
pleasures in visiting the museums in the Reserve is the admiration
we feel for the ingenuity of these pioneers in improvising to satisfy
their wants. We see at the Western Reserve Museum at Cleveland or at the beautifully kept museum at Burton choice examples
of the handicraft of men who were seldom expert artisans, but who
became under necessity fairly competent craftsmen. Here are
frontier-made chairs, tables, beds, and cradles; shoe benches and
churns; looms, spinning wheels, and combs; apple peelers, sausage
grinders, toasters, and trivets—all roughly but usefully made by
hand from crude materials on the Reserve.

These objects point up several facts about our story. Even the wealthier pioneers had to travel light, and the poorer families brought even less than minimum essentials. It was prohibitively costly to buy these things from the Eastern markets and have them hauled in. Few of the families would have had the cash to pay for them in any event. They had to rely on their own improvisations or do without. They were as completely as possible in modern times self-contained and self-sufficient. But such an economy inevitably condemned its members to a low material living standard, and the American economy was moving rapidly away from simplicity toward intense specialization and exchange.

The local handicrafts did stimulate manufacturing in Ohio at a very early date and laid the foundation for the diversified industrialization which has always been characteristic of Ohio and the Reserve. The settlers, however, were by no means content with their lot. They, too, held to the American dream of better things next year, better opportunities for the children than those enjoyed by the fathers and mothers. That was, in fact, the driving motive behind the migration in the first place. People wanted to get ahead, and they went west to find better opportunity for advancement. A crude log room with homemade furniture and implements was endurable as a camp for the first season or two, but always because there lay behind the hardships of this year the expectation of converting the log cabin into a kitchen for a neat frame house next year, and a bigger and better one a few years later. At no time have Americans felt that they have reached the proper economic level or standard of living, or felt content with the prospect of their children reproducing and reliving the pattern of the fathers in the manner of a French peasant, an Arab clan, or a Chinese gardener.

The two things that were holding back the development of the Reserve were transportation and a medium of exchange—money and credit. It would have been out of character for these pioneering Americans to fail to overcome these obstacles.

The complex story of the origin and growth of Ohio banks, of turnpikes, canals, and railroads, is rooted in this primary need of our forefathers and in their determination to progress and to succeed. We have just seen how with their energetic canal building they began to open transportation routes to market, though we must remember that the canal, useful as it was, was only a shallow channel across the middle of the Reserve—an area 120 miles wide. Of almost equal and central concern were the problems of creating banks and getting money and credit to do business with.

The point is insistent. An Ohio drover would get together a herd of cattle to drive on foot across the mountains into the feeding grounds at Chester and Lancaster counties, Pennsylvania, for the Eastern markets. The pace of the drove was slow. It took from thirty-five to forty days to make the trip. If the drover pressed his cattle into a month's trip, they bunched, got lame, and many of them had to be left behind on rented pasture until the next drove came through. Robert Murray of Burton, a noted drover, recorded that in 1832 he got from $25 to $50 a pair for oxen, and $10 to $15 a head for steers. The expenses of the trip amounted to from $1.50 to $2.50 a head. He might possibly get cash or goods to bring back with him and the transaction would be complete. He could pay his taxes, get some yard goods for his wife, buy some more cattle, and reduce his mortgage. Many new families in the Reserve managed to hold onto their farms and make a living in this way.

But if they were selling pork, butter, or cheese, the best and most accessible markets were the Ohio River towns or New Orleans. Harvey Baldwin and Royal Taylor and his brother Samuel of Ravenna bought several dairies at Bainbridge and Auburn in the 1820's and manufactured cheese and butter for this market.[1] Baldwin hauled 2,000 pounds by wagon to Beaver in 1820, transferred it to a pine skiff, and floated down to Wheeling, Marietta, Maysville, and Louisville, selling as he went. Taylor took thirty tons down the river in 1826. The trip required over six months. Their activities were typical of the day. Now it happened that many of these larger operators wished to buy in New York, Baltimore, or Philadelphia after selling in New Orleans, and for this

---

[1] Reserve cheese competed poorly with imported cheese in this period because of wild leeks in the pastures. All the dairy products were tainted with this disagreeable pungent plant until the land was finally fenced in and "sweetened."

three-cornered exchange they needed a smoothly operating system of banks to handle their transactions.

It took a half century of trial and error, of service and selfishness, speculation, fraud, and investment, to get a reasonably sound system of banking in operation. Ohio worked on the problem continuously. Almost every session of the legislature tried to improve the situation. It began with its first meeting. Recognizing the need, it chartered the first bank on April 15, 1803. The institution, known as The Miami Exporting Company, was granted the right to issue notes "payable to the bearer." The nature of the Ohio economy of the period is revealed in this item in a Cincinnati newspaper for July 21, 1806: "The Miami Export Company, will receive stall fed beef-cattle on foot, corn fed pork, tallow, lard in suitable kegs, flour and kiln-dried corn-meal inspected, cordage of particular descriptions, hemp, spunyarn, pot and pearl ashes and tobacco—towards the produce instalments of shares the approaching season . . ." The bank served the Cincinnati area very well and prosperously until the general collapse of the country dragged it under in the panic of 1818-1819.

The first bank in the Reserve was the Western Reserve Bank at Warren. It was chartered on February 20, 1812. Warren on the Mahoning River in the southeast portion of the Reserve was geared to Pittsburgh and the Ohio River trade and was at that time more thriving than Cleveland. The bank was capitalized at $100,000. Under its able president, Simon Perkins, it became a notable institution. It had for its stockholders and directors some of the most capable and progressive men in the southeast portion of the Reserve, including the great Elisha Whittlesey of Canfield. In the hard days of 1818, when banks all over the country were closing and the agents of the Bank of the United States were in Ohio trying to redeem the circulating paper in specie, the Western Reserve Bank was able to pay out $40,000, leaving only $10,000 unredeemed. Its position was so exceptional that the agents accepted the settlement. By the year 1835, when things were looking up in Ohio, this bank had accumulated a capital of $144,057, specie to the amount of $50,816, a circulation of $149,175, and loans and discounts of $232,115. It served its region well throughout the wild period of its existence—a period which experienced all the vicissitudes known to banking.

The second bank in the Reserve was chartered in Cleveland on February 23, 1816, under the "Bonus Law" of that year.[2] It was organized under the name of the Commercial Bank of Lake Erie with Alfred Kelley as president and Leonard Case, Sr., as cashier —two of the rising young men of Cleveland and future leaders in the Reserve and in the state. This bank was the beginning of Cleveland as the great banking center of the Reserve, and one of the centers in the state and nation.

The records of the Commercial Bank neatly penned in four large books, covered with brown leather, have been preserved. They are often on display in one of the cases in the east end of the great entrance hall of the Western Reserve Historical Society Library in Cleveland. They were presented to the Society in 1877 by T. P. Handy, cashier. He wrote on the flyleaf of one of the volumes his own brief firsthand account of the institution.

This ledger, with the two journals and letter-books, are the first books used for banking in Cleveland. They were made by Peter Burtsell, in New York, for the Commercial Bank of Lake Erie, which commenced business in August, 1816,—Alfred Kelley president, and Leonard Case [Sr.] cashier. The bank failed in 1820. On the second day of April, 1832, it was reorganized and resumed business, after paying off its existing liabilities, consisting of less than ten thousand dollars due to the treasurer of the United States. Leonard Case was chosen president, and Truman P. Handy, cashier. The following gentlemen constituted its directory:

Leonard Case	Alfred Kelley
Samuel Williamson	David King
Edward Clark	James Duncan
Peter M. Weddell	Roswell Kent
Heman Oviatt	T. P. Handy
Charles M. Giddings	John W. Allen
John Blair	

---

[2] This law provided that banks receiving a charter from the state should set apart for the state one share in each twenty-five of its capital stock. The dividends on the state's share should accumulate until the state owned one sixth of the total stock; thereafter it was to receive its share of the dividends. In return the banks were exempt from state taxes and their charters were good until 1843.

Its charter expired in 1842. The legislature of Ohio refusing to extend the charter of existing banks, its affairs were placed, by the courts, in the hands of T. P. Handy, Henry B. Payne and Dudley Baldwin, as special commissioners, who proceeded to pay off its liabilities, and wind up its affairs. They paid over to its stockholders the balance of its assets in lands and money, in June, 1844. T. P. Handy was then appointed trustee of the stockholders, who, under their orders, distributed to them the remaining assets in June 1845. Its capital was five hundred thousand dollars. The books were, prior to 1832, kept by Leonard Case, cashier.

These two banks at Warren and Cleveland were the only ones in the Reserve for the next thirteen years. The story of banking in the nation during those years is a sorry tale which we have no need to try to retell here. It is the story of the long and bitter fight over the United States Bank in Jackson's day, of wildcat banks, swindles, inflated paper, unauthorized shinplasters, of outright counterfeiting, of booms and panics. The Ohio banks were caught in the interlinking national operations. The system itself was defective. The most important asset of a new bank seemed to be a printing press. In many cases the stockholders had put in no money at all; they had merely given their promissory notes for the stock, and the banks had then issued bills on this promise. They were really borrowers rather than lenders of money. The Bank Commissioners of Ohio summed it up neatly in their report for 1842 when they said that

the great and fundamental error in the banking system may be traced to the want of individual liability of the directors and stockholders, to pay the debts they contract, and redeem the paper they put in circulation.—The same man, in his corporate capacity, might be poor, but, as an individual he might be rich; and his wealth, in a great measure, drawn from the profits or spoils of the corporation of which he was a member.

Our concern is with the more general problem of how the citizens of the Reserve worked their way through all this tangled web, in most cases keeping their honor and their solvency, to form and operate a system of banks that would meet the need of their expanding commercial enterprise. They needed more banks. The businessmen of Painesville petitioned the legislature to issue a charter for the Bank of Geauga. It was granted in 1829, and was capitalized at $100,000. That made three banks in the eastern portion of the Reserve, but none in the west. This omission was corrected in February 1831 when a charter was granted to the Bank of Norwalk, the growing town in the center of the Firelands. Its capital was $100,000. John Gardiner of Norwalk, later to become a noted banker in the Firelands and a promoter of railroads, was a clerk in this bank. The handsome Gardiner house, still in possession of the family, is on a spacious lawn on tree-arched West Main Street. Like other banks of the decade, its chief function was to issue notes to expand credit circulation. At one time it served twenty counties in north and central Ohio. The distress for money at this time was stated with withering irony by a Cincinnati writer. He said that the need was "greater than can well be imagined. . . . Money can be lent upon mortgages on good city property at from 12 to 15¢ when the security is unquestionable and worth at least 100% more than the amount loaned. . . ! "

The opening of the Ohio-Erie Canal, as we have seen, lifted Cleveland suddenly into prominence and importance as a trade and commercial center. Its new position was immediately reflected in the demand for wider banking facilities at this terminal port. On March 3, 1834, the Bank of Cleveland was chartered with capital stock set at $300,000. Within five weeks this authorized capital was oversubscribed by $93,200—a good omen for the Western Reserve. A Dayton newspaper commented:

The promptness with which the stock of this bank has been taken up, is a flattering indication of the continued prosperity of the country. . . . The time for opening the books was the most unfavorable that could be, yet with all the cry of pressure and panic, there seems to be no lack of money when a profitable investment is to be made.

On the same day—March 3, 1834—a second bank was chartered in the Firelands at the rising port city of Sandusky. The

Bank of Sandusky was capitalized at $100,000. The Western Reserve was now provided with six banks in five counties in 1835. Their total circulation was listed at $867,579 against specie of $241,394. The population figures are worth scrutiny. Trumbull County, served by Warren, had 32,130; Lake, served by Painesville, about 13,000; Cuyahoga, Cleveland, 18,440; Huron, served by Norwalk, 18,637; and Erie, Sandusky, about 12,000—a total of around 94,000. These figures look cold and dry, perhaps even forbidding, on the printed page. But they spring to warm human life when we see them as symbols of the vision and hard work of individual citizens of the Reserve trying to develop their land and find ways of doing business with one another.

In view of the many shortcomings of the system incorporated in the charters of these first banks, the legislature decided not to renew them when they expired in the early years of the 1840's. Many of them had been forced to close their doors and suspend payment at one time or another. Time and again the depositors had lost their money through bank failures. The newspapers of the entire period are filled with stories of collapses, worthless bank notes, and runs on the banks. The bank commissioners in their report for 1842 now declared that

public opinion is adverse to the present unrestricted system of banking . . . both the interests of the public and the future solvency of the banks would be better secured by the incorporation of new banks than by the renewal of the old.

After months of arduous study, of acrimonious debates and party divisions, the legislature of 1845 voted to wipe the slate clean. The expiration of the charters had left only eight authorized banks in the state in 1844. There were only two in the Reserve and both of them were in the Firelands at Norwalk and Sandusky. The statement, however, is misleading, for the situation was not so bad as it sounds. Actually several of the old banks were immediately reorganized. They died under one charter or one name and were reborn under a new charter and sometimes under a new name. The metamorphosis was so rapid in some instances that it is profitless to try to follow it. We note, however, that both the Bank of Geauga and the Western Reserve Bank were specially authorized to reorganize in 1845, and they continued to do business almost without interruption.

The new banking laws were framed largely by Alfred Kelley. He was continuing his great public service to Ohio by serving as chairman of the Currency Commission. In presenting the bill to the Senate in January 1845, his committee said that it

> entertains no doubt that a very large majority of the people of the State anxiously desire the enactment, by the present General Assembly, of some law authorizing the establishment of banks which will furnish them with a safe and convenient currency, afford reasonable facilities for obtaining money to meet the wants of commercial and manufacturing operations, and at the same time hold out proper inducements to those who have money to invest in banking institutions.—In framing this bill the committee have constantly in view the great landmarks of entire security to the bill holder, reasonable security to dealers with the banks, and proper inducements to the capitalist, whether great or small, to invest his disposable means in banking.

The bill was passed by a narrow margin. It provided for a State Bank of Ohio, capitalized at $6,150,000, with branches distributed according to plan throughout the state; and for a new class of Independent Banks. Five of the branch banks and six independent banks were located in the Reserve between 1845 and 1850. The banking act and the new charters made careful provision against the more obvious abuses of the old system which we have already described. A board of bank commissioners supervised the operations. Cleveland was represented by John W. Allen, a long-time associate of Kelley. He came out from Connecticut in 1825, aged twenty-three, studied law and was admitted to the Cleveland bar. He had been president of the village of Cleveland, mayor of the city, a state senator, and a member of Congress. He was prominent in banking as a director of the Commercial Bank of Lake Erie, and later as the first president of the Society for Savings. He was a leading figure in the early development of railroads in the state. He was a notable, but typical, example of the quality of men who were laying the foundations and building the superstructure of the state and the Western Reserve in these formative years of the second and third quarters of the nineteenth century.

Two of the new branch banks were located in Cleveland. The Merchants' Branch was organized in July 1845 with P. M. Weddell as president and Prentis Dow as cashier. It later became the Mercantile National Bank. The other was the Commercial Branch, organized in November, with William A. Otis, the ironmaker, as president, and T. P. Handy, whom we have met in the Commercial Bank of Lake Erie, as cashier. Its business was taken over by the Commercial National Bank when its charter expired in December 1864. Other branches were the Summit County Bank at Cuyahoga Falls, chartered in November 1845, the Norwalk Branch in May 1847, and the Farmers' at Ashtabula, in February 1848.

There were six independent banks in the Reserve: the Bank of Geauga, the Canal Bank and the City Bank of Cleveland, and the Western Reserve Bank at Warren, all chartered in 1845; the Sandusky City Bank, organized in 1846; and the Mahoning County Bank at Youngstown, chartered in 1850. Altogether they were able fairly satisfactorily to carry on the business of the Reserve through the mid-century and the Civil War.

In addition to these conventionally operated banks, the Western Reserve also acquired another banking institution of unique origin and purpose. In his centennial *History of Cleveland*, J. H. Kennedy wrote:

While there is much that might be said in high praise of all the banking institutions now under consideration, and while the majority of Cleveland banks have been managed with fidelity, honesty, and satisfactory results to their stockholders, it is permissible to make special reference to this one, which has made a remarkable record—especially as it was founded on what was, in those days, an experiment in western finance. The Society for Savings differs from most banks and savings and loan associations, in that it has no capital, and that its profits go to the depositors.

The *Cleveland Daily True Democrat* in 1849 carried a series of notices. On March 24 it announced that the "Bills to incorporate a Savings Institution, and also to incorporate a Mutual Insurance Company in this city, have passed both houses and are now laws. These institutions will prove of much benefit to our people." On June 2 it was reported that W. A. Otis, H. W. Clark, and S. H. Mather were appointed as a committee to draft bylaws for the corporation of the Society for Savings. On June 29 the paper announced: "The Society for Savings in this city incorporated by act of the last legislature, is now fully organized and will soon be ready to commence business. . . . The object of this society is to enable industrious persons to invest such part of their earnings as they can conveniently spare, to advantage." And on July 25, "The Society for Savings will be ready to receive deposits on August 1. Its offices are at 4 Bank St. Depositing hours from 5-7 PM Wed. & Sat."

Behind these statements lay an interesting story. One day in the summer of 1848 Charles J. Woolson was in the law office of Samuel H. Mather. They were both from New England and their conversation centered around their native state. They talked about the New England savings banks, the service they were rendering, and the success they were having. And then, like a good New Englander in the Reserve, Woolson said, "Why not have a savings bank in Cleveland? I believe one could be established here that would be a success and a great benefit to the community. Now, you think of this, and see some of our businessmen. I believe they will take an interest in it and be ready to aid in its organization."

Woolson's hunch was correct. Mather consulted a number of Cleveland men. They not only approved, but offered their active services. Senator F. T. Backus and Representative Leverett Johnson carried the proposal to the legislature, and on March 22, 1849, the act to incorporate the "Society for Savings in the City of Cleveland" was passed. The name was suggested by that of a similar institution in Hartford, Connecticut. It was designated as "a benevolent institution, without capital, managed by trustees without salary, in the interest of depositors only, to whom profits are paid, or for whose benefit they are accumulated and received." There were no stockholders, and the trustees had no personal interest in the funds except as they themselves were depositors.

Many prominent Cleveland men helped with the organization and direction of the business, including Mather and Woolson, William A. Otis, John W. Allen, J. F. Taintor, and Mayor Flavel W. Bingham. Allen was president, Mather secretary, and Taintor treasurer.

The office was a room at No. 4 Bank Street on the same corner where Kelley, Case, and their associates opened the first bank in Cleveland. The odd business hours noted by the paper—five to seven on Wednesday and Saturday from May to November, and four to six from November to May—were set to make it possible for Taintor to receive deposits after he had finished his work as teller in the Merchants' Bank. Mrs. D. E. Bond called on August 2 to make the first deposit in the Society. It was $25. During 1850, 131 people deposited a grand total of $9,537.99 with the Society. The expenses for the first 18 months were $47 of which $3.00 was for a sign.

These banking institutions of the mid-century, or their successors, have grown to such enormous size and they are now housed in such palatial quarters that we have difficulty in re-creating them as they were a century ago in the days of their beginnings. In the first years of its life the Society for Savings conducted its business in a small room at the rear of the Merchants' Bank. Here were housed also the offices of Mather and of an insurance company. When Taintor resigned early in 1852, Mather took over the job of treasurer. At the close of the day Mather would place the assets and the cash on hand in a long tin box and lock it up in the vault of the Merchants' Bank. Some evenings he would carry it home and place it under his bed for the night.

Under the managing leadership of these outstanding citizens, the idea of the savings bank gradually took strong hold on the people of Cleveland and of the Reserve. By 1855 the number of depositors had grown to 1,490 and their savings had reached $181,875.52. Two years later the Society moved to new quarters on Bank Street (West Sixth) in a ground-floor corner room of the Weddell House—one of the leading hotels in the west a century ago. It had been erected in 1847, and part of it still stands there

THE MORMON TEMPLE AT KIRTLAND

THE WILLIAMS HOUSE
Situated two miles north of Wellington

HARPER HOUSE (Shandy Hall)
Now the property of the Western Reserve Historical Society

on the northwest corner of Sixth and Frankfort. Lincoln stopped here on his way to his inauguration and spoke from the second-story balcony to a vast crowd gathered in the street below.

During the ten years the Society was quartered in the Weddell House the number of depositors grew to around 6,000 and their savings amounted to nearly $2,000,000. By that time the Society was able to put up its own building on the northeast corner of the Public Square. Still the number of its depositors soared and their savings mounted. When the Society moved into its present building on the west corner of the block in June 1890, 41,378 people had on deposit $19,145,276.60 with the Society for Savings. That is a fair index of the growth of the financial structure of the Western Reserve. We quote once more from Kennedy: "In a financial sense, the Society was long since counted one of the strongest and most successful of the banking institutions of the West."

The banking reforms which we have noted greatly improved the situation in the Reserve, but they did not end all the troubles. In the difficult decade preceding the outbreak of the Civil War, banks collapsed all over the nation. Some of the weaker institutions in the Reserve were caught in the train. Failures were common enough for the papers of the day to report them casually, stoically, and, at times, ironically. The *Plain Dealer* used above the frequent announcements in its columns a cut of a log cabin being blown to pieces sky-high—a picture which it had previously used during Harrison's Log-Cabin and Hard-Cider campaign in 1840. When the Canal Bank exploded like the log cabin in 1854, the *Plain Dealer* wrote:

About the Canal Bank, yesterday, there was not only a large, but a greatly interested crowd. The bill holders, who got the gold for their notes, were arrayed in smiles, and contrasted, most ludicrously, with the grim-visaged depositors, who got nothing.

A couple of incidents that grew out of this failure will help us understand the men and the temper of the time. Captain Grummage, who had finished a season sailing on the lakes, had just deposited in the bank all the money he had—$1,000. When he learned that the Canal Bank had failed, he got a gun, made his way into the bank, and ordered the cashier to give him back his money or be shot. He got the money, with no more questions asked either by the bank or the law.

Dr. H. C. Ackley, a trustee of the State Insane Asylum at Newburg, had deposited with the Canal $9,000 of the institution's funds. His own personal account was also with this bank. He made no issue over his own money, but he did demand the return of the state's funds to care for the hundred insane patients. His demand was refused. He thereupon swore out a writ of attachment, and, accompanied by the sheriff, went back to the bank once more. He asked for the keys to the vault. He was, of course, refused. Surrounded by an excited crowd of sympathetic spectators, the good doctor proceeded to smash open the vault. Sheriff Spangler helped. He called in some deputies, armed them with sledge hammers, and they broke down the brick work surrounding the inner vault. Bank officials could find no way to stop the demolition. All through the afternoon the sledge hammers fell against the vault. Finally that night the officials of the bank decided to capitulate to prevent further destruction. The doctor and the sheriff took the keys, opened the vault, and took away the money that was there—$400 in gold and $1,460 in bills.

CHAPTER TWELVE

THE MORMONS AT KIRTLAND

In the early nineteenth century the Western Reserve, like other portions of the country, was violent with religious fervor. Odd sects of every variety of belief and practice flourished among the lonely and isolated villages on the frontier. Larger brotherhoods, like the Baptists for instance, split off into numerous camps, each stressing some unique point of difference—Free-will Baptists, Six-Principle Baptists, Seventh-Day Baptists, United Baptists, etc. Some sects specialized in foot washing, some in jerking and rolling, some in unknown tongues, some in celibacy. They separated from one another on the basis of their differences. The Universal Church became a welter of antagonistic fragments and not a brotherhood of believers.

Alexander Campbell, a notable orator in frontier pulpits, believed that this fragmentation weakened the cause of the Kingdom. He proposed to unite the divergent sects on the simple, primitive plan of the early New Testament church. They would take for their creed the specific statements of faith and practice of the first church, and they would adopt the name of Christian, as the followers of Jesus were first called at Antioch. Every man should be able to agree to brotherly union on that solid platform. Campbell preached this doctrine widely and effectively throughout the Reserve and won many converts.

Campbell discovered, however, that the simplicity of such a creed was deceptive and open to a variety of interpretations and emphases. What, for instance, about communism as practiced by the first Christians? The book of Acts was disturbingly specific

131

on the point. In the second chapter it recorded: "And all that believed were together, and had all things common; and sold their possessions and goods, and parted them to all men, as every man had need." Should this practice be adopted as a part of the present-day Christian church? And was the second coming of Christ imminent as the early Christians believed?

Alexander Campbell said no to both questions. The most brilliant of his converts, Sidney Rigdon, said yes. And Rigdon happened to be the most popular and successful evangelist in his new brotherhood on the Reserve. He was thirty-seven years old in 1830, a serious, handsome man, given to periods of brooding and susceptible to the more esoteric experiences of fasting, swooning, and seeing visions. He broke with Campbell over the issue of communal property. Many believers followed his leadership. He led them to Kirtland where they founded a colony with communal property. Instead of uniting the Christian sects, Campbell had created two more.

Among Rigdon's own converts to the Campbellite faith was a volatile young man of twenty-three named Parley Pratt. He was immediately touched with the vision and himself became a zealous evangelist. He went about preaching the new gospel. He decided that he should go off to New York to propagate the faith. The region around Palmyra where he went was, at that moment, kindled with spiritual excitement. It was the holy ground of the Smiths and the rising new sect of Mormon. The strange, God-smitten young Joseph Smith, wandering among the hills of Palmyra in 1823, had been guided by the spirit to a spot where there was revealed to him, and to him alone, a lost scriptural record of Mormon and a new dispensation recorded on plates of gold. To him also, and to him alone, was divulged the secret of its translation. Joseph, though unlettered and unlearned, labored for two years and rendered into English the sacred *Book of Mormon*. It was published at Palmyra in 1830. It became one of the pillars for the new brotherhood to be known as the Church of Christ of Latter-day Saints. A small band of believers quickly formed around Joseph Smith. They too were zealous missionaries. Among them was Joseph's older brother Hyrum. And it so happened that Parley Pratt, who had gone to preach to the New Yorkers, stayed to listen to Hyrum. He was seized with conviction and converted again—this time to Mormonism. And with augmented fervor he turned right around and went back to Ohio to win over the Campbellites to this still newer revelation. He arrived in the Reserve shortly after Rigdon's feud with Campbell and the founding of the Kirtland colony of communal Christians.

Rigdon, as it turned out, was in a softened and receptive state of mind. He listened attentively to the amazing story as told by the bubbling Parley Pratt: how Joseph Smith had been guided to the golden plates, how he was given the secret of their language, how he made the *Book of Mormon,* how he formulated the articles of faith and became the prophet of Mormonism. It was a remarkable and complicated story, but it was confirmed by an angel of the Lord who appeared before Rigdon; he believed, and was converted and baptized in the faith. Again his colony trusted his leadership and followed him into the new religion. Thereupon Rigdon made his own pilgrimage to New York to see the Prophet face to face. It was a dramatic meeting of two unusual and strangely different men: Rigdon a learned man, a scholar, and already established as one of the great preachers of his day; Smith an ignorant man, only twenty-four years old, still unsure of himself and feeling his way. Smith was inwardly flattered and magnified by the homage of this noted religious figure from the Western Reserve who now presented himself as Smith's follower. He welcomed Rigdon. He humbly confessed that the Lord had called him to be His prophet because he was "unlearned and despised." He invited Rigdon to investigate for himself all the wretched calumnies and scandals through which Smith had already passed, and to read his new *Book of Enoch,* a revelation concerning the city of Zion, the perfect city of God. The irrepressible Rigdon investigated, believed, and accepted, and became the number-two man in the forming organization of the Mormons.

When two such powerful personalities meet and form a union, however, neither is obliterated, for each has a corresponding impact on the other. Rigdon accepted Smith as his prophet, but Joseph Smith also fell under the influence of Sidney Rigdon. Rigdon persuaded him to leave New York and transplant his church to the Reserve at Kirtland. His urgings were supported by a vision and a revelation to the Prophet in which God commanded the community to go to this region on the east of the Promised Land, a land flowing with milk and honey. And thus it came about that the Western Reserve of Connecticut became for most of one colorful decade the home of the Mormons during their critical, formative period.

In January 1831 Rigdon drove the Prophet in a sleigh from New York to the Reserve. They pulled up in the snow at Kirtland in front of Gilbert and Whitney's store. With his generally infallible sense of drama befitting a Prophet, the tall, striking young Joseph Smith jumped out of the sleigh and marched impressively and confidently into the store, straight up to Whitney, a total stranger, and stunned him with the greeting, "Newel K. Whitney! Thou art the man!" Whitney replied that he had no idea who was addressing him. "I am Joseph the Prophet. You've prayed me here, now what do you want of me?"[1] Whitney took Smith into his house, and became one of his devoted and lifelong followers.

Joseph Smith found gathered about Rigdon in the vicinity of Kirtland about one hundred and fifty converts, most of them reasonably prosperous landowners. Their confidence in Rigdon led them to accept Smith as their Prophet and Rigdon as the first minister of Mormonism. About fifty of the New York families left such little property as they possessed and followed Smith to the "Stake in Zion." They preached and proselyted along the way, and entered Ohio with songs and prayers and millennial rejoicings. Their arrival at Kirtland, and the emotional orgy among them and Rigdon's flock which followed, created a furor among the nonbelievers of the region.

We have a graphic picture of the activity of this period from the pen of a neighbor and eyewitness, Eber D. Howe, founder and editor of the *Painesville Telegraph*. He wrote:

---

[1] Fawn M. Brodie, *No Man Knows My History: The Life of Joseph Smith, the Mormon Prophet*, New York, 1945, p. 98.

They pretended that the power of miracles was about to be given to all those who embraced the new faith, and commenced communicating the Holy Spirit by laying their hands upon the heads of the converts, which operation at first produced an instantaneous prostration of body and mind. Many would fall upon the floor, where they would lay for a long time, apparently lifeless. They thus continued these enthusiastic exhibitions for several weeks. The fits usually came on during or after their prayer meeting, which was held nearly every evening. The young men and women were more particularly subject to this delirium. They would exhibit all the apish actions imaginable, making the most ridiculous grimaces, creeping upon their hands and feet, rolling upon the frozen ground, going through with all the Indian modes of warfare, such as knocking down, scalping, ripping open and tearing out the bowels.

At other times, they would run through the fields, get upon stumps, preach to imaginary congregations, enter the water and perform all the ceremony of baptising. Many would have fits of speaking all the different Indian dialects, which none could understand. Again, at the dead of night, the young men might be seen running over the fields and hills in pursuit, as they said, of the balls of fire, lights, etc., which they saw moving through the atmosphere. Three of them pretended to have received permission to preach, from the skies. One of the young men referred to freely acknowledged, some months afterwards, that he knew not what he did for two or three weeks.

Howe published his observations in 1834, three years after the arrival of the Latter-day Saints, in a book called *Mormonism Unveiled.*

The news of the Mormon migration into New Connecticut headed by the Prophet himself, the man who had converted the great Sidney Rigdon, spread far and wide. People from all around came to watch their religious ceremonies. Kirtland on its hill above the rugged and beautiful Chagrin River Valley swarmed with arriving converts and the idly curious. Some who came only to mock were stunned by the Prophet's miracles and remained to join the brotherhood. The New Testament, of course, has much to say about miracles and lays considerable stress on Jesus's power to perform them and on his transfer of that power to his apostles. Joseph Smith had been anointed with this power.

He gave an awe-inspiring demonstration of it when the Reverend Ezra Booth, a Methodist minister on the Reserve, brought a group to Kirtland to hear the Prophet. Among them was Mrs. John Johnson of Hiram, about thirty miles southeast of Kirtland. Her right arm had for years been paralyzed and useless. As the conversation with Smith turned inevitably to the subject of miracles, one of the party pointed to Mrs. Johnson's arm and asked Smith if he, or anyone on earth, had been given the power to heal her. Smith remained silent for a long time. Then, according to authentic report, he walked to the afflicted woman, took her hand, and said, "Woman, in the name of the Lord Jesus Christ, I command thee to be whole!" He said no more, turned, and left the room. The startled company turned their eyes on Mrs. Johnson. She lifted up her arm with ease and from that moment forward, it is said, had full and complete use of it. Reverend Booth and the Johnson family counted this a revelation of God and were immediately converted to Mormonism. The news of this miracle spread, and still more converts flowed into Kirtland from New York, New England, and Canada. The colony grew and extended over the rolling hills and valleys around Kirtland.

Smith now began to show his remarkable powers of organization and leadership. It had never been his intention to make the Reserve the center of his church. Kirtland was to be only an intermediate way station on the road to the real Zion. He revealed to his people that the holy city of God would be created at Independence, Missouri. To this end he had sent forth his emissaries into the Missouri frontier to prepare a place and found a colony. And while Smith was molding the converts into order at Kirtland, the brothers in Missouri were struggling to prepare a better place. They had their troubles. The nonbelieving settlers in Missouri resented the Mormons. Tension mounted as the colony grew. Then incensed and antagonistic mobs began to use violence and commit arson against them. When this failed to dislodge the Mormons, the mobs drove them away by force. These heartbreaking experiences caused Smith to postpone his plans for going farther west and led him to make more secure the venture in the Reserve.

Eventually the magnificent temple which he envisioned would rise in Missouri, but in the meantime there must be erected here at Kirtland a worthy and imposing house of worship at the temporary center of Mormonism. It would dramatize the growing spiritual power and numerical strength of the movement, and it would give the Prophet a proper setting for his leadership of his church. Like all the important steps in the life of Joseph Smith, the decision to erect the temple at Kirtland came to him as a directive from God through a revelation to His Prophet on May 6, 1833. This one was quite specific, including, as in the case of the Ark, exact dimensions for the structure. Its auditorium was to be fifty-five feet wide and sixty-five feet long. The building was to be three stories high, crowned with a spire that would be lifted high into the heavens and visible throughout the countryside.

The site was admirably selected—on the level crown of a high bluff overlooking the rugged valley of the east branch of the Chagrin River. It dominates the sky line from all approaches to the village. The grounds surrounding it are spacious and well kept. Smith either had architectural visions or some good carpenters, artisans, and stone masons among the converts, for the building has stood since the middle 1830's and its workmanship throughout is still substantial and pleasing. Joseph Bump, a convert from Silver Creek, New York, was the master builder, but he got instructions each evening from the revelations of Smith for the next day's work.

The Mormons, struggling to make a bare living for themselves, began work on the temple with some reluctance. It was a communal enterprise, financed by tithes and built by the brotherhood. Each man donated one day of work each week. The Prophet himself was foreman in the quarry. Those who had teams hauled the stone from the quarry to the building site. The others got out the stones, prepared them for use, and erected the walls. As the foundations rose layer by layer and the building took form, their enthusiasm kindled. Here would be no common frontier meeting-house, but an enduring mansion to God in the wilderness and a monument to Zion. Under the preaching of Rigdon it became the symbol of the welfare of the Church and the salvation of the world.

The building of the temple was begun with the laying of the cornerstone in July 1833. It went forward under the contagious enthusiasm and exhortation of Smith and Rigdon. The ecstatic Smith poured out prayers and blessings as the stones were brought up to the yard, hoisted to the rising wall, and swung into place. The emotional Rigdon would pace the walls at dusk, raising his hands and lifting up his face to Heaven while he invoked the choicest blessings of God on the temple and its builders. His emotions would overcome him, he would weep with joy and allow his tears to fall upon the sacred masonry. The womenfolk did their humble part. Heber C. Kimball wrote that

our women were engaged in spinning and knitting in order to clothe those who were laboring at the building, and the Lord only knows the scenes of poverty, tribulation, and distress which we passed through in order to accomplish this thing. . . . Almost all the sisters in Kirtland labored in knitting, sewing, spinning, etc., for the purpose of forwarding the work of the Lord.

Three years of toil went into the making of the temple, and when it was finished it was, as it has since remained, one of the most striking pieces of architecture in the Western Reserve. Joseph Smith's vision was strongly influenced by the New England builders of the late colonial period. When you see the tower from a distance, you suppose that you may find among the trees another characteristic white church facing the village green. Instead you see a temple individual in design and unique in its adaptation of a familiar pattern. It is two-stories-and-an-attic high with two rows of Gothic windows, and a row of dormers in the gently sloping roof. You may not notice at once that the walls are made of thick rough limestone because they are plastered over with faded blue stucco. The stucco was then marked, a little crudely, with lines in imitation of masonry. It is said that the women crushed glass and china to mix with the stucco to give the surface the glistening effect that is particularly noticeable when the sun falls upon it. Over the entrance doors and the large window centrally placed in the façade

above them are the elliptical arches common in colonial style
houses from Connecticut across New York into Ohio. Set off as they
are by two Gothic windows on each side over near the stone quoins
that form the corners of the building, they are arresting but not
inharmonious or displeasing.

You enter into a vestibule. A fine stairway at each end winds
engagingly up to the second and third stories. Under each of them
is a small vestry room. A courteous young member of the congregation will probably emerge to greet you and offer his services to
explain what you are about to see as you pass on through the vestibule into the apostolic floor. If you look only at the rows of pews
you will think you are in one of the old New England churches.
There are four rows of them—two in the central section, and one
across each of the two aisles. But the individuality even of the
pews is soon evident. They are really a series of stalls with mov-
able benches which may be turned to face the west or the east. The
stall doors can be locked from the outside. The pews, however,
are not likely to be the first things you will notice. Your eye will
be caught and held by the big central window with its elliptical
arch and by the unique arrangement of the pulpit for which it
forms the backdrop. And not the pulpit but the pulpits, for there
are twelve of them after the vision of Joseph Smith. They are
constructed in four tiers of three pulpits, each tier rising above the
one in front of it. Like the rest of the interior they are painted a
luminous white. Each is marked with gold initials indicating the
titles of the hierarchy of the priesthood who occupied them during
services. Two flights of steps, one on each side, give entrance to
the pulpits. Facing them are two blocks of elevated boxes, like
the choir boxes in other denominations, for lesser officials of the
church.

The ceiling over the central pews is arched like the big window.
Eight pillars along the aisles support the low flat ceiling over the
side pews. They are square but beautifully fluted. The brethren
hitched oxen to the large planes and drove them along the timbers
to carve out these grooves. These square, white, fluted and ornamented pillars, however, are merely the outer casing; they enclose

and decorate giant yellow poplar logs which run all the way up
from the basement to the attic. All the molding and carving are
particularly fine. Talbot Hamlin included this interior in his study,
Greek Revival Architecture in America, and called it "unusual in
its late use of extraordinarily rich Late-Colonial type detail."

Having contemplated all this loving effort to create on the Ohio
frontier a house worthy of the Lord, you turn to face back to the
east. And there you see against the same kind of window the same
banks of pulpits. You glance back to the west again to make sure
that you are not turned around. The pulpits and their arrangement
are identical except that those on the west are lettered *M* and those
on the east are lettered *A.* They symbolize the elaboration of the
hierarchy of the church and the new discipline which Smith had
introduced into the Order. Smith had been shrewd enough to see
that the uncontrolled behavior of his followers as described by
Eber D. Howe would bring his church into disrepute and ridicule;
and that the organization would be weakened, if not plunged into
chaos, if everybody saw visions and preached as he saw fit in
strange tongues. He tightened his central control over his followers by forbidding unauthorized and unordained converts from
preaching Mormonism. He did wish to preserve the enthusiasm
of his followers, however; and he made all of his male converts
members of the priesthood under his own supreme authority. He
conferred upon them appropriate titles drawn from the New Testament: apostles, bishops, elders, priests, deacons, and teachers; and
he arranged them into successive ranks up which the good and
faithful could hope to climb in influence and responsibility.

John the Baptist had appeared to Joseph Smith in a vision back
in New York to restore to him and his followers the Jewish order
of Aaron. Smith thereupon ordained the "Priesthood of Aaron."
The twelve ranking members of the Order occupied the east pulpits. If the meeting on the apostolic floor was temporal, the priesthood of Aaron presided and the faithful in the pews reversed their
benches and faced east. In another vision at Kirtland, Smith
received from God Himself the admonition to restore to the earth
"the higher order of Melchizedek." This enigmatic Melchizedek

is mentioned cryptically in Genesis as "the priest of the most high God," and the order is referred to in the Psalms: "Thou art a priest for ever after the order of Melchizedek." Paul in the epistle to the Hebrews had reasoned out a tenuous argument to demonstrate the superiority of this order over that of Aaron, and had shown that only Melchizedek and Jesus had enjoyed its privileges. Now the vision of Joseph Smith had elevated him and certain designated Mormons to its high mysteries. The west pulpits were occupied by the priests of this order. If the meeting was spiritual, if was conducted by the Melchizedek priesthood and the faithful in the pews turned their benches to the west.

After you have viewed the apostolic floor, the second or church floor seems less spectacular though the arrangement is much the same. The pulpits are plain, and the pews have a drop leaf at the front and back which could be raised and used for writing. In this room the converts were instructed and missionaries trained. The top floor is partitioned into ten classrooms for similar use. The temple cost $60,000. All the materials except the glass and the hardware were taken from the forests of walnut, white oak, and cherry and from the quarries in the vicinity of Kirtland.

The cornerstone had been laid on July 6, 1833, and it was now ready for dedication on March 27, 1836. The ceremonies must be in keeping with the extraordinary character of the enterprise. Smith planned them with care, giving attention to *décor* and minute stage business of the ritual. He called together his inner circle and drilled them in the technique of anointing the head with oil as practiced by Jesus and the apostles. He taught them how to pour oil into their left hand, to raise the right hand and intone the blessing, then anoint the subject and again pronounce appropriate blessings. Done in the proper pace with ritualistic cadence, the ceremony was impressive to the onlookers. Smith would go from room to room on the third floor of the temple where his elders were gathered together and drill them in the parts which they were to play at the actual dedication. The spirit of God came mightily upon them, and they felt the fire of the Holy Ghost aflame in their bones. They made a joyful noise unto the Lord.

The dedication was one of the memorable events in Kirtland. The brotherhood itself had grown to a thousand or more converts. People from the surrounding region came in. A thousand souls, it was said, crowded into the white-walled auditorium facing the twelve carved pulpits decorated with red velvet and stamped with gold letters to designate the rank of the occupant. Another thousand gathered round the doors outside in the spacious temple yard. The services began quietly in the morning. The Prophet offered a prayer of dedication. In the evening the women were excluded, 416 elders, priests, deacons, and teachers gathered in the temple, and the service rose in pitch. The Spirit descended and Smith urged the saints to let themselves go. George A. Smith jumped up and began to make glorious prophecies of the wonders to come. Then, Smith wrote in his journal:

All the congregation simultaneously arose, being moved upon by an invisible power; many began to speak in tongues and prophesy; others saw glorious visions; and I beheld the Temple was filled with angels, which fact I declared to the congregation. The people of the neighborhood came running together (hearing an unusual sound within, and seeing a bright light like a pillar of fire resting upon the Temple), and were astonished at what was taking place.

The frenzy continued for two days. The men stayed in the temple fasting and praying, prophesying, and seeing visions. The climax was Smith's transportation, like Elijah and Moses, into the Divine Presence. He ordered the veil to be lowered around his pulpit and that of Oliver Cowdery. Hidden from the awe-inspired congregation, they prayed in silence for a space of time. Then the veils were parted and the congregation saw the two men, transfixed, pale, shaken, gazing raptly toward Heaven. The Prophet began to speak:

We have seen the Lord. He was standing upon the breastwork of the pulpit, before us, and under His feet was a paved work of pure gold in color like amber. His eyes were as a flame of fire, the hair of His head was white like the pure snow. His countenance shone above the brightness of the sun, and His voice was as the sound of a great waters, even the voice of Jehovah, saying—"I am the first and the last, I am He who liveth, I am He who was slain, I am your advocate with the Father. Behold, your sins are forgiven you, you are clean before me, therefore lift up your heads and rejoice. . . . For behold, I have accepted this house, and my name shall be here!"

Smith continued to address the people in this vein for some time. Then he told how Moses appeared before him, and Elias, and Elijah, committing to him the keys of this dispensation and announcing that "the great and dreadful day of the Lord is near, even at the doors."

For days after these ceremonies the Saints lived in spiritual ecstasy as though the Kingdom were indeed at hand.

With rare exceptions, only the poor and the indigent took kindly to the communal doctrines of the nineteenth century. A few firmly and sincerely believed that the millennium was so near at hand that it was pointless to lay great value on worldly goods. The nineteenth-century sects in this respect paralleled the experience of the early church. The second coming was postponed day after day, week after week, year after year while the hard daily business of living and making a living went right on. The industrious brethren labored in the fields to bring in stores for the common use, and the idle and lazy brethren ate the fruits of this labor. Invariably, whether it was in the day of Saint Paul, who had to lay down the order that he who did not work should not eat, or in the day of Joseph Smith, this arrangement produced severe friction.

Rigdon urged Smith to give to his people a new revelation. It was called the United Order of Enoch. Under this order the brethren must consecrate unto the Lord by covenant and irrevocable deed all their properties to be administered by the bishop—Edward Partridge.[2] The bishop would then give back to the steward

---

[2] "Behold," said the Lord, "thou shalt consecrate all thy properties, that which thou hast unto me, with a covenant and a deed which cannot be broken, and they shall be laid before the bishop of my church." *Book of Commandments*, Chapter xliv, verse 26. Brodie, p. 106.

whatever was necessary for the support of himself and family. The surplus was church property to be used or distributed as the authorities saw fit.

Even in so devout a brotherhood, however, there was no way of getting around the differences between the rich and the poor. During the fervid hours of devotion in the temple, when thoughts were turned to Zion and visions of the millennium, all might be equal co-sharers in the kingdom; but in the hot afternoons of labor in the fields, to one swinging a scythe in the meadow or a cradle in the wheat, worldly property still held its temptations. The established Ohioans, who by their sweat had cleared the lands along the Chagrin River, had to place a great strain on their generosity to accept the New York emigrants and the converts from abroad. They did not take kindly to the command to hand over to the United Order of Enoch a deed to their land which they could not reclaim if their faith should waver—as in many instances it did. Some refused. As in all the other communistic colonies, the system broke down. It broke rapidly among the Mormons at Kirtland, and was formally abandoned on April 10, 1834. Thereafter the brethren were required only to give to the Lord their surplus after meeting their own needs.

The problem of dividing the property was a troublesome one which Joseph could solve only by another revelation. It was easy enough to hand back titles to farms where the original owner had continued to live and work while giving into the common storehouse the produce of the land. It was not simple in the case of the temple grounds, the new tannery and steam mill, and the print shop. The revelation awarded these properties respectively to Smith himself, Rigdon, and Cowdery. In addition, the church leaders got the properties on which they were living, and Joseph became the owner of two lots in Kirtland and a fine 140-acre farm with a good house on it near by. The generosity of the early converts who deeded away their land and gave their money gladdened the heart of the Prophet, himself a man with no property or substance. Ezra Thayer and Leman Copley gave at half value 1,000 acres on which the New York converts might settle as members of the United Order. Newel K. Whitney, who became a bishop in the church, made his store into a commissary for the Order. John Tanner, a wealthy convert who had sold his lands and had cash in hand, lent the church $13,000 to pay the mortgage on the temple, and made a personal loan to Smith of $2,000; the Prophet was never able to repay him and Tanner made the loan a gift.

There was never enough money, and bishops were hard pressed to find land or work for the stream of indigent converts who kept on coming to Kirtland. Smith went heavily into debt for goods to keep the Order going. He borrowed wherever he could. He got $350 from the Painesville Bank, $10,000 from Charles Holmes, $5,000 from Timothy Martindale, $1,150 from Winthrop Eaton, $3,000 from the Bank of Geauga. He also got $5,600 from Halstead Haines and Co., of New York, in addition to a credit for $60,000 worth of goods there, and another $30,000 worth in Cleveland and Buffalo. This extensive indebtedness was ultimately to bring disaster to the whole Kirtland enterprise, as we shall see, but the immediate effect of all this flow of money and goods was to give to Kirtland a breezy atmosphere of profit and boom.

As the inevitable day of reckoning came nearer, Smith tried to rescue himself and his church from financial ruin by setting up a bank. That was quite the thing to do in the 1830's. Banks were springing up all over the state and they seemed to be making money in huge quantity for everybody concerned. It was all very easy. Except for the expense of printing notes with the bank's name on them, and renting a banking office, almost no capital was required. In 1836 there were thirty-three chartered banks and nine unchartered ones issuing bank notes and doing business in Ohio. So great was the speculative boom in real estate in the mid-thirties that all these banks did not satisfy the demand for more and easier money. It was quite natural that Smith should conceive of the idea of a bank for his own brotherhood. He organized it early in November 1836 under the solid name of The Kirtland Safety Society Bank. He ordered a quantity of crisp new bills and notes from New York and Philadelphia engravers. He announced that its capital stock would be no less than $4,000,000. Subscriptions, secured by Kirtland real estate inflated to fantastic values, ranged from $1,000 to $500,000. At this time Smith valued his own holdings, consisting of the temple lot, the farm, and some other parcels at $300,000.

The bank opened in January 1837 when the bank notes arrived in Kirtland. Ominous news arrived from Columbus on the same day. The Ohio legislators got agitated with alarm over the uncontrolled banking practices in the state and nation. Disaster was certain if the condition continued unchecked. They observed that the circulation of the authorized banks had jumped over 70% in a single year, and that loans and discounts had jumped almost as far between 1835-1836. The legislature had petitions before it to establish banks in thirty-four places. Smith's petition for Kirtland was among them. The legislature, after due deliberation, refused to grant any further banking privileges until a sounder general position had been attained. The Kirtland Bank did not get a charter. This was the news that came to the Mormons along with their new notes.

The Mormons had already grown accustomed to persecution. Their natural reaction was that they were being discriminated against because of their religion. Smith thought of a way out of the impasse. He had stamped on the notes in very small letters "anti" before the engraved word "BANK" and "ing Co." after it, thus converting the company into "The Kirtland Safety Society antiBANKing Co." A large collection of these notes in various denominations may be seen at the Western Reserve Historical Society in Cleveland. The Mormons now had plenty of money. Smith paid off the big debts for the goods he had purchased. After the first few weeks of easy-money exuberance, people began to wonder about the security behind the circulating paper. Smith and Rigdon met this challenge by opening the bank vaults to the skeptical for inspection. There on display were rows of boxes, glistening with silver coin, and marked with the sign $1,000. All suspicions were temporarily allayed. The holders of the bank notes did not know that under the bright layer of silver was a box full of sand, gravel, lead, and scrap iron.

The inevitable run on the bank began a few weeks after the opening. New York banks refused Kirtland paper from the outset. Cleveland at first accepted it, and about $36,000 was circulating there before the break came. Rumor moves fast when a bank is under suspicion. Cleveland merchants stopped taking Kirtland bills. Holders of the bank's paper rushed in to redeem it in specie. There wasn't enough gold and silver to redeem even a fraction of the outstanding notes. The "antiBANKing Co." ceased payment and closed its doors. Outraged and incensed losers sought redress in the courts. Since Smith was operating the bank outside the law, he was subject to a fine of $1,000, and anyone presenting evidence leading to the conviction of a violator would receive a share of the fine. Smith was haled into court in March, tried, and convicted, despite his lawyer's plea that the bank was organized before the law was passed. At this point a trusted officer of the church, Warren Parrish, for a short time cashier of the bank, resigned his offices, left the church in bitterness and castigated the Prophet. The collapse was complete and disastrous.

Actually the fiasco at Kirtland was only a part of a larger, national picture. The entire country was rocked by the panic of 1837, which began on May 10 when the New York banks suspended specie payments. By the end of the month 800 banks were closed and the nation was in the grip of a severe depression. There was little consolation for Joseph Smith in the fact that his misery was being shared by others. Enemies, apostates, creditors turned upon him and closed in through the courts. Numerous suits were filed against him, he was arrested seven times, and saved from jail only by valiant efforts of his faithful followers who managed to raise $38,428 for bail. Others were not so faithful. Six of the twelve apostles rebelled against him. Many members left the fold in bitterness of spirit. All the petty hatreds and annoyances that had been accumulating flared up under the provocation of money and property. Some of the debts were settled, others went by default. Smith and the organization were bankrupt. The Prophet went away on a missionary journey and sent some of his sorely pressed brethren on a mission to England to relieve the tensions during this stormy period. But in his absence no miracle occurred, and he found his enterprise still in virtual ruin. A meeting of the brotherhood resulted in a schism and confusion. The rebellious members withdrew and set up their own congregation.

The persecution of Smith grew more bitter. Scandal, whispered about through several years, became open gossip and accusation. It centered about his personal life as well as about his management of the bank. In the eyes of his many enemies he became a carnal monster indulging in orgies of immoral relations with women. A new warrant for his arrest was issued. Smith felt now that the situation was hopeless. In January 1838 he prepared to flee from Kirtland. He must have relived all too vividly in those last threatening days his near-fatal sufferings at the hands of a riotous mob in Hiram.

In 1832 Smith had gone with Rigdon to the Johnson house in Hiram to revise the Bible. Feelings soon rose against him. The Johnson boys became disgusted and left the church. The Campbellite minister, Symonds Ryder, a man of considerable fame as an evangelist in the Reserve, had been converted to Mormonism because of the miracles wrought in the early days at Kirtland. His faith wavered, however, when his name was misspelled in one of Smith's revelations. He became one of the chief persecutors of his former leader. He led a mob to the house of John Johnson on Saturday night, March 24, 1832. They broke into the house and seized Smith and Rigdon. Smith was asleep in a trundle bed when the mob grabbed him. They tore off his clothes, beat him, and tore his skin. They cut his lips with a glass vial which broke when they tried to force it into his mouth. Then they smeared his body with tar and covered him with feathers from a pillow which they had ripped open. They dragged both of them out into the cold night, bumping them over the frozen ground, and finally left them unconscious in the field. Smith regained consciousness and removed some of the blood, tar, and feathers from his face and body. He crawled back to the house. His wife Emma fainted when she saw his hideous body in the doorway. The womenfolk scraped away the tar during the night and bound up his wounds. That morning, on the appointed hour of the Sabbath, Smith appeared before the Mormon congregation. Several members of the mob were there. They were amazed to see the Prophet, still more bewildered when he preached quietly and eloquently as though nothing untoward had occurred. The whole experience increased his prestige, and, despite the enmity that continually surrounded him, he was not again molested. The emotional Rigdon became insane for a time following the harrowing night.

Now in the winter of 1838 the bitterness had become so intense that Smith feared for his life. He had done all he could and it was not enough. He remembered the admonition of Jesus: "When they persecute you in one city, flee ye to another." He fled from Kirtland. Here are his own words:

A new year dawned upon the church at Kirtland in all the bitterness of the spirit of mobocracy, which continued to rage and grow hotter and hotter, until Elder Rigdon and myself were obliged to flee from its deadly influence, as did the apostles and prophets of old. . . . And on the evening of the twelfth of January about 10 o'clock, we left Kirtland on horseback to escape mob violence which was about to burst upon us under the color of legal process, and to cover their hellish designs and save themselves from the just judgment of the law. The weather was extremely cold, and we were obliged to secrete ourselves sometimes to elude the grasp of our pursuers, who continued their race more than two hundred miles from Kirtland, armed with pistols, etc., seeking our lives.

In this inglorious fashion Joseph Smith and Sidney Rigdon left the Reserve, and closed one of the strangest chapters in its religious and economic history. But Smith had fled one mob only to encounter another. He died in the Carthage, Illinois, jail under a rain of bullets from an attacking mob while awaiting trial on a charge of treason. A branch of the church accepted the leadership of Brigham Young, the Vermont painter and glazier who read the *Book of Mormon,* was converted, and came to Ohio in 1832 to pay homage to the Prophet and become his faithful follower and disciple. His polygamous rule was not accepted by the church at Kirtland. This congregation carried on in the tradition of Joseph Smith under the name of the Reorganized Church of Jesus Christ of Latter Day Saints. They claimed title to the temple on the grounds that they were the true continuation and descendants of the organization which built it, and that the Church in Utah was a fragment of the true Church. The Lake County Court of Common Pleas decreed in favor of the Kirtland church, and in 1880 legal title to the property passed to it. A large sign on the front of the temple proclaims these facts. There are about a thousand members of the Church in the vicinity of Kirtland. The temple, still standing serene and dignified among the trees on the bluff south of the Chagrin River, is well kept and unchanged. Only two other remnants of the days of Joseph Smith remain in the quiet crossroads village—the modest house of Hyrum Smith, and a part of one of the cottages across the street from the temple yard, now incorporated into a modern small apartment.

CHAPTER THIRTEEN

HIGHWAYS AND TURNPIKES

THE journalism in the Cleveland papers between 1830 and 1860 is not brilliant. Many of the columns must have been dull even to the readers of those days who got the papers fresh from the press. But as one perseveres, turning the fading pages of news about the weather, the shipwrecks and drownings, the coming and going of stagecoaches and distinguished visitors, the lawsuits and judgments, the price of wheat, corn, and hogs, the dilapidated state of the fences around the Public Square, the dust bowl and the boggy mire of Superior Street and Euclid Avenue, the need for street lighting, public water, sewage disposal, police and fire protection, the menace of cows and hogs on the street and the Square, the occasional robbery, rape, and murder, the growth of population, and the new homes, banks, commercial houses, and manufactures, the editorial and letter comment on the past, present, and future of the Reserve—as one turns the pages the prosaic bones of these columns begin to take on flesh, to come to life, to evoke, like a documentary film, a fascinating community of turbulent, living, breathing, struggling men and women. They are, in the turning of these pages, not dead, not static, but erect, leading their lives day by day, planning for the future, emerging, evolving from their isolated village on the Cuyahoga into the proud metropolis of the Reserve. Their vision is also on the goal of becoming one of the beautiful cities of America. And when the last page is turned and we reflect on the spectacle we have just witnessed, the recurring theme, like the basic melody in a symphony, is Roads, Roads, Roads—turnpikes, trams, rails—transportation—brotherhood, trade understanding through communication.

151

"Get the farmers out of the mud!"

Travel in the Reserve in the first half of the nineteenth century was a wearisome and hazardous business. We have recorded Melish's experiences on horseback as an early sample. The stump-cluttered mud bogs which he encountered along the township lines continued, with little improvement, to be the only highways interlinking the Reserve towns. The narrow trail from Youngstown to Sandusky, used in ancient days by the Indians and later hard-trodden by the pack horses of the early traders, was unsuited to wagons and only grew worse with traffic. Sleds were serviceable during the frozen winter, but the rest of the year it was a choice between clouds of dust in midsummer and axle-deep mud in spring and autumn.

Stagecoach travel was inaugurated around 1816 to connect Cleveland with Buffalo, Pittsburgh, and Columbus. The Buffalo line served the towns along the northeastern end of the Reserve. The Pittsburgh route led diagonally across the Reserve to Wellsville on the Ohio, where passengers transferred to a boat. The trip required thirty hours.

A turnpike company, under legislative charter, had constructed a clay toll road from Sandusky across the western edge of the Firelands to Columbus in 1834. We now drive this route in a couple of hours. The Reverend Mr. Read traveled over it the year it was opened. He had spent a stormy night at Sandusky in an unclean inn. He had found the lower element among the Sandusky citizens intemperate, and he "heard more swearing . . . than I had before witnessed." The town still had large pine stumps in the main street. He departed by stage before daylight. A heavy rain had poured in through the broken glass in the coach doors, the dirt had stopped up the drain holes in the floor, and the Reverend Mr. Read, stepping into the coach, splashed his feet in mud and water. He was the only passenger. For hours the only sounds he heard were "the call of the driver, the screeching of the wheels, and the song of the bull-frog." The wind blew in through the broken panes, and the side curtains flapped in his face. As for the condition of the new road, Read wrote with ministerial restraint:

All that had been intimated about bad roads now came upon me. They were not only bad, they were intolerable; they were rather like a stony ditch than a road. The horses on the first stages could only walk most of the way; we were frequently in up to the axle-tree, and I had no sooner recovered from a terrible plunge on one side than there came another in the opposite direction. I was literally thrown about like a ball. Let me dismiss the subject of bad roads for this journey by stating, in illustration, that with an empty coach and four horses, we were seven hours in going twenty-three miles. . . . Yet this line of conveyance was advertised as a "splendid line, equal to any in the States."

The minister did find a few pleasant spots in the Firelands. Russell's Tavern, a good house on a fine farm, served him breakfast of eggs and coffee. The proprietor owned three books—a gazeteer of Ohio, a geography, and a well-used Bible. German families were beginning to settle in the region. The deadened trees on the farms were still standing and the corn was growing up among the pine and oak trunks: "Life and desolation were never brought closer together." He grew rapturous in the Wordsworthian manner as he passed through the miles of forest in all its

stages of growth, decay, dissolution and regeneration; you must see it pressing on you and overshadowing you by its silent forms, and at other times spreading itself before you like a natural park; . . . you must travel in it in *solitariness,* hour after hour, and day after day, frequently gazing on it with solemn delight, and occasionally casting the eye round in search of some pause, some end without finding any, before you can fully understand the impression.

Other passengers out of Cleveland were not so romantic. They complained about the manners of their companions and the clouds of dust that suffocated them. They particularly resented the irony of buying a ticket to ride in the coach, only to find themselves walking much of the way with a rail on their shoulder to pry the coach out of the endless mudholes.

Bad as it was, people still had to travel over whatever roads they found.

In 1824 a state road had been laid out along Kinsman Road

from Cleveland eastward through Warrensville and Orange Center —our present U.S. 422. At the eastern end of the Reserve a turnpike had been opened in 1828 from Warren to Ashtabula Creek to give a connection between Lake Erie and the Mahoning River. When oil was discovered in upper Trumbull County just before the Civil War, the fifteen miles of road between Warren and Mecca were crowded with coaches, hacks, and wagons carrying workers and speculators and hauling oil back to the shipping center. Another pike connected Cleveland with Medina and Wooster. It was a toll road operated by a private company, but it was so rough and disagreeable as late as 1843 that irate citizens smashed the tollgates in protest against the charge for every ten miles of travel.

The wheat road, as it was familiarly known, led up through Fitchville, Olena, and Norwalk to Milan in the Firelands on the Huron River where, in 1839, a canal was opened to Lake Erie. For about a decade it was one of the busiest roads in the Reserve. Lake schooners came up to the mile-long docks at Milan; "land schooners"—the big grain wagons—came in from the wheat fields with grain. At the height of the harvest season 365 wagons arrived and unloaded at the wharves. The teamsters stopped at night at inns along the route. Mr. Angell, tavern keeper at Olena, provided bed and breakfast for a hundred teams and teamsters on a single night at fifty cents for a man and four horses. They were on their way to Milan with grain. Milan tried to protect this lucrative business by refusing to the Lake Shore and Michigan Southern Railroad a right of way through its precincts. The railroad dropped south to Norwalk, the trade coveted by Milan followed it, and in the late 1850's the port at Milan decayed.

The roads to the east through Willoughby and Painesville, and west through Elyria and Oberlin, or through Lorain to Sandusky were in the same condition. It was easier to sail on the lake than wade through the mud by land to the Lake Erie port towns. From Sandusky west to Toledo, the Western Reserve and Maumee Road, opened in 1839, carried coaches and wagons across the swampy region which had formerly been virtually impassable. The road from Cleveland to the mouth of the Huron River was

built by Lorenzo Carter, Nathaniel Doan, and Ebenezer Murray
along the old Lake Erie beach. It is still known as the Detroit
Road.

These were the main roads of the Reserve until well into the
1840's. There were, of course, hundreds of miles of township
and county-line bogs, technically called roads, but they were,
during most of the year, more of a barrier than a connection. The
farmers who called for outlets from their isolated lands and their
small towns wanted transport to the canal, the lake, or the nearest
railroad station.

Two methods of getting the farmers out of the mud were hopefully introduced. In the late 1830's, a few miles of macadam
roads were constructed. Gravel was spread over the clay surface
and rounded away from the top for drainage. This was a marked
improvement. From 1838 to 1843, Ohio built more miles of macadam roads than any other state.

The other method, which excited the Reserve for several years,
was the plank road. Lumber was the cheapest material on the
frontier. Thousands of acres of it were cut and burned. Men of
that day invariably spoke of "the inexhaustible supply" of timber.
Why not lay a smooth floor of planks along the roads for the
coaches and wagons to run on? It seemed like such a good idea
that companies were formed in many of the towns and in Cleveland
to pave the roads with planks. The enthusiasm was at its height
in 1848-1849. The Cleveland papers surmised that plank roads
to Wooster, Warren, and Ravenna would increase the trade of
Cleveland "more than all the railroads in contemplation." "Push
them along in every direction," said the *Daily True Democrat* on
April 24, 1849; "let the Reserve be vamped over with them. The
increase of the value of lands along their lines will pay for them
over and over again." A reporter for this paper had observed and
counted the previous December eighty-six teams struggling along
the four miles of road between Doan's Corners and Cleveland,
and concluded that plank roads "will be good stock."

In this spirit of optimism plank roads were projected from
Cleveland to Chagrin Falls, to Jefferson and Sandusky; from

Warren up to Fairport, and from Rockport to Elyria. The construction from Cleveland to Chagrin Falls was to be the first of its kind in northern Ohio. It was estimated to cost $20,000. Chagrin Falls would pay half of it, if Cleveland would pay the other half. The *Plain Dealer* (December 12, 1848), declaring that "Ohio is the worst state in the Union to travel in, especially northern Ohio," expressed its opinion that the plank roads "fully answer all the purposes the most sanguine claim for them."

For the next few years planks spanned the mudholes in all directions. The big heavy wagons, covered with canvas, rumbled over them in long lines. They were loaded with produce from the Reserve farms, with salt and coal, and with manufactured goods moving in and out of Cleveland and the lake-port towns. But the roads failed to meet the *Plain Dealer's* sanguine claims. The timber, buried in the muck, exposed to sun and rain and frost, and ground under heavy wheels and shod horses, rotted quickly away. The plank roads were not kept in repair. Within a few years they were like a washboard, and almost as unpleasant for travel as the dust and mud. Moralists also complained in 1851, when the planks were still reasonably sound, that the new roads were doing Cleveland more harm than good because they brought into the "saloons and other resorts" undesirable characters who disgraced the community. The increasing traffic into Cleveland also began the continuing era of traffic hazards. The procession of wagons jammed the narrow roads, the stagecoaches had trouble getting through and around and provoked much shouting and swearing, teams got frightened and ran away. The planks did not extend into Cleveland. In 1857 there was one mile of paved street in the city, but no planks. Euclid and Superior were wide expanses of dust or mud, and helpless pedestrians waited on the corners for a fighting chance to get safely across between the teams and carriages.

It became increasingly obvious that, while turnpikes were necessary for the short hauls, they were not the answer for heavy transportation in large volume and for fast passenger service. That would be a job for the oncoming network of railroads and the improvement of lake steamers. Roads would have to wait for another seventy-five years and the era of motorcars and trucks to realize the dreams of the farmers of 1850. Pending their temporary relapse, however, these turnpikes were the scene of one of the most turbulent and colorful eras in Western Reserve history. The teamsters and stagecoach drivers were tough and hardy men of the open road. They could smoke, chew, spit, swear, and fight with the best of the canalboat men. They would sit aboard their ponderous wagons or high on their coach boxes, reins skillfully gathered in one hand, a long whip in the other, and, like the captain of a schooner, pilot their craft rapidly along over the rough and tortuous routes across the Reserve. At night they would curl up in a blanket on the floor or perhaps share a bed with two or three other men.

The stagecoach companies advertised their "fast" schedules and praised the appointments of their rigs. Some of them were lavishly upholstered, with folding steps and polished side lamps, and with the body swung on leather straps for easier riding. Well-fed and sleek, groomed horses waited in the stables at the inns every few miles along the main routes to replace the tired teams that had made the run of the previous relay. The drivers would blow their long brass horns when they were still a few miles away to warn the landlord to have the fresh team ready. At mealtimes and in the evenings the taprooms of the inns were lively and rowdy with teamsters, coachmen, and travelers drinking, gambling, and swapping yarns. People from the lonely farms sometimes came in to enjoy a spirited evening in their company. Around this life and rigorous form of travel much lore has accumulated. Literature re-creates the colorful characters and flavorsome speech of the coachmen and the landlords. The museums preserve samples of the coaches, the harness, horns, and whips, and the costumes of the drivers.

In more recent years, as the hardships of stagecoach travel recede and the lost days become romantic in retrospect, many of the better old inns in the Reserve have been restored to their original state and made inviting with their fireplaces, kitchens, taprooms, and four-poster beds. The Dunham Tavern on Euclid

Avenue, once well out in the country toward Painesville, was opened in 1842. For years it was one of the fine inns on the coach road. It is now a museum, and its old kitchen with the big oven, the dining rooms, and taproom, refitted with period relics from the Reserve, are occasionally used for group dinners and meetings. The stone smokehouse and the huge stable, forty by fifty feet, stand at the rear of the house.

The famous Rider Tavern[1] in Painesville, built by Goldsmith about 1822, was another of the distinguished inns. It is built after the general pattern of Washington's home at Mount Vernon. It was restored in 1922, and it re-creates with its period furniture some of the atmosphere of the stagecoach era in graceful style. Its large new dining room added to the old house serves the automobile tourists of the country. The Old Tavern at Unionville, erected about the same time, is built on the same model. It, too, has been restored. In the 1840's as many as thirty stagecoaches were seen stopping at this tavern on the east-west coach route. The Singletary House facing the green at Streetsboro, across from the severely beautiful Doric Congregational Church, was for many years a tavern on the Cleveland to Wellsville coach line. The Stone Tavern at Poland, a two-story house made of sandstone, was another of the inns on this route. It is one of the oldest in the Reserve, erected in 1804 by Jonathan Fowler, a man certified to the first governor of Ohio as "a suitable person to keep a publick house of entertainment." The Brecksville Inn, built in 1839, over-looking the village green, is still standing and open for business. Its black walnut siding is three feet wide; the nails were handmade.

These are a few splendid samples, surviving into our day, of the hostelries which served the Reserve a century ago before the railroads concentrated travelers in the large city hotels. Now that the automobile and modern highways have again put much of the traveling population on the roads, many of these inns come again to life to serve them bed and board.

---

[1] Now Lutz's Tavern.

CHAPTER FOURTEEN

BUILDING THE RAILROADS

Before the canal system in Ohio was well under way, men were already talking about railroads. They continued to talk about them for a generation. The canals were serviceable but slow—eighty hours from Cleveland to Portsmouth. Reckless drivers of stagecoaches had been known to reach a speed of eight miles per hour. Imaginative men like the citizens of Sandusky and of Cleveland looked into the future and predicted that the time would come when trains would hurtle across the surface of Ohio at a speed of fifteen miles an hour. One Ohio city refused to allow a debate on this issue in 1828 with the simple statement, "If God had designed that his intelligent creatures should travel at a frightful rate of fifteen miles an hour, by steam, he would have told it through His holy pamphlet. It is a device of Satan to lead immortal souls down to Hell." Twenty years later trains out of Sandusky actually ran sixteen miles per hour.

Sandusky had taken the lead in railroad-mindedness among Reserve towns. It had lost its strong bid for the lake terminus of one of the canals. These had gone to Cleveland and to Toledo. Toledo likewise had the first railroad in the west—a thirty-three-mile-long stub of oak track to Adrian, Michigan, opened in 1836. Not wishing to be completely by-passed in this internal development of Ohio, Sandusky men sponsored the idea of a railroad running south between the two canals to the Ohio River via Bellevue, Tiffin, Carey, Kenton, Springfield. There it would join the Little Miami Railroad and achieve through service to Cincinnati. They got a charter from the legislature on New Year's Day,

1832, for the enterprise which they named the Mad River and Lake Erie Railroad. The proposal created excitement and enticed subscribers to buy its bonds. One of them was Ralph Waldo Emerson, who invested some of his lecture money in the venture.

Amid great festivities the first earth was ceremoniously turned in September 1832. The beginning was premature. The 1830's were difficult years, culminating in the great panic of 1837 when many of our citizens were on a dole of a shovelful of potatoes for a week's allowance. Nontheless the Sandusky people kept at work, and by 1839 they had a few miles of usable track. By 1841 they had succeeded in pushing their rails back across the low ground south of Sandusky, following an old fur traders' trail through the forest walls and up over the old beach ridges to Bellevue, a distance of sixteen miles. In that year there were only thirty-six miles of railroad in Ohio. The rails were sawed white oak with a thin strap of iron spiked to the surface. The construction was crude. The ends of these iron straps would work loose, and sometimes actually jab through the floor of the cars and injure a passenger.

By 1842 the road was opened to Tiffin. Charles Dickens that year, after his most unhappy stagecoach trip from Columbus to Upper Sandusky, during which he thought he would be killed or at least have most of his bones broken, was pleased to board the cars at Tiffin for the rest of the journey to the lake. In his *American Notes* he wrote, "At two o'clock we took the railroad; the traveling on which was very slow, its construction being indifferent, and the ground wet and marshy; and arrived at Sandusky in time to dine that evening." Recalling Read's journey south from Sandusky by stagecoach, we note the improvement in travel. The citizens of Cleveland waited another seven years to see the first train enter their city.

In the 1846 edition of Henry Howe's *History of Ohio,* enlivened by nearly two hundred of his own quaint sketches of people, towns, and roads, there are but two pictures of trains—one in Xenia and the other at Kenton. The Mad River Line, still inching its way south, had just reached Kenton. Howe shows a tiny, wood-burning engine drawing four small, four-wheeled cars through the village.

NORTH SIDE OF CLEVELAND'S PUBLIC SQUARE ABOUT 1895

CLEVELAND'S WATER FRONT IN 1864

The Great Lakes boat, built by T. W. Kennard, is docked in the Cuyahoga River at the foot of Superior. The original picture belongs to William Walster of Meadville, Pa.

MODERN ORE CARRIERS IN THE CUYAHOGA

The engine had been shipped by canal and lake from the East to the port at Sandusky. All the early locomotives had names like ships. This one was called the *Sandusky*. It was the first to run in the Reserve. The directors were so proud of it that they fired its boiler and blew its whistle for hours even though no track was ready for it to run on when it arrived in July 1838. Those in use on the Cincinnati end of the line—the Little Miami Railroad—had come up the river by way of New Orleans. These two roads made connection late in 1846; they provided a more rapid 211-mile route from Lake Erie to the Ohio River.

Not content with this progress; the enterprising Sandusky men planned and began construction on another route cutting through the richer wheatlands of the Reserve by way of Monroeville to Mansfield, a distance of 56 miles. The road reached Mansfield in 1846 with one accommodation and one express train each day. On January 8, 1851, it entered Newark. Sandusky for this achievement received the high distinction of editorial acclaim from her rival Cleveland. The *Daily True Democrat* wrote, "Sandusky deserves every praise. No city of her size has shown more enterprise or done more." It was largely through the efforts of Sandusky that the miles of track in Ohio had lengthened from 36 in 1841 to 299 in 1850.

Cleveland seemed to many people to have gone to sleep. The newspapers of the era are constantly enlivened with indignant or ironical outbursts from their readers. They say it is time for Cleveland to stop talking and build roads. When the Mad River and the Little Miami railroads met, one citizen wrote wryly that Clevelanders could now go from the lake to Cincinnati by rail— by sailing over to Sandusky City to catch the train! The temper of the Clevelanders may be gauged by this flavored item from the *Daily True Democrat* on April 4, 1848:

Not far from this city may be seen, and could have been during all the past winter, a solitary man, with pickaxe and spade, digging into the bowels of the earth. Every now and then he would raise his eyes to the task before him and groan in agony. And, reader, what do you think is his object? Why, he is building a railroad from Cleveland to Columbus! Poor fellow! To keep the charter alive, he is obliged to labor on without "cessation." Surely the prospect brightens; and the citizens of Cleveland may soon expect to ride to the Capital on a railroad.

These criticisms were, as they usually are, quite unjust. They ignored the gigantic risks, and the difficulties of finance, right of way, charters, management, and materials faced by the sponsors. They did not know how earnestly and farsightedly the Cleveland leaders were working on these problems. What they did know, of course, was the stupendous failures already made in a day when there were no precedents or experience to serve as a guide, when each venture had to learn about railroad building the bitter way.

While Sandusky was putting down track to link itself with Cincinnati, Cleveland had built what it optimistically and generously called the Cleveland and Newburgh Railroad. It was opened for traffic in 1838. It ran from a stone quarry near the present Adelbert College down Euclid Avenue to the Public Square. The road was nothing more than a tramway down a rutted, dusty, or mud-soggy street. The grandiose charter authorized this great railroad to carry passengers and freight "by the power and force of steam, animals, or other mechanical force, or by a combination of them." Two horses, as a matter of fact, furnished the propulsive force. And two trips a day exhausted all the demand for transport. A single passenger coach accommodated all the passengers. The freight was stone and lumber which was dumped into the Public Square. The road was soon abandoned, but the ties and rails lay in the street and rotted in the mud. It was an inauspicious beginning for the rail center of the Reserve.

The Reserve had also witnessed the catastrophe of a second undertaking in which its citizens lost heavily. This was the mad scheme to build on stilts the Ohio Railroad. The story reads like a concoction in some boys' romance, but it is a matter of record and may be read in detail in C. P. Leland's Western Reserve tract, *The Ohio Railroad: That Famous Structure Built on Stilts.* A group of sixteen prominent citizens, including John W. Allen, P.

M. Weddell, Rice Harper, Eliphalet Austin, Charles C. Paine, and Herman Ely, organized the company at Painesville in April 1836. They thought they could avoid the heavy expense of grading and graveling a railroad bed by placing the tracks on two rows of piles driven into the ground and sawed off to grade. The new road would run from the eastern edge of the Reserve to the mouth of the Maumee River. Two great trade centers would be built, one on the Grand River near present Fairport, and the other on the Maumee.

The legislature granted them a charter and extraordinary privileges. They could issue money like a bank—and they did, with a loss of several hundred thousand dollars to the holders of their paper. They were also granted the backing of state credit—with a loss to Ohio of $249,000. The ease with which the company got pledges of support of almost two million dollars indicates the spirit of speculation of the age. The people were so eager for transportation that they willingly believed that any scheme, however fanciful, to move people or goods through the mud and forests would certainly succeed.

The engineering on the road was also in keeping with the vigorous but blundering imagination of the 1830's. A pile driver with a half-ton iron hammer pounded the two rows of poles into the ground. A circular saw cut the tops off at the proper height. A sawmill followed along behind the pile drivers preparing stringers eight by eight inches and fifteen feet long for the rails. These were laid on crossties held in place by cedar pins. Iron straps were laid on the stringers. Workmen labored away on this contraption west of Fremont and in the Reserve between Cleveland and Huron while the management worried through the panic of 1837 and the mounting troubles that brought on the complete collapse in 1843. For its pains and its money the Reserve got fifteen miles of stilts which rotted so slowly that they continued to stick up out of the ground like grim tombstones through the next half century.

These experiences, however, did not stifle the energies of the Reserve. The ambitious villages in the interior—Ravenna, Hudson, Jefferson, Medina, Elyria—continued to cry for outlet. Few

people were thinking of a continental network of railroads. They
were still in the stage of trying to connect their own towns and
counties with a Lake Erie port, the Ohio River, or the canal. In
Ohio their thoughts ran north and south rather than from east to
west. Cleveland, as the center of the Reserve, was the logical
terminal and natural leader. Why, they demanded again, doesn't
Cleveland do something?

Cleveland was doing something. The papers kept announcing
still another meeting to be held in the courthouse to discuss ways
and means. Good men were formulating the plans. There was
John W. Allen, that prominent and tireless public servant of the
city, whom we have already met as banker. Despite his connection with the two railroads just mentioned, he was one of the
leaders in the proposal for a railway to Columbus and Cincinnati,
and became president of the C.C. & C. There was Henry B.
Payne, one of Cleveland's leading citizens. He had come out from
Hamilton, New York, in 1832 as a young lawyer. He was interested in all sorts of enterprises, and was a director or stockholder
in eighteen companies. He worked with Allen for city improvement and public waterworks. He married a Cleveland girl, the
daughter of Nathan Perry, himself the son of one of the first
Reserve families and owner of large areas of Cleveland and Lake
County real estate. Payne was a director of the proposed C.C. & C.
Railroad. There was Leonard Case who became president of this
road. He had migrated to a farm in the Reserve near Warren as
a boy. He had been crippled by illness, but he went on to become
a surveyor, land agent, and a lawyer. He came up to Cleveland in
1816. He became president of the Commercial Bank. He foresaw
the growth of Cleveland and he invested wisely in real estate downtown and in the suburbs. He was president of the village of Cleveland from 1821 to 1825. The vast fortune which he accumulated
passed to his son Leonard, Jr., who in turn founded and richly
endowed the Case School of Applied Sciences, now Case Institute
of Technology, and gave to Cleveland many cultural benefactions.

There was Richard Hilliard who had come out from New York
to the Reserve in the 1820's to go into the dry-goods and grocery

business. He prospered mightily. He became president of Cleveland in 1830. He saw the usefulness of the Flats and bought up a large share of this land to be developed for manufacturing. He worked with Allen, Payne, and others to improve the city, and now he joined them in the effort to get the C.C. & C. started. There were also Alfred Kelley's capable brother Thomas, and Cyrus Prentiss, who became president of the Cleveland and Pittsburgh road, and many other such men vigorously promoting the railroads.

These men were not easily discouraged or defeated; they conceived large ventures, and they were trusted by their fellow citizens. They got their railroads for Cleveland and the Reserve. The charter granted by the legislature in 1836 had been forfeited— one reason for the vexation of the citizens expressed in the newspapers. It was revived in 1845. For the next three years the directors tried to get together enough capital to begin the work. Subscriptions were slow in coming. Various people suggested that if Alfred Kelley would take the presidency they would subscribe. In August 1847 Richard Hilliard and Thomas M. Kelley went to Columbus to see Mr. Kelley. The physical trip itself was all the argument anybody needed to establish the urgent need of rail connections between Cleveland and the state capital. It could be made only by stagecoach or by canal and it required two days over rough roads. Winter closed the canals and discouraged all but the most pressing travel by road.

They found Kelley in his handsome and comfortable Greek-revival stone mansion which he had built on East Broad Street in 1836. (It is still there.) He was looking forward to some years of leisure and peace, and a chance to reorganize his private affairs which had suffered for the public welfare. His brother and Hilliard talked with him late into the evening urging him to accept the presidency of the C.C. & C. Kelley said no. Mrs. Kelley also said no. She thought she and her children were now entitled to see something of Mr. Kelley. As Hilliard was leaving, he said to Kelley, "I appreciate your reasons for declining our request, and I admit we have no claims on you. This project, however, is very important to Cleveland and the State, and should it fail because you decline to take hold of it, will it not be a source of regret the residue of your life?"

Kelley became president a few days after this meeting and just three years and six months later he rode the first through train into Cleveland from Columbus.

Those years were almost as strenuous for Kelley as his canal-building days. He held a meeting in Cleveland to explain the program for building the road. Subscriptions poured in. They soon reached $3,000,000 worth of stock. Cleveland itself put up $200,000. Kelley, grown so familiar with the lay of the Ohio land, helped the engineers to locate the 145-mile route and the right of way. On September 20, 1848, he and a dozen others went down to the terminal site in Cleveland and turned a few spadefuls of earth to symbolize the beginning of the project. While he organized all the intricate details of the contracts, finances, and materials, that lone man ridiculed by the paper was continuing to keep the charter valid. Kelley himself went to Wales to get some of the iron for the rails. Some of it was shipped in by way of the St. Lawrence River and the Lakes. He bought 7,000 tons in the East, and the *New York Tribune* announced that the price had gone up from $3.00 a ton to $5.00. Kelley had this road built not of oak with strap-iron surface, but with the new solid iron T rails of the general type now standard.

Once the construction got started, the parallel rails marched down across the Reserve at a good rate. Two trains each day were running down to Wellington in midsummer 1850. By the end of the year the road had reached Crestline. By the end of January the Cleveland papers were dramatically reporting from day to day the approaching completion of the C.C. & C. On January 31, 1851, they announced "only thirteen more miles to go"; on February 18, "last mile of the C.C. & C. completed." Kelley and Mayor William Case of Cleveland had laid the last two joining rails and hammered in the last spike while a crowd looked on and cheered, a cannon fired salutes, and the whistle of the little engine tooted. The first train then moved across the rails and into Cleveland at seven o'clock that evening.

Such an epoch-making achievement, of course, called for a full-dress celebration. Since it wasn't the Fourth of July, the next best date was selected. That was Washington's Birthday. The city firemen, after rehearsal, the Cleveland bands, and the local militia in full uniform turned out to greet the special train from Columbus. It bore 428 officials, dignitaries, and private citizens, headed by the governor, Cleveland's own Reuben Wood, affectionately known as "the tall chief of the Cuyahoga." They were greeted with cheers, cannon salutes, and band music, and then conducted to the Public Square for the speeches. The *Herald* summed up the general spirit in the flowing periods of that day.

On Saturday, as we saw the Buckeyes from the banks of the Ohio and the rich valleys of the Miami and the Scioto mingling their congratulations with those of the Yankee Reserve, upon contemplation of an improvement, which served to bring them into business and social connection, and to break down the barriers which distance, prejudice, and ignorance of each other had built up, we felt that the completion of the Cleveland, Columbus & Cincinnati Railroad would be instrumental in accomplishing a good work for Ohio, the value of which no figures could compute.

During the three months ending June 1, the intercultural and commercial link carried 31,679 passengers. The cars were drawn by engines manufactured in Cleveland by the Cuyahoga Steam Furnace Company. On September 22, this rising concern delivered the eleventh locomotive for the C.C. & C. road.

The construction of the C.C. & C., in addition to bringing Alfred Kelley back to his old home town, was the occasion for the arrival of a man who was to become one of the city's great figures. He was Amasa Stone, general benefactor and special patron of Western Reserve University. This Massachusetts farm boy had become famous while still a young man as a builder of railroads and the Howe Truss Bridge which he helped to design. He had joined with Frederick Harbach and Stillman Stitt to build railroads in New England. Kelley persuaded him and his company to undertake the entire contract for the Cleveland to Columbus trackage. He accepted the job of superintendent of the road and moved to Cleveland in 1850. From then on until his death in

1883, he was a director in several leading banks, president of many railroads, and restlessly engaged in ironworks, woolen mills, and a dozen other manufacturing activities. He designed and built the old Union Passenger Depot. He was a friend and counselor of Abraham Lincoln. He became a multimillionaire. His only son, Adelbert, was drowned in the Connecticut River while he was a student at Yale. In his memory, Amasa Stone gave to Western Reserve College, then located at Hudson, a half-million dollars on condition that it move to Cleveland and name its college of liberal arts Adelbert College.

Judging by the emphasis of the Cleveland newspapers, the Reserve was even more interested in the proposed rail line between Cleveland and Pittsburgh. A charter had been granted for it in 1836, but it had shared the same troubles which the other companies had encountered, and, like them, did not get organized until 1845. Construction began down at Wellsville on the Ohio in July 1847, and at the Cleveland end in February 1849. Exactly two years later the road had reached Hudson. In celebration, the delegation that had come to Cleveland for the opening of the C.C. & C. were taken for an excursion ride over this portion of the C. & P. to visit the village of Hudson. The track, not yet ballasted, was rough and the travel slow. The train on the return trip jumped the rails and was delayed until late that night. Hudson had not been able to feed all its guests, and they arrived in Cleveland weary, famished, and less sure of the benefits of steam locomotion. Ravenna, thirty-eight miles from Cleveland, greeted the opening of the road into its precincts in March 1851. During the first week of April, 1,363 passengers were carried on the new coaches. The following year the two sections were joined and a through road opened to the southeast. The trip required thirty-six hours.

These roads were all geared to the south. To connect the Reserve from east to west and with Erie, Buffalo, and New York, the Cleveland, Painesville, and Ashtabula Railroad Company was organized. Alfred Kelley was one of the directors and later president of the road. Amasa Stone was the builder, as well as a director and later the superintendent. The rails reached Painesville on November 20, 1851. A big delegation of Cleveland people in "two fine cars" rode over for the grand opening. The mayor made a speech. As the line neared completion to the Pennsylvania border, the *Daily True Democrat* again voiced the spirit of the day. On comes the iron band linking us closer, it said. "The Reserve, as glorious a land, and as free as the sun shines upon, will wake up to new life under these railroad openings." At the same time the line to the west was edging its way to Berea and Elyria, through Lorain County and the Firelands, and across the swamps toward Toledo.

This rapid account of progress minimizes some of the troubles Kelley was having to realize his dream of free-flowing rail traffic from Michigan and Cincinnati through Cleveland to New York. One of his difficulties must be recorded as a part of essential railroad history as well as an illuminating insight into the character of this driving personality. It came about in this way.

When Stephenson designed and built the first locomotive in England, he chose for no apparent reason at all to set the axle length at four feet, eight and a half inches. That caprice determined the distance between the rails on the first tracks. The Pennsylvania Main Line, the B. & O., and the New York Central to Buffalo adopted the English gauge. A southern road across New York terminating at Dunkirk had laid its tracks six feet apart. Other early roads chose gauges of four feet three, four feet seven, four feet nine, and five feet. The engine *Sandusky* was built to a four-feet ten-inch gauge. It set the standard in Ohio, for the legislature made it unlawful to build any other gauge in the state. Kelley's roads, therefore, were laid with rails four feet ten inches apart. All this variety caused inconvenience to travelers and expense to shippers for they had to unload themselves or their goods at the end of one line and load again on another. It cost as much to make these transfers as it did to run a train an additional fifty miles. But many workers had jobs at transfer points.

The Cleveland, Painesville, and Ashtabula was supposed to extend into Pennsylvania to Erie, there to connect with the two roads for New York. The New York Central had used the English standard gauge to Buffalo, but wished to extend its line to Erie to meet the Ohio road on the four-feet-ten gauge. The city of Erie was determined to preserve a difference in gauges in order to get the business of unloading and reloading all the passengers and freight that passed through. It passed a "gauge law" requiring that all roads running from Erie to the New York state line be either four feet eight and a half inches or six feet wide, and all between Erie and Ohio four feet ten. Because Kelley took the New York Central's side in the controversy, he was refused authority to continue the C.P. & A. into Pennsylvania.

Kelley was not one to accept defeat from such a narrow and provincial attitude. The larger ends of the Ohio railroads were dependent on Eastern connections. Kelley explored all the possibilities. He discovered that the Franklin Canal Company of Pennsylvania had a charter which gave it the right to construct a railroad instead of a canal if it chose to do so. Kelley then bought a controlling interest in this company, transferred it to the C.P. & A., and went on building his railroad. Erie got an injunction against him. When the court examined the charter, it found that it was in order—except for the first five miles from the Ohio line. Kelley was stopped again. He went through the five miles, made friends with the landowners, and succeeded in buying a right of way through most of the area. In some cases he personally bought whole farms. He got from the local officers of the townships the right to cross highways with his tracks. And in November 1852 he ran the line into Erie.

The citizens there threatened to mob him if he came to town. He promptly drove into Erie and walked about the streets. One brick was thrown, but Kelley was not molested. The heated opposition of Erie continued for a time, and they actually tore up track to prevent the roads from joining. But time was on Kelley's side, the union was effected, and by 1854 the law was adjusted to protect these steps on the road to progress. Kelley thereupon retired from active railroad business, again to seek a period of rest after seven of his most strenuous years. He had the satisfaction of seeing the main routes through Ohio served by a fair net-work of canals and railroads with Cleveland as the center. The entire lake front from Bank Street (West Sixth) to the Cuyahoga was taken over by the railroads, and long docks reaching into the harbor joined the rails with the steamers and schooners of Lake Erie.

One other important road was completed before the Civil War despite vicissitudes as great as those just described. This was the Cleveland and Mahoning Valley Railroad, chartered in 1848, and completed to Youngstown in 1857 just as this section began to take on primary importance as an iron center in the midst of a region of coal. It ran through Newburg, Solon, Aurora, Mantua, and Warren. By this time, too, the small roads were being gathered into larger units which during the reconstruction period became the great New York Central, the Pennsylvania, the Baltimore and Ohio, and the Erie systems. " 'Consolidation' is the order of the day," the Canal Board wrote in 1855. "The immense railroad system of Ohio is rapidly becoming a unit." It was reaching into every county of the Reserve to stimulate manufacture and trade. Before the Civil War stopped construc-tion, Ohio had 2,788 miles of railroads. No other state had so much.

When we get to thinking about these great systems with their present luxurious cars, we forget just what the first trains were like. A glance at the early prints brings us back to the reality. The engines look like old-fashioned sawmill boilers on wheels. The tall ornate smokestacks pour out smoke from the acres of forest cut down to feed them. The engineer, standing on an open platform unprotected, except for his stovepipe hat, drives the train along the uneven track at fifteen to twenty miles an hour dragging a few swaying carriages behind him. The slaughter of wild life and livestock along the way is so heavy that it causes protests and cries for protection in the newspapers, and soon brings about the "cowcatcher" on the front of the engine and cattle guards at country lanes. The passengers sit on hard seats on elongated stagecoaches, some of which have observation platforms. The engine puffs smoke and cinders back into their faces. People get killed up there when they fail to heed the warning of the conductor and get knocked off by a low bridge. And inside, some of the passengers are so annoyed by the undisciplined children whose parents take them out "for an airing of a few hundred miles" that they write a letter of protest to the papers. They don't think little boys and girls should be permitted to climb uninvited into ladies' laps, soil their dresses, eat molasses candy and wipe their fingers on gentlemen's trousers, or climb noisily over the backs of the seats in the cars. Can't such behavior be stopped?

It couldn't be stopped, but nonetheless more and more passengers rode the ever-lengthening coaches behind ever-bigger and more powerful engines over heavier, safer, and smoother tracks. And increasing wealth for Cleveland and the Reserve rolled in on the new iron wheels.

CHAPTER FIFTEEN

SHIPWAYS ON LAKE ERIE

LAKE ERIE sweeps west-southwest to form the entire northern border of the Reserve. Moses Cleaveland coasted along the shore peering into the mouths of the streams at Conneaut, Ashtabula, Fairport, and Cleveland. He found them clogged with sand, but well favored and protected. They would need only to be dredged and marked to make excellent harbors for future port cities. The lake was cut off from direct connection with Lake Ontario by the Niagara escarpment, but the Welland Canal would in 1831 lift and lower ships around the Falls, and the Erie Canal in 1825 would connect the lake with the Hudson River, New York City, and the broad Atlantic. In the meantime the lake was a ready-made natural highway to Detroit and Buffalo; all it needed was boats designed to sail across these temperamental waters.

That was not so simple as it appears. For the early settlers in the Reserve, Lake Erie was, in its way, a wilderness even more vast and formidable than the miles of forest along its shore. With few exceptions, the pioneers preferred to cross to the Reserve by land, breaking their way through the forest a few miles a day, on foot, by wagons, or by sleds, driving with them a few cows and some oxen to drag logs and to plow among the stumps of their clearings. Rarely in those first years did they trust their family and goods to the inadequate boats on the lake. The casualties among those who did attempt it were relatively heavy. The lake, which looked so serene and inviting on a windless sunny day, could in a few moments roar and howl with a storm. The winds

173

chopped up the shallow waters, tossed the sturdiest boats wildly about, and all too frequently capsized them, or drove them ashore on a harborless bank.

The record through the years, right down to this day, is made sorrowful by such tragedies. The *Annals* of the Early Settlers' Association preserve many of them. Early in 1808, when only a few families clustered about the mouth of the Cuyahoga, Joseph Plumb, Stephen Gilbert, Adolphus Spafford, William Gilmore, and a woman domestic servant took out an open boat to go over to Black River. A squall capsized the boat a half mile off Dover Point and drove the wreckage ashore upon a rocky beach under a high, overhanging cliff. All but Joseph Plumb were drowned. He was found by his son who spotted the wreckage of the boat and let himself drop from a sapling over the cliff to his father lying exhausted on the beach.

The Hunter family attempted to make the journey from Buffalo to Cleveland by open boat. Just as they came in sight of the mouth of the Cuyahoga, a quick storm rose and struck them. The entire family was drowned. Eleven of the first eighteen deaths during the first decade in Cleveland were by drowning.

It is not surprising, therefore, that the early settlers did not find Lake Erie the convenient highway between Buffalo and the Reserve that the Ohio River was for the streams of immigrants going down from Pittsburgh. The river flowed gently along at two or three miles an hour. A man could load his family and goods into anything that would float, and drift, almost without effort, down to Cincinnati. There was no current on Lake Erie. It was toilsome work to row a boat on it, and the winds were generally adverse for westward travelers. The first settlers did not even accumulate about the ports. They moved back from the lake to the high ground, and they thought more about turnpikes than about schooners, more about railroads than about steamboats. Proximity to Lake Erie, nonetheless, was one of the greatest and most valuable assets of the Reserve; within a few decades it would give to the lake ports superior advantages over the river towns and shift the area of concentration of people in Ohio from the south to the north. The immediate need was technique and facilities for building ships for the lake, skilled captains and sailors to manage them, and harbors to receive them. All were forthcoming.

The first craft on the lake were Schenectady rowboats augmented with sails when the wind was favorable. A few enterprising men at the port settlements put their heads to work on the art of ship construction, knowing full well that the demands for transportation in the Reserve would far outrun any roads through the forests, and that no mode of conveyance yet devised by man was more economical than boats and water. The first of them at Cleveland was Lorenzo Carter, who figured so prominently in the struggling founding years of the village. He had come out in May 1797. When malaria drove other settlers back to Newburg, Carter refused to budge. Instead he erected his historic log cabin down by the river, and traded with the Indians. He built a ferry to take people and goods across the Cuyahoga from the foot of Superior Street. In 1808, only four years after Buffalo had launched its first schooner, the twenty-five-ton *Surprise,* Carter began Cleveland's shipbuilding industry by launching the thirty-to-forty-five-ton *Zephyr.* He built it up on the riverbank and hauled it down to the water with oxen. It was of shallow draft, and it sailed poorly, but it was useful for short trips along the lake. Joel Thorp, another of the first settlers at Cleveland, built the following year the little five or six-ton schooner *Sally,* and Alexander Simpson launched the *Dove,* about the same size as the *Sally.* In 1810 Murray & Bixby put into service their big sixty-ton *Ohio.* It joined Commodore Perry's squadron in the War of 1812 as a supply boat. It was on duty in another part of the lake when the battle was fought. Several others with interesting names like *Contractor, Washington, Adams, Good Intent* were built in these first years. The *Cuyahoga* was built at the mouth of the Chagrin River from the good timber in that region. She was commandeered by General William Hull for his march on Detroit in the War of 1812, and was captured, fully loaded, by the British.

Levi Johnson, famous early housebuilder in Cleveland, also entered the shipbuilding business and sailed on the lake for many

years. He had arrived in 1809. He had built the old log courthouse and jail on the Public Square, Judge Walworth's house—
the first frame house in the village—and many other dwellings.
Later in his career he also built the old lighthouse on the point,
and the government pier on the west bank of the river. His own
house was in the woods on the Euclid Road east of the Square. In
1814 he used this timber to build near his house the schooners
Ladies' Master and *Pilot*. He placed rollers under them, engaged
farmers to bring in their oxen, and with twenty-eight yoke
dragged the boats down Superior Street, broke a jug of whisky
over their bows, and launched them in the Cuyahoga. The *Pilot*
sailed to all the Lake Erie ports carrying troops and stores for
the United States Government. He built the *Neptune,* this time
choosing to lay his ways among the timber along the river at the
foot of Eagle Street. Her maiden voyage was down to Buffalo in
1816. She was used in the fur trade by the American Fur
Company.

The appearance of this little fleet did not mean that ships were
now sailing in and out of the Cuyahoga. We get a graphic glimpse
of the harbor facilities in 1813 from the "Reminiscences" of
Melinda Russell.[1] Her father came out from Connecticut in
1812, driving a team of oxen and himself walking all the way.
He went back for his family in 1813, and brought them to Cleveland by boat. Even this small craft could not get into the Cuyahoga. Its passengers came in by rowboats, landed, and pulled
themselves up the bank of the river "by the scrub-oaks, which
lined it."

The ninety-four-ton *Union* dropped anchors offshore at Cleveland in 1816 to take on a cargo of some 800 barrels of pork. While
these barrels were being rowed out to the ship in small boats, a
storm began to rage across Lake Erie. It lasted, as they often
did, and do, for two nights and days. All loading had to be
suspended. On the second night one cable broke and the *Union*
began to drift toward shore. The mate weighed anchor and let

---

[1] *Annals,* Early Settlers' Association, No. 4, p. 65.

her run with the storm. She was blown to Put-in-Bay, fifty-five miles west. In that protected harbor she was repaired and on the next day sailed back to the mouth of the Cuyahoga to finish loading. Incidentally we note that a small ship like the *Union* made that year a net profit of $6,000 carrying chiefly farm produce across the lake.

Year after year small new schooners went into the lake from the Cleveland yards, built of the timber in the Cuyahoga forests. Leonard Case's brother-in-law, William Gaylord, built the *Lady of the Lake* in 1815 and placed her in service between Cleveland, Detroit, and Buffalo. Philo Taylor, one of the incorporators of the Commercial Bank of Lake Erie, built the *Prudence* in 1821. Nobel H. Merwin, owner of the Mansion House Hotel, and a Clevelander from Connecticut since 1816, launched his forty-four-ton schooner in 1822, broke the usual jug over her bow, christened her *Minerva* for his mother, and sent her off to faraway Mackinac with provisions for the garrison there. She sailed the round trip in just four weeks.

At Conneaut, Ashtabula, in the protected river mouths of the Grand and the Chagrin, on west at Black River, Vermilion, Huron, and Sandusky these same scenes were being enacted. Captain Sam Ward began his career of shipbuilding for the lake by launching at Conneaut in 1818 a twenty-seven-ton schooner, the *Salem*. He later moved on to the mouth of Belle River, above Detroit, turned out ships from his yards there, and was at one time owner of the largest fleet sailing on Lake Erie. Extensive shipyards were set up at the mouth of the Black River, where the wide, deep stream makes a sweeping curve paralleling for a distance the shore of the lake, forming an excellent harbor. These yards prefabricated timber from the Black River forests and shipped them to Lake Superior where they were put together to make the *John Jacob Astor*. It sailed the upper lake in Astor's fur-trading enterprise.

Vermilion, among its lagoons, had a fair harbor and fleet, including the schooner *Ranger*. Its prospects were so favorable in these early years that Captain Alva Bradley, one of the great builders and owners of lake ships, passed Cleveland by and settled at Vermilion. He built a small vessel, gathered a cargo for it, sailed it himself, and gradually built up an immense fortune as captain-owner. This pattern of activity was common in the sailing days.

Huron, with its small, compact harbor at the mouth of the Huron River, was particularly industrious and progressive. The village had the disadvantage of being near enough to well-favored Sandusky to cause rivalry. Vessels crossing Lake Erie often refused to stop at Huron because its approaches were shallow and exposed. They went on to Sandusky, and Huron—or Huron River—passengers had to go back overland to reach their destination. Captain Augustus Walker of Buffalo, one of the notable sailors of his day, took his boats in and captured much of the lucrative trade that came down from the Firelands. He joined a company of local citizens to erect a shipyard here. They built the *Huron* and many other sailing vessels. Walker said that in 1817 there were nineteen of these small American sailing vessels on Lake Erie. When steam came into use, Huron also built the *Sheldon Thompson,* one of General Winfield Scott's troop ships in the Black Hawk War which carried a cargo of cholera-smitten troops across the lake in 1832.

Almost any kind of boat with a sail is attractive to the eye as it moves over an expanse of blue-green water with a gentle wind spreading her canvas in the sun. These Reserve-built boats delighted visitors and spectators from the shore, but they were generally dull sailers. They were open boats, long, shallow and flat-bottomed. Some of them, according to Captain Walker, "could hardly crawl off shore under canvas." Yet they had to be kept of slight draft because of the shallow harbors. Designers tried to compensate for this by adding leeboards to be lowered over the side of the boat in deep water and raised as it came into port. They were unpopular because of their awkward appearance and because Lake Erie storms sometimes carried them away and left the boat tossing out of control. The centerboard and drop keel replaced the leeboards.

The early ships also had an open, unprotected deck. The seas washed over it in heavy weather. The builders of the *Red Jacket* added a "bulwark" around the deck, to offset her lack of side above water when loaded and to prevent seas from breaking over the deck. The Church & Jones yards at Huron carried on experiments in ship design and rigging to meet the requirements of Lake Erie. By 1825 they were building boats that were wider in proportion to their length, and of greater carrying capacity and more graceful appearance than any previously seen on the lake. By placing the foremast close to the bow and the mainmast nearer to the stern, they got greater spread to the foresail, more open space amidships, and easier handling in the wind. During the golden period of the sailing ships from 1830 to 1860, the Lake Erie schooners were both beautiful and practical. Though they carried grain and lumber, whisky, pork, and cheese, when the cargo was stowed and the canvas spread, one of these schooners running before the wind past the expanding lake front of Cleveland might have been the *Golden Hind* itself putting out for the fabulous East.

Only a decade after Carter launched the *Zephyr,* the first steamboat on Lake Erie dropped anchor outside the Cuyahoga sand bar and lightered in its passengers. On that late August day in 1818 most of Cleveland's four-hundred population were out on the point to see this strange new sight, this portent of the future. They saw riding at anchor a trim, schooner-rigged, 330-ton ship with a bust of Oliver Hazard Perry for her figurehead. Her carved taffrail was brilliant in white, green, and gold paint. A smart awning was spread over main and quarter-deck, and passengers lined the rail. But these appointments were hardly noticed. What really caught the attention of the spectators was the incongruous smokestack just aft the foremast, with its thin wisp of blue-white wood smoke rising into the rigging and drifting with the wind into the mainmast; and the big half-circle box amidships enclosing the paddle wheel. Around it they could read the bold lettering: WALK-IN-THE-WATER. The *Register* had its own way of expressing the enthusiasm of the day. About two months after this spectacular event it wrote:

The facility with which [the *Walk-in-the-Water*] moves over our lakes warrants us in saying she will be of utility, not only to the proprietors, but to the public. She affords to us a safe, sure, and speedy conveyance of all our surplus products to distant markets. She works as well in a storm as any vessel on the lakes, and answers the most daring expectations of the proprietor.

Her engines pushed her along at a speed of about eight miles an hour without the aid of sails. She would reach Cleveland from Buffalo at the close of the second day, stopping at Dunkirk and Erie, and possibly calling at other ports on the way.

From this maiden voyage to the end of her career in a storm just out of Buffalo in October 1821, *Walk-in-the-Water* carried Cleveland and Western Reserve people, goods for the mercantile houses, and the United States mails. A prominent Cleveland man had attended her launching at Black Rock. He was Eber D. Howe, pioneer printer, founder in October 1819 of the *Cleveland Herald*, the second newspaper in the town. He happened to be at Black Rock in August 1818. He left us in his autobiography an account of the launching and of his experiences as a passenger on the famous steamer. He wrote:

I was present at Black Rock and saw the first steam-boat launched, that entered the waters of Lake Erie. It was called "Walk-in-the-Water," and was a memorable event of that day. At this time there was no harbor at Buffalo of sufficient depth of water for a craft of that size, and owing to the crude manner of constructing engines at that time, she had very great difficulty in getting up the [Niagara] river into the lake, consequently she was obliged to wait for a "horn breeze," as the sailors term it, and hitch on eight or ten pair of oxen by means of a long rope or cable, and together with all the steam that could be raised, she was enabled to make the ascent.

Howe also experienced an Erie storm while aboard the *Walk-in-the-Water* which might have been a portent of the one on that fatal night of 1821. He had taken passage on the steamer at Black Rock for Cleveland. They had fair sailing and arrived off the mouth of the Cuyahoga beyond the sand bar on the evening of the second day under a heavy northwest gale of wind, and a heavy sea. At that time there was no entrance to the harbor, except for very small craft and lighters. It was soon discovered that the boat could proceed no farther against the wind, and could not put back without great peril. Finally all the anchors were cast, with the alternative of riding out the gale or going onto the beach, and I think the latter was most expected by all on board. The gale continued for three nights and two days without much abatement, and on the morning of the third day, the passengers were taken ashore in small boats. . . .

Newspaper editor Howe was quite conscious of travel time because in 1819 the mail came in by horseback once a week from Buffalo and Pittsburgh.

On this same voyage culminating in the distressing storm was young, twenty-five-year-old Reuben Wood with his wife and child. He had come to Cleveland in 1818 to practice law. He became governor of Ohio from 1850-1851. He must have enjoyed the experience on the *Walk-in-the-Water,* at least in retrospect. For, many years later he suddenly resigned his post of minister to Valparaiso, Chile, where he found the climate too calm and sunny, and the people too ignorant and indolent, and came back home "that he might once again be a sharer in the activities of a wonderfully progressive intellectual people, and again enjoy the sight of a wild, howling storm on Lake Erie." His home was "a noble farm, 'Evergreen Place,' on the margin of the beautiful lake he loved so well."

The *Walk-in-the-Water* was, indeed, "safe, sure, and speedy" in the Lake Erie meaning of those words, and she did work in a storm as well as any other vessel on the lakes in 1818. This did not save her when the howling storm struck her as she began what proved to be her last voyage. Among the seventy-odd passengers, which included a company of missionaries going west to labor with the Indians, a gentleman from Detroit and his bride, were Orlando Cutter and George Williams, of Cleveland, and John S. Strong, a cattle dealer from Strongsville, a few miles to the southwest. Strong had taken a drove of cattle to the Eastern market, and was bringing home in his saddlebags the cash from the sale. He decided to ease his journey by taking passage on the "safe, sure, and speedy" steamboat. Cutter, who had often sailed the schooners, decided to try out a steamer on his way back from the East.

When the furious gale hit the ship, many of the passengers were terrified, and the missionaries sang hymns to comfort them. Williams long afterward remembered that Strong "lay in a berth near the companion way, his saddlebags under his head. When asked how he could lie there so quietly, he nonchalantly replied, if he was to be drowned he might as well be drowned there as anywhere." Cutter was so seasick from the tossing that he lay indifferent to any further fate that might await him. Captain Rogers used every resource to ride out the storm and save the ship. He could not get back into Buffalo. He dropped three anchors but they would not hold. Toward morning he let the ship loose and sent her to the beach broadside on. He ordered a rope stretched from the boat to the beach, and ferried all his wet and weary passengers safely ashore in the ship's boat.

This breakup of the first steamer was accepted as a routine expendable operation on Lake Erie. The following April the Black Rock yards had a bigger, faster, safer, more elegantly appointed steamer ready to replace the *Walk-in-the-Water*. She was the *Superior*, and she carried the still growing trade and passenger list for Buffalo, Cleveland, and Detroit without accident. She was soon joined by the *Henry Clay* in 1824, a ship fitted with cheap quarters forward designed for the increasing flow of immigrant passengers moving now by steamer from Buffalo to the west. While this steamer was making its first voyages, the intrepid and versatile Levi Johnson, with the Turhooven brothers, was building at Cleveland the 250-ton steamer *Enterprise*. The 60 to 70 horsepower, wood-burning engine was built at Pittsburgh and hauled to the Cuyahoga. The steamer was ready for service in 1826, while the ditch for the canal to Akron was opening along the Cuyahoga. She sailed to Buffalo and Detroit with Johnson himself as master. Huron launched the steamer *Sheldon Thompson*. By the time the Ohio canal was completed, Lake Erie had 11 steamboats and a large fleet of schooners ready to bridge the 180 miles between it and the entrance to the Erie at Buffalo. They carried 50,000 passengers westward from Buffalo, many of them to the Reserve. Steamers arrived and departed at Cleveland at the average rate of 7 a day. All this activity did not seriously arrest the urge for railroads and turnpikes, but it did help bring to the Reserve the wealth with which these competing and expensive modes of transportation were constructed.

From 1833 on to the Civil War, the story of the growth of the Lake Erie marine is the story of engineering progress. Each year the boats were lengthened, widened, accelerated, and made more comfortable. They slid in increasing numbers down the ways of the shipyards in the ports of the Western Reserve. Huron was especially proud of its greatest and most famous steamer, *Great Western,* which entered upon her long career in 1838. She had two smokestacks, and three masts for her sails, augmented by an outer jib. Two enormous side paddle wheels moved her swiftly and gracefully through the water. A smart pennant with her name across it flew from the foremast. She was the first steamer on the lake with cabins above the main deck. She had two tiers of them with promenade decks between them and the railings. Her forward quarters below deck were fitted for the mass immigrant trade. She carried thousands of passengers back and forth across Lake Erie.

The Cleveland yards proceeded to outdo their rivals at Huron. They were expanding rapidly. Seth W. Johnson had opened a yard on the Cuyahoga in 1835 for repairing boats. He soon advanced to shipbuilding. From his yards came 2 fine ships, the *Constellation* and the *Robert Fulton,* and for a quarter of a century his firm continued to launch stout ships for the lake trade. At the same time Quayle & Moses, later Quayle & Martin, were building at a fast rate in their Cleveland yards—in a single year they launched 13 boats to keep up with the mounting demand for transportation for the Reserve. Peck's yard produced the 200-ton *Jenny Lind* and many others. Cleveland's pride was the 1,136-ton, 260-foot *Empire,* the longest yet to appear on Lake Erie.

The ambitious builders said that they could have made her even longer if the curving Cuyahoga River could have contained her. She had a luxurious dining room 230 feet long, cabin space above decks almost the full length of the ship, separate saloons for ladies and gentlemen, and dormitory quarters for the immigrants. She carried Cleveland people on holiday cruises, with an excellent band to entertain them. She carried profitable cargoes of flour and package freight in addition to her heavy passenger list. Some idea of the volume of travel developing on the lake may be gained from the fact that in the first year of the *Empire's* career 20,244 passengers sailed from Buffalo to Cleveland.

The spirit of the times may be savored from this rhapsody printed in the *Herald* as a salute to the appearance of the *Empire* on Lake Erie:

... Who can keep pace with the marvels of Steam. Scarce twenty-years ago the "puffs" of "Walk-in-the-Water," first broke the primeval stillness brooding on the waters of the vast Mediterraneans of the New World, and already they are hourly furrowed by a fleet of swift steamers of unrivalled excellence. Civilization and enterprise have changed the broad wilderness of the West into the most fruitful granary of earth—young commerce has but waved her magic wand and the Empress of the American Archipelagoes now proudly points to her unequalled Empire.

Ashtabula in 1846 had about a dozen vessels in the lake service. The queen of their yards had been the *Washington*. Capital for her construction had been subscribed out of the small savings of many of Ashtabula's thousand citizens. One June night in 1838, at two o'clock as she was steaming past Silver Creek on her way with a heavy passenger list from Buffalo, she caught fire in the engine room. Within a few minutes the ship was a roaring inferno. Men, women, and children wakened from sleep in panic and rushed for the railings. Many were caught in the flames and burned to death. Others got to the ship's sides and jumped. Several of them were drowned. A honeymoon couple struggled in the water, and soon went down in each other's arms. One man threw his two children into the lake, then jumped with his wife. She was saved; he and the children were drowned. Captain Brown tried to run the vessel ashore. The cables controlling the rudder burned in two and he could not steer the vessel. She was adrift and burning fiercely, while the passengers screamed in terror. The flames shooting up into the night sky could be seen at Silver Creek, from along the shore, and for miles across the lake. The *North America* saw them and steamed to rescue. Forty of the passengers had burned to death or were drowned. The waves of Lake Erie were tossing hats, bonnets, baggage, boxes, and bits of burned wreckage all around the scene of the tragedy. The disaster was reported in the newspapers, those immediately affected mourned the loss of lives and property, and still more people booked passage on the steamers.

General Harrison came over to Cleveland for his campaign speech at the American House aboard the steamship *Sandusky*. Dickens came east to Cleveland from Sandusky aboard the *Constitution,* and Clevelanders must have taken a mischievous satisfaction when he wrote that he had been seasick. The growing list of lost ships, however, was too formidable to be ignored. Each season in the mid-nineteenth century left from 300 to 500 boats sunk, burned, or wrecked on the shores of the lakes, many of them on treacherous Lake Erie. Handsome and elegant, swift and "safe" as they were, all the same they were wooden boxes coated with inflammable paint and varnish, a powder keg for a stray spark or a bit of carelessness. And once the keg was lighted, there was little chance of avoiding a tragic conflagration. Cleveland people saw such a disaster just east of their harbor in the early morning hours in June 1850. The *G. P. Griffiths,* one of the popular steamers of its day, was nearing port when a fire started near the engine room. Most of the passengers were still asleep. Dawn was breaking, the shore and harbor were in sight, and the captain was not alarmed. Neither were the passengers who arose and dressed as the word was passed. Then the vessel ran aground on a sand bar and stuck. Panic swept through the ship, people completely lost self-control and began to scream and hurl themselves overboard. One hundred and fifty-four bodies were recovered or washed up on the beach.

Accidents could not be eliminated, but there were two things men could do to lessen their number. They were to continue to improve the structure of the vessels, and to deepen and mark the channels and light the danger points. Both were done, and further improvements are made each year. Safer construction was a slow engineering development depending on the design of better engines, elimination of fire hazards, and the coming of the iron and steel ships. Guideposts for sailing only required the doing. The first vessels out of the Reserve ports were navigated largely by the watchful eye of the captain or the mate who kept the boat in sight of land, and took note of inlets and harbors as they sailed along. They watched for signs of storms, observed the winds, and ran for cover when danger threatened. There were no lights along Lake Erie, no harbor markings of any kind at the ports until the year 1818. The shallow, oxbowing rivers which constituted the harbors along the Western Reserve were all blocked by the sand bars. Even Sandusky on its magnificent bay was blocked by the shallows between Cedar Point and Johnson's Island, and the larger vessels had to drop anchor outside and send passengers and cargo in by small boats. Until it was deepened after the opening of the canal, the harbor at Cleveland was usually only about three feet deep.

The first light there was erected in 1820. Shortly afterward lighthouses were set at Conneaut, Ashtabula, and Fairport. The lighthouse marking the rocky point at Marblehead, and guiding vessels into Sandusky Bay, was built in 1821. It is still standing, and it is a pretty sight from the channel and the islands when the morning sun catches its white tower. The floor of Lake Erie was then charted, and through the years, as the ships grew longer and of deeper draft, the channels have been dredged to receive them. The markings are now so detailed and thorough and the navigation equipment on the ships so complete and sensitive, that a captain must take a long gamble with the weather dispatches or become careless indeed to run into trouble on Lake Erie.

The story of the ships and shipping on Lake Erie since Moses Cleaveland's surveying expedition is long and fascinating. We have set down enough of it here to show how the people of the

Reserve, having first avoided the lake, soon began to use it lavishly to develop the potentialities of their venture into the Ohio wilderness. And by the end of the first half century, lake commerce was one of the most important elements in the economy of the region. The railroads threw a scare into the shipbuilders and owners. When the rails began to span the shore line along the old beach ridges between Buffalo and Cleveland, between Cleveland, Toledo, and Chicago, there were many who tolled the bells and prepared the shrouds for the Lake Erie ships. The lake shipping industry did have its moment of suffering in the first months of excessive enthusiasm for the new steam railroads. It was only temporary. Railroads cost a mint of money; vessels were comparatively cheap and the tracks across Lake Erie were free. Railroads were not free from hazards either. Some of the same citizens who saw their fine ship *Washington* burn, also saw the horrible wreck at Ashtabula when the railway bridge collapsed on a cold December night in 1876, plunging eight cars into the river seventy-five feet below. Eighty-five people were killed and everybody on board was injured. The wreckage also caught fire and burned to death those who were pinned by the crash.[2]

Neither did the railroads at first make the profits predicted by the sponsors. Many people went bankrupt. In the meantime the shipbuilders caught their breath, and after 1853 began to build faster than ever. In the next three years the Cleveland yards alone turned out thirty-seven new vessels. The others were relatively just as productive. The passenger trade did fall off, and though it revived, it never again recovered its dominance. Ore was soon to take its place. In 1852 the *Baltimore* had brought down to Cleveland from Lake Superior six barrels of iron ore.[3] No one in Cleveland valued the ore enough to pay the shipping charges. Three more years passed. Then, in August 1855, the little schooner *Columbia,* Justice Wells, Master, sailed into harbor

----

[2] The bridge was built by Amasa Stone, against the protests of other engineers. He was censored by the coroner's jury. Loss of sleep and brooding over this tragedy led Stone to die by his own hand.

[3] The original bill of lading is in the library of the Western Reserve Historical Society.

through the Cuyahoga and tied up at the Crawford and Price docks. She had come down from Lake Superior, through the newly opened Sault Canal, and she had aboard 132 tons of ore from the Marquette iron range consigned to the Cleveland Iron Mining Company. Her arrival was hardly noted among the ships coming and going on that day. And yet that voyage, and that tiny bit of cargo, were portents of the greatest single change that affected the Reserve from Moses Cleaveland's day to this—the beginning of the giant iron and steel industry of modern Cleveland, and the ore and coal trade of Conneaut, Ashtabula, Fairport, Lorain, Vermilion, Huron, and Sandusky.

CHAPTER SIXTEEN

MOLDING NEW CONNECTICUT:
East of the Cuyahoga

WE return to the settlements in the Reserve to see what was happening to them during these pre-Civil War years while the transportation and banking systems were evolving. Their growth was not sensational or feverish. If their history were to be summed up in a sentence, it would be simple: Until the middle of the century the growth of the Reserve towns was slow or imperceptible, and the pattern of their life in a rural atmosphere of an agricultural economy was relatively unchanged. Another generation would see the Reserve rise to prominence as a manufacturing and commercial region. It would see streams of Irish, German, Norwegian, Finnish, Italian, and Polish immigrants flow in through Ashtabula, Painesville, Cleveland, and Sandusky, and fan out into the Reserve to expand the farms, man the factories, work in the oil, coal, and bog-iron fields, lay the crossties and rails, and build, load and unload the ships in the Lake Erie harbors. But the old way of life, still unswervingly New England in character, lasted out the first half century in most of the Reserve and has continued into the present in a few of the villages.

Conneaut and Ashtabula, first village sites in the Reserve, had begun, after long slumber, to develop as important port towns for the eastern portion of the Reserve. They were the closest connecting links with Warren, Youngstown, and the upper Ohio River. Each had reached a population of about one thousand by 1850. Piers and lighthouses had been built for the lake vessels, and several forwarding houses were doing a good business receiving produce from the interior and shipping it to Detroit, Buffalo, and Canada. Citizens of both towns owned and operated several ships on the Great Lakes. The Public Square at Ashtabula was an open space crossed by paths and fronted by the Greek revival city hall and the Baptist Church. The coming and going of the ships and the stagecoaches broke the monotony of the isolation.

Fourteen miles south of the lake was the little county-seat town of Jefferson which Joshua Giddings and Benjamin Wade were making famous. Their little law offices, still preserved, suggest something of the atmosphere of the time. We can, in imagination, see the distinguished Congressman Giddings, six feet two inches tall, home to Jefferson after a hard session in Washington, walking about the village at his ease, barefoot, shirt-sleeved, in old brown linen pants, chatting with his fellow citizens, or discussing the law or Greek literature with his partner Wade. They were leading citizens in a village whose simple living was graced by a high cultural and intellectual tone which William Dean Howells' father, editor of the *Sentinel,* praised in superlative terms:

The little village of Jefferson, which then counted hardly more than seven hundred inhabitants, was the home of Giddings and Wade, and was the center of a most extraordinary amount of reading and thinking. Outside of Massachusetts, I do not believe that an equal average of intelligence could have been found among all sorts and conditions of men, who were there of an almost perfect social equality.

The courthouse with its six Greek columns, the hotel, the four churches and the seventy-three dwellings were gathered about the Square, and its three stores served the farming population of the surrounding townships. It was still frontier New England.

Geneva, later to become a manufacturing center, was still a small country town on the Cleveland-to-Buffalo road, and was noted as the home of Platt R. Spencer, who made his neat and flowing penmanship famous through the copybooks in the nation's schools. A monument to his memory stands in the village cemetery. The favorable soil and the climate tempered by Lake Erie made the farmlands here and around Madison especially productive for fruits, shrubs, and flowers.

Kinsman, in the northeast corner of Trumbull County, had the advantage of the continuing interest of the Kinsman family, descendants of wealthy John Kinsman, who founded the town. It remained the small center of a good farming region. Its prosperity in the 1820's and 1830's made possible the fine houses which still distinguish and give interest to the village. The Allen House, on the outskirts, built in 1821, the Congregational and Presbyterian Church, built in 1831-1832, the Kinsman House on the Public Square, built about 1823, and other fine buildings of the period which are still standing, were erected by workmen brought from Connecticut. They were, indeed, bits of the best of New England set among the forests in the eastern end of the Reserve. A good school, known as the Kinsman Academy, was established in 1842-1843. Mrs. John Kinsman and her brother also gave generous donations to keep open in the 1840's the struggling little Western Reserve College at Hudson.

While Kinsman was continuing in its New England tradition, the village of Newton Falls was becoming a portent of the new era which would supersede it. When the branch canal was opened from Akron, it became a shipping and manufacturing center with a woolen mill and paper mill. Within a decade it rose from nothing to a village of 900 people. Warren, the county-seat town, was likewise becoming a manufacturing and commercial center in a small way for a rural area. We have noted the founding and growth of its first bank and the coming of the branch canal in 1839. It was from the beginning a mill town. George Loveless dammed the Mahoning at the foot of East Market Street in 1803 and constructed a race to his gristmill. Other mills soon rose along the banks of the river to saw lumber for the new houses, and to grind corn and wheat for the settlements. We find James Van Gorder advertising in the *Chronicle* in 1830 for 5,000 bushels of wheat "to be delivered at either my upper or my lower mill." In 1817 Benjamin and Charles Stevens introduced a carding machine and began to manufacture "satinet and fulled cloth." The carding mills were popular among the settlers because they produced a finer quality of yarn without the long hours of effort around the family fireplace. This seemed to some of the conservative citizens a dangerous evolution that produced idleness in the home and encouraged them to go to a store to buy what they wanted. The paper moralized on the occasion of the agricultural exhibit in 1819:

Idleness is destructive to every social as well as moral principle. If family fabricks were made of better material, with more care and pride, foreign stuffs would soon be out of fashion and of course out of use.

In the 1830's Warren was also making wagons, and fitting them with tires fashioned from the charcoal iron furnace that was opened at near-by Hubbard in 1836.

Warren, like Kinsman, had good leadership in its civic interests. *Brown's Cincinnati Almanac* for 1810 announced:

At a neat frame school house the learned languages are taught by Mr. Gad. H. Towner, who has at present, the charge of several students of the first respectability in that part of the state. There is a public library and a number of genteel persons residing in the neighborhood.

Ten years later Warren built a fine brick building to house its academy. William Holmes McGuffey of the *Readers* fame, then fresh out of Washington College, Pennsylvania, applied for the post as teacher. The distinguished Yale men who conducted the examination adjudged McGuffey a miserable failure and refused to appoint him.

The social life of one of these early communities may be best seen through an extract from a letter written in 1806 by Yale man and lawyer John Stark Edwards. His house, built in 1807, and known as the Webb House, is the oldest building still standing in Warren. Edwards wrote to his friends in Connecticut:

We are but just through the 4th of July. It was celebrated at Warren with great splendor. About one hundred citizens of Trum-

DOWNTOWN CLEVELAND WITH TERMINAL TOWER GROUP IN FOREGROUND

CLEVELAND MUSEUM OF ART
Across the pond in Wade Park from University Circle

·   SEVERANCE HALL
Home of the Cleveland Symphony Orchestra

bull sat down to a superb dinner provided for the occasion. Seventeen toasts were drunk in flowing bumpers of wine under a discharge of firearms. The whole was concluded with a feu de joie and a procession. . . .

In the evening we attended a splendid ball at which were present about thirty couples. You would have been surprised at the elegance and taste displayed on the occasion, recollecting that within seven years, on the same spot of ground, the only retreat from the heavens was a miserable log house, sixteen feet square, in which I was obliged to take my lodgings on the floor, wrapped in my blanket. . . .

So much for New Connecticut. Do you think now we live in the woods, or is it surprising we forget that we do?

Brown's Almanac reported that there were about fifty frame houses and log buildings, "several of them on an elegant plan" in Warren in 1810. The price of lots had gone up in six years from $50 to $250. "Presbyterian and Baptist churches have been formed, but no minister is settled. In the town there are several stores. Cattle are driven from this place to the Onondaga Salt Works to be exchanged for salt." By 1850 its population had reached to nearly 2,000, and its mills, stores, bank, and county courthouse were busy with the development of the southeast corner of the Reserve.

Five miles down the river at Niles, much the same type of activity was under way. This village, named in honor of the famous Baltimore editor of *Niles' Register,* began in 1806 when James Heaton built a gristmill, a sawmill, and an iron furnace on the banks of the Mahoning. The gristmill, somewhat altered, still stands. Heaton made the first bar iron in Ohio in 1809 at his blooming forge, named "Maria Furnace" for his little daughter who lighted the first fire. The ore was hauled in from the bogs and made into stoves, kettles, and other articles in demand on the frontier. This milling and manufacturing attracted other settlers. One of these was James Ward, who in 1842, after the opening of the canal, built three more furnaces to produce bar iron, horseshoe and tire iron, and sheet iron. The industry attracted many Welsh ironmasters to the banks of the Mahoning. William Mc-

Kinley's parents moved here, and the future twenty-fifth President was born in the village on January 29, 1843.

On down the river in Mahoning County, Youngstown was developing as a third among the mill towns. Until the middle of the century it was about the same size as Warren and with quite similar interests. The Heatons set up a crude smelter on Yellow Creek in 1802. Many others were soon flourishing. Then in 1826 the first coal mine was opened. The Mahoning coal proved to be capable of reducing the iron ore from the local bogs. These two resources soon set the pattern over which Youngstown and vicinity would develop. We have already spoken of Governor David Tod's mine and of the introduction of coal to Cleveland. Because of Youngstown's location on the Mahoning River with easy access to the Ohio, it was more closely geared to Pittsburgh and the iron area of western Pennsylvania than to the Reserve. Even to this day, despite its use of the Lake Erie ports, this relationship with Pennsylvania still continues, and Youngstown is the most difficult of the Ohio cities to reach from the center of the state. By the time the railroads were built to Youngstown, the village was operating a rolling mill to make nails, spikes, rod and hoop iron, and other articles, and it was projecting the manufacture of the new T rails coming into use on the railroads. Youngstown never became particularly New Connecticut in character. Mr. Frary in his fine book *Early Homes of Ohio*, emphasizing the peculiar style of the Reserve, found none to mention in Youngstown.

At near-by Poland and westward in Canfield the contrast was marked. Though a superior grade of limestone abounded in the vicinity of Poland, and there were considerable quantities of coal and iron, the village was not industrialized. Henry Howe, after visiting it in the 1840's, reported that

it is one of the neatest villages in the state. The dwellings are usually painted white, and have an air of comfort. Considerable business centers here from the surrounding country, which is fertile. . . . Poland contains five stores, one Presbyterian and one

Methodist church, an academy, an iron foundry, one grist, one saw, one oil and one clothing mill, and about 100 dwellings.

Dr. Jared Potter Kirtland of Wallingford, Connecticut, a graduate of Yale Medical School, came here in 1823 to practice medicine. He was one of the great naturalists of his day, a true scientist, and an outstanding physician. He went up to Willoughby in 1837 to teach in the medical school and later moved to Rockport (Lakewood).

From the day of its founding, Canfield, the county-seat town, took on a New England air which it still retains. In the earlier days the Lombardy poplars surrounding the gracefully sloping oval village green could be seen from far away by the stagecoaches approaching the village on the turnpike from Cleveland to Pittsburgh. There were about 300 people living in the village. The Elijah Wadsworth house, built in 1800, stood, as it still stands, at the south end of the green. Almost facing it was, and still is, the little one-story brick office with the flat roof and heavy shutters which served the distinguished lawyer of Canfield, Elisha Whittlesey, during his long and busy career. Just back of the office on higher ground stands Whittlesey's house, beautifully executed in the Greek revival manner inside and out. It is now one of the show places of Canfield. At the north end of the green was the home of Judge Eben Newton, onetime law partner of Whittlesey, which he built in 1822. It, too, is still there. These famous Reserve men set the tone for the village. The courthouse, erected in 1842, served the county until 1879 when the seat of government was moved over to Youngstown. Its presence here at the end of the village green attests to the prominence of Canfield during the preindustrial era of the Reserve.

The Portage County towns were more isolated and developed slowly. Too far west for easy transport to the Mahoning, too far south of the lake to reach the ports, and lying off to the east of the Ohio-Erie Canal, they remained scattered and small for a half century. Deerfield, Edinburg, Campbellsport, Streetsboro were on the Cleveland-to-Pittsburgh road, but around these township centers only a few people settled. A good many incoming families acquired farms in the townships, cleared away the forest, cultivated pastures, and made much of the county into one of the cheese centers of the Reserve. It was from this region, especially around Aurora, that Baldwin, Taylor, and others gathered cheese to be marketed down the Ohio River in the 1820's. The flour and woolen mills were built at Kent, then known as Franklin Mills, on the Cuyahoga River where two falls, one seventeen feet and another twenty-five feet, furnished water power to turn the mill wheels. The township was originally purchased by Aaron Olmstead of Hartford, Connecticut, for twelve and a half cents an acre. It had a voting population of twelve in 1815. The village, scattered along and back of the river, had only about 400 inhabitants in 1850. There were then about 1,500 in the entire township. The fairly even distribution of the families over Portage County is indicated by the fact that in 1840 they ranged only from 756 in Atwater to 1,649 in Randolph, which was then larger than Ravenna. And of the twenty-one townships, only seven increased slightly while fourteen declined in population in the next few decades. The branch canal brought temporary increased activity along its route across the middle of the county.

Aurora and Streetsboro were untouched by any of the changes which transformed the Reserve. Aurora's few houses under their trees, spread along the crossroads, and Streetsboro with its famous church and village green are not very much different from the villages through which the stagecoaches passed a century ago— except for the black-top highways which have replaced the dust of the old turnpikes.

Hiram, on its hill overlooking some of the most beautiful terrain in the Reserve, likewise grew very slowly and remained a highly stable community, centered since 1850 around the rich influence of the Western Reserve Eclectic Institute, which in 1867 became Hiram College. James A. Garfield was one of its first students. He worked as a janitor in the old building in the center of the wooded campus, and later returned as president of the college.

Benjamin Tappan's town at Ravenna, which he had laid out in

1808, was coming along as the county seat. First the Presbyterians, and then Congregationalists, Universalists, Disciples, and Methodists had built churches. Jesse R. Grant, father of the general, had moved there and established a tannery, Dr. Isaac Swift had opened an apothecary shop, an academy was founded, and two newspaper and printing shops were set up. The courthouse and jail and several stores faced the square. As the roads were improved, the village began to manufacture carriages. It was in 1850 an unhurried country village in the interior of the Reserve set on the rim of the divide between the rivers that flow to the Ohio and those that go north to Lake Erie. The branch canal was off a little way to the south. According to Whittlesey many of the settlers in the earlier days moved on over to the more idealistic community at Tallmadge, driven out of Ravenna "by the systematic oppression of a large proprieter [sic] and agent, Benjamin Tappan."

The charming town of Hudson cultivated from the beginning its New England concept of distinction. We have already observed its village green, its church, and old houses which have been cherished with care and arrested in time by descendants of the original settlers. David Hudson had fostered the development of his village until his death in 1836. In 1890 his daughter celebrated in the Congregational Church her ninetieth birthday. She had been the first white child born in the almost unbroken forests of Summit County in 1800. Howe described the social tone of the village in the 1840's as "elevated."

If we were seeking a village to represent ideally the best New England tradition it would probably be Hudson. After the clearings were made and a few log cabins erected, Hudson built a school and organized a Congregational Church, both in 1802. The father of John Brown, who lived in several of the Reserve villages, set up a tannery in 1805. The young abolitionist agent spent fifteen years of his youth here working for his father. Except for a few stores, there were no commercial enterprises at Hudson. Instead it became an intellectual and educational center. Besides its two female seminaries, it was noted as the seat of the Western

Reserve College. This influential institution, later to become Western Reserve University, was founded in 1826 and conducted by Yale men who had come out to the wilderness of New Connecticut. It was long known as the "Yale of the West." Its fine old buildings and spacious, tree-embowered New England style campus to the north of the village are now a preparatory academy for boys. Colonel Porter and his son Simeon were brought to Hudson to erect the first building, now known as South College. The chapel was built in 1836. The Loomis Observatory (third in the United States) and North Hall were built in 1837, and the Athenaeum in 1840. Many other interesting buildings are preserved to show the quality and character of the village in its early days. Hudson's own house, built in 1807, may now be seen restored to its original appearance. The Connecticut house at the northeast corner of the square, now the library, dates from 1837. The Hosford House with its rare (in the Reserve) gambrel roof was built in 1832.

Melish and Hawley in their reports on the Reserve missed all these fine things that were developing at Hudson because of the impassable roads which isolated this New England village.

Tallmadge was allotted at the drawing of the Connecticut Land Company in 1798 to a company of members. The eastern half of the township was acquired by Colonel Benjamin Tallmadge and Ephraim Starr. It remained as a few lines on the surveyors' map until 1807 when David Bacon, a missionary with colonizing zeal, acquired it and built a log cabin in the midst of the township forests. He encouraged Congregational Christians to join him in a religious settlement. They came rapidly and in large numbers from Connecticut and from other less favored settlements in the Reserve. They lived by a rigorous Puritan moral code. But no man has yet devised a scheme to hold permanently together a group of human families under a single code. Money and minor points of doctrine, together with clashes of personalities, always shatter the brotherhood. This happened with Bacon's settlement after five years of enthusiasm. Bacon and his colonists could not get on together and they could not get enough money to meet their mortgage payments. Bacon departed in 1812, and much of the land went back to the proprietors who resold it at a profit.

The stamp of its New England settlement, however, remained with the survivors and was passed on by the newcomers. About a dozen of the leading men and women united in 1809 to form the Christ Church of Tallmadge. Other families joined. In 1821 they began to build on the village green itself the celebrated Congregational Church. The men spent the day before Christmas, a Monday, in dragging up the logs which were to be sawed into lumber for the imposing structure. Amadeus N. Sperry got the first log to the green at one o'clock that morning. All the shingles were hewed from a single chestnut tree. The four serene columns at the front were shaped from solid walnut logs. The lovely church was opened and properly dedicated in 1825. The accretions which disfigured it during the latter part of the century were removed and the windows and pine sash restored for the centennial meeting in 1925.

Though the wide green is now circled by paved highways, and traffic flows around it, it has not been harmed. It is a rich experience to go out there in the late evening, stand by the great elm trees, and look at the church, its columns, the windows, and its white, poised tower shining in the moonlight.

A glance at a highway map shows eight roads radiating from the village green. They are a monument to Bacon. At considerable expense, which contributed to his ultimate failure, he caused the township to be resurveyed into what he called "Great Lots"—sixteen of them, each comprising 1,000 acres. Along each lot he ran a sixty-six-foot road, east and west, north and south. Then from each corner of the green he ran intersecting roads, after the pattern of the capital at Washington, to the four corners of the township. Double rows of elms were planted along these "arterial" routes into Tallmadge, making this the village most conveniently accessible to the surrounding township in the entire Reserve.

Farther north the village of Twinsburg was founded by Moses and Aaron Wilcox, twin brothers, in 1818. In the second quarter of the century it was a flourishing educational center. Samuel Bissell, who had come as a small boy to the Portage County wilderness with his father, had gone back to Yale for his education. He returned to the Reserve in 1828 to minister to the Congregationalists at Twinsburg and teach school in a small log house. Families who could afford it paid him two dollars a term for tuition. The poor were instructed without charge. His school grew with the years. It became known as the Twinsburg Institute, had a staff of seven teachers, and in the 1840's had enrolled 300 pupils from all over the Reserve. Many of them were Indians. From the Institute many of its lawyers, doctors, ministers, and other professional men went out into the life of the Reserve. We read with regret that the institution went bankrupt during the Civil War, but the devoted Mr. Bissell, having lost his money in philanthropy to the Institute, continued in his seventies to teach school for his living.

The handsome, well-proportioned Congregational Church facing the six-acre green was erected in 1848. The old Wilcox house stands back of the bank.

These were the more peaceful villages, unaffected by the changes in transportation. Down at the Old Portage and the falls of the Cuyahoga River two young villages had sprung up with the opening of the canal. They were developing intense rivalry for population, prestige, and the honor of being chosen as the seat of Summit County which was formed in 1840.

Akron, as we have noted, was on the high point of the divide, and on the eight-mile portage path used by the Indians in going from the Muskingum over to the Cuyahoga. It was not a spot likely to be chosen by settlers looking for good farm land. Joseph Hart had chosen Middlebury, now East Akron, for a settlement in 1807, and Miner Spicer had cleared a farm in 1811 out on present Buchtel Street where the University of Akron now stands. When the commissioners decided to run the canal across the portage, General Simon Perkins of Warren (one of the commissioners) formed a partnership with Paul Williams, and bought up 1,000 acres for a trifling sum of money. They laid out the beginnings of Akron in 1825 and reaped a rich harvest. The Irish who came west to dig the canal put up a hundred cabins in the village. In 1827 when the canal was opened about 600 people were living in Akron. It was in the Reserve, but it was in no wise New Connecticut. It was on its way to becoming a cosmopolitan industrial town. The clay deposits in the neighborhood proved excellent for stoneware and sewer pipe. In 1847 the Barber Match Company opened a factory. Blast furnaces were set up to utilize the local ores. Gristmills and sawmills were erected to take advantage of the abundant water supply. Then in 1841, after much controversy, Akron was made the county seat. It was a bustling, sometimes rowdy, town of less than 2,000 people, at the junction of the Ohio and the Branch Canal, with hundreds of boats in the basin.

Cuyahoga Falls was even more an overnight town, stimulated by the two canals. The location seemed favorable. At this point the Cuyahoga River falls 200 feet in two and a half miles and offered cheap water power for the pre-steam-age industry. The village was not laid out until 1837, when a promoter with the unusual name of Birdseye Booth saw the possibility of rivaling Akron. Within three years the town had grown so rapidly that it made a strong bid for the courthouse—and almost got it. In less than a decade it had 1,200 people amid a sprawling collection of paper, saw, and flour mills, two furnaces and two tanneries, a fork and scythe factory, a starch factory, and the usual group of stores, warehouses, and churches. Expanding Akron, however, soon embraced Middlebury, and outdistanced Cuyahoga Falls which fell into the business orbit of its larger neighbor.

Geauga County, which dates from 1805, was the second county formed in the Reserve. It begins a dozen miles south of Lake Erie and rises to the high and rolling ground at Chardon and Burton where the Chagrin, the Cuyahoga, and the Grand River form to take their separate sweeping routes to the lake. In the early settlement days the farms of Geauga County were among the most isolated and lonely on the Reserve and some of the harshest suffering of pioneer life was experienced by the first settlers. The settlers were almost all farmers. They made quantities of cheese, and, among the maple forests around Chardon and Burton, they made maple syrup. No large towns grew up in the county and no important manufactures were established. The population gradually reached a sparse peak in 1840, and then as gradually leveled off. During the next forty years every township in the county except Burton and Montville showed a slight decline, and Burton changed only from 1,022 to 1,130 in those four decades.

These general observations prepare us for James A. Garfield's remarks about this portion of the Reserve, at a meeting of the Geauga County Historical Society at Burton in 1873, within sight of the belfry of Hiram College where he was educated. He said:

On this Western Reserve are townships more thoroughly New England in character and spirit than most of the towns of New England today. Cut off from the metropolitan life that has been molding and changing the spirit of New England, they have preserved here in the wilderness the characteristics of New England as it was when they left it in the beginning of this century. This has given to the people of the Western Reserve those strongly marked qualities which have always distinguished them.

Garfield might have been speaking of Burton itself, for even to this day, despite a noisome factory just north of the green, a few filling stations, and lunch shacks, it clings to its somewhat decayed glory as a New England community. It was settled largely by families from Cheshire, Connecticut. Its splendid museum at the south end of the green preserves the physical setting of the pioneer life by-passed by the industrial era. The green itself retains to an unusual degree the charm of the old village. It is generously proportioned and is dark and cool in summer with its thick forest of maple trees. A log cabin for maple-sugar making, owned by the village, is in the middle of it. Graveled walks cross the Square. It is, indeed, a museum piece.

Chardon, on the other hand, though retaining its eleven-acre Square and its row of post-Civil War business houses facing it from the west, is more of a modern town. The green is sleek and trim with many walks and few trees. Many of the village people commute to Cleveland where they work in the factories. In the past century its population has increased only from about 400 to its present 2,000. It was laid out in 1808 and named for Peter Chardon Brooks, proprietor of extensive acres in the township. Settlers were attracted by the beautifully rolling farmland along the hills and valleys surrounding the village. It was good dairy country. The New Englanders were especially delighted with the sugar-maple forests which abounded in the county. From the earliest days to the present, in February and March, when the cold nights and warm days cause the sap to flow freely, the farmers have hung out their pails under the metal spouts on thousands of trees to catch the sweet liquid. A spirit of festivity enlivened the county during the season of boiling and evaporating the sap into high-quality syrup and sugar. For many years the product was shipped east by the carload to be sold to help meet the demand for Vermont syrup. As produced by the best makers, it was equal to the finest product of New England.[1] The demand is now so heavy that the entire output is marketed in the region, some of it from roadside stands.

Chardon celebrates this further link with the pioneers and the New England tradition by holding a Maple Festival usually during the first days of April. The crude pioneering methods of rendering the sap in kettles are seen in contrast with the modern vats at the larger groves. People from miles around come to the Festival.[2]

It is in these gestures, and the relative leisure of this county seat and farm trading center, that the early Reserve is perpetuated at Chardon.

Painesville during the first half century became a port of

---

[1] Through bad husbandry in many of the groves the trees have declined in quality and their yield has been reduced. Experts from the agricultural experiment stations are attempting to show the present-day farmers how to improve and care for their trees.

[2] In 1948 the governor of Ohio and the governor of Vermont were guests at the Festival. They were to settle the long vexing question which state had the superior product. Each governor, blindfolded, tasted samples from each state. Each playfully and courteously pronounced the syrup of the rival state the better. The question is still open.

entry, by way of Fairport Harbor and the Grand River, for many settlers in the Reserve. It became the seat of Lake County when it was formed in 1840. It was an important village on the road from Cleveland to Buffalo, a center of trade, and a seat of learning. The surrounding land, protected from early and late frosts by its proximity to Lake Erie, was favorable for farming and for fruit and vegetables. Some of the outstanding business and professional men of the Reserve settled at Painesville. It was for a time the home of Governor Samuel Huntington. The artist William H. Beard was born here in 1825, and his more celebrated brother James spent his early years in Painesville. Thomas W. Harvey of textbook fame came out in 1833 at the age of twelve, and later became superintendent of the Painesville schools. The Painesville Academy was a respected institution of learning a century ago. The Lake Erie Female Seminary, now Lake Erie College (for women), was founded on the beautiful New England campus of forty acres at the west end of the village in 1857.

We have noted Painesville's part in promoting banks and railroads. This interest was a reflection of the business acumen and the accumulating wealth of the community. The prosperity and the taste of these early founders and settlers may still be seen in the surviving houses of the town. Painesville was fortunate to have the noted architect-builder Jonathan Goldsmith come to the village in 1811 and live there until his death in 1847. His fine taste and skill produced for Painesville and the neighboring villages of Willoughby and Mentor some of the handsomest and most interesting houses in the Reserve. His own lovely cottage, which he built in 1841, with its low-pitched roof and its typical frieze, ornamented with grilles, was unfortunately burned in 1927. He built the splendid house on North State Street in 1829 for Dr. John H. Mathews, another for Stephen Mathews in 1831, one for Albert Morley, and two for Isaac Gillett's daughters—all of which are still standing. The Rider Tavern, already mentioned, was another of his many buildings. The appearance of family dwellings like these in less than a decade after Doctor Hawley's visit to the Reserve is the best witness we can summon to show how the region along the lake was faring in these years.

Neighboring Mentor and Willoughby a few miles to the west toward Cleveland were developing over a somewhat similar pattern—with the exception of the lake-port and county-seat activities—but more slowly. Willoughby was the medical center of the region. The Willoughby Medical College was opened in 1834. It was for a decade a flourishing school, turning out doctors for the Reserve. Like several other such schools of that day, however, it had its troubles in getting cadavers for its 175 students to use in the dissecting room. The trade of grave snatching flourished. The public was sensitive to this practice. The Willoughby College was suspected of taking the body of Mr. Tarbell from its grave. The irate citizens stormed the college buildings and broke up equipment. The school closed in 1847—some of the professors moving to Cleveland to establish what later became the medical school of Western Reserve University and others to Columbus to found the Starling Medical School, now the medical school of the Ohio State University.

CHAPTER SEVENTEEN

OUT OF THE WILDERNESS:
West of the Cuyahoga

As we have noted, the territory west of the Cuyahoga was not surveyed for settlement until several years after the eastern portion of the Reserve because of the uncertainty of the claims of the Indians. The first settlers established themselves near the Black River around 1810, in what later became Amherst, Ridgeville, and Eaton; but they could be counted on the fingers of both hands until after the close of the War of 1812. At the mouth of the river, which provided a good harbor, there was only the trading post of Nathan Perry and Azariah Beebe. After the war, ships for the lake trade were built alongside the river, and a village spread along the banks. It received a good quantity of wheat for shipment during the 1830's. By 1836 there were enough people there to incorporate the village which they named Charleston. The wide deep river offered such an excellent harbor close to the grainfields that the village had a natural expectation that it would be the focal lake point for the Reserve. The canal commissioners thought differently. Then the railroads selected a more southerly route, leaving Charleston (Lorain) twice disappointed, and cut off from the stream of traffic. The village declined and all but disappeared until the radical change in economy and transportation in the 1870's once more brought it to life with the new name of Lorain.

Elyria became the center of the county. Heman Ely purchased 12,500 acres along the forks of the Black River at the falls. Like the other colonizing holders of vast acreages, he at once built a gristmill and a sawmill to supply the first essential wants of settlers. He sent out axmen to clear a portion of the forest for farms and houses. Then he sold it off to the settlers for a small down payment and a four-year mortgage. He laid out the town and coined its name by adding *ria* to his own, at the same time relishing the corrupted classicism of the resulting Elyria. Enough people had come by 1822 to form a county, under Ely's lobbying, with his village as the county seat. It was incorporated in 1833. Quarries of good building stone were opened here and at Amherst, beginning an important industry in the county. Amherst stone was used in many Ohio buildings, such as those at Oberlin College, and was shipped in quantity across to Canada. The Parliament buildings were made from it. Flour mills were built, a furnace and machine shop were set up, the lumber mill grew, and by the time the railroads reached Elyria, it had become an industrial town of some 1,500 people as well as the trading center for a slowly developing cattle, dairy, grain, and fruit-growing countryside.

Wellington was a quiet country town in the heart of the dairy section. At one time it was the second village in the nation in the production of cheese. Substantial houses, well back from the tree-lined main street, spread southward from the business block. Its citizens were ardent prohibitionists and abolitionists. Kelley's C.C. & C. Railroad linking it with Cleveland did not alter its rural character or appearance.

Oberlin was, as it still is, the distinguished college town of the western portion of the Reserve, and its development has been governed by the influence and free intellectual tradition of Oberlin College. It had been hacked out of a dense, unbroken wilderness in the damp plain eight miles from Elyria in the winter of 1832-1833. One wonders what spirit or vision led the Reverend John J. Shipherd, after a hard ride over the district on a hot August day, to select this unprepossessing spot as the site for a college. Perhaps it was in part at least a pledge from some New Haven men of 500 acres for the erection of a college. A twelve-acre square was blocked out as a campus and village green. The board of trustees held its first meeting here in 1832. The legislature granted them a charter, and in December 1833, in a log building, the doors of the college were opened to the first students.

The venture was viewed with disfavor by the people of the county because of its radical views and fanatic program for educating women as well as men, Negroes as well as whites. It was antitobacco, antiliquor, anticlassics, antislavery, and ardently missionary. In its early years it was often referred to as the people's college because it gave poor boys and girls of good mind and character full opportunity for a Christian education. In fact it laid strong emphasis on the dignity of manual labor and service as a complement to intellectual and spiritual discipline.

Its abolitionist sentiment was intensified by the arrival in Oberlin in 1835 of freedom-loving students and faculty from Lane Seminary in Cincinnati where they had been forbidden to associate with Negroes or debate the issue of slavery. In the 1840's Oberlin enrolled over 500 students each academic year. And from its halls went forth a stream of teachers, ministers and missionaries of both sexes not only to the Reserve, but to the uttermost parts of the world. Several papers were published here, the professorial houses spread along the gracious streets, and the village assumed an air of confident leadership which it has never surrendered.

The region about Medina was an exceptionally heavy forest. Prior to the end of the War of 1812 the few settlers were seven to a dozen miles apart, each family in its own clearing. Joseph Harris had cleared a block of forest near the south edge of the Reserve in 1811, seventeen miles from the nearest family. The Burr family came the following year. Indians were still passing by their cabins along their ancient trail through the county from Sandusky to Tuscarawas. A few more Connecticut families came in 1813. Others came after the war, raising the population to several hundred, and the county was organized in 1818. There were so many wolves in the woods that the settlers could not keep sheep. Their pens would be raided and wiped out at the very door of the cabin. Bears ate up their pigs. One of the memorable experiences of the first settlers was the organized drive to exterminate these wild animals. It was known as the Hinckley Hunt, in honor of Judge Hinckley, the great landed proprietor of the northeast townships. On Christmas Eve 1818, about six hundred men and boys from all over this section of the Reserve—from Cleveland, Newburg, Brecksville, from Bath and Granger, from Medina, Brunswick, and Liverpool—assembled at Hinckley with guns, axes, knives, and dogs. They came on horseback, sleds, and on foot. They spread with military organization along lines blazed on the trees to drive the game into the center. When the results of the slaughter were computed, they found seventeen dead wolves, twenty-one bears, three hundred deer, and uncounted turkeys, foxes, coons, and other small animals. The game was divided among the men of the hunt.

Medina became one of the great wheat and corn-producing districts of the Reserve. The grain piled up profitlessly in the 1820's because it could not be taken to a market. The opening of the canal, followed by the stage road from Columbus to Cleveland, gave outlet to the farms and the people began to prosper. They rapidly cleared extensive areas. The magnificent virgin timber forming a solid canopy of foliage high above the forest floor was so free of underbrush and low limbs that the settlers could drive horses and sleds through the woods. When they cleared the land they cut only about halfway through the bole of each giant tree over the space of several acres. Then, when the wind was right, they felled the trees on the windward edge, crashing them against the slashed trunks in the plot, and tumbling hundreds of trees to the ground like a row of dominoes. The "inexhaustible supply" of the world's finest timber was burned to expose wheat fields to the sun. In our day of bulldozers, tractors, and power saws it is hard to conceive of the years of immense, backbreaking manual labor, of farmers and their sons swinging axes and pushing saws by hand, to clear the slashings and the stumps from their farms and villages on the Western Reserve.

In the midst of this farming country the little town of Medina, twenty-eight miles from Cleveland, and now closely geared to the metropolis, grew up slowly as the market, trade, and governing center of the county. It was laid out in 1818 by Captain Badger around its intimate Public Square and was for a time called Mecca. It accumulated along with its 600 inhabitants the usual collection of a half-dozen churches for the different denominational beliefs of its citizens, several stores, and a newspaper printshop, all centering about the county courthouse and the fenced-in Square. On the outskirts were, in 1840, a woolen mill, a flour mill, an ax factory, and a furnace. To the south of it were the farm villages of continuing charm—Wadsworth, Leroy, and Lodi. Leroy is still a small, authentic New England village, with graceful white churches, an inn, and well-kept homes on large lawns about the wooded green.

Over in the Firelands the villages of Norwalk and Milan, after a late start, were making their way energetically forward, surrounded by the good farming townships of Lyme, New Haven, New London, Greenwich, Berlin; and served by the port towns of Vermilion, Huron, and Sandusky on its magnificent bay. The high and pleasant ridge where Norwalk stands was selected as a village site in 1815 by Elisha Whittlesey who had come over to the Firelands on law business. With Platt Benedict of Danbury, Connecticut, and Frederic Fallig, he formed a partnership to develop a town there. Benedict rode horseback to Connecticut and purchased the land for $2.15 per acre. The village was laid out in 1816, by Almon Ruggles, and in 1817 Platt Benedict built there the first log cabin. He was a four-year-old boy when his family suffered the burning of Danbury, and now at last he had land and a home in the Sufferers' Tract. Whittlesey got the legislature to make Norwalk the seat of Huron County. He caused to be planted along wide Main Street the rows of maple trees whose successors still give to the avenue, the most beautiful in the Reserve, its charm and peace. Also under Whittlesey's leadership the village founded an academy and erected a three-story school building. It was still famous in the 1830's and 1840's for the quality of its work and the capable men it educated. President

Hayes, Governor Foster, and General McPherson were among the notable men who went forth from the Norwalk Academy.

Like Hudson, Canfield, Painesville, and a few other distinctly (and distinguished) New England communities on the Reserve, Norwalk had from the beginning many well-to-do citizens who accumulated wealth in the third and fourth decades of the century and built for themselves the handsome houses which still stand, neat and well-kept, on the zealously cultivated, deep, wide lawns on West Main Street. The white Fulstow House, at 99 West Main, with its green shutters, its four two-story, octagonal columns, and its oval sunburst was built by Thaddeus Sturgis in the early 1830's. The Stewart House at 6 South Church, also classical revival in style, was erected in 1833. The Georgian-style brick house at 54 West Main, now known as the Martin House, was built in 1831 for Moses Kimball. The brick house at 114 West Main, with its simple Greek lines and its two fluted columns flanking the doorway close to the front walls, dates from 1848. It was built as a Presbyterian school for girls during Norwalk's heyday as an educational center. H. M. Wooster made it into a residence in 1858, and it is still owned and occupied by his descendants. These are but a few representative houses of the period of the early prosperity of this town in the heart of the Firelands.

Norwalk was on the main turnpike from Cleveland and the railroad line to the west. It developed the diversified small industries common to most of the county-seat towns: flour mills, sawmills, sash and door factories, carriage works, foundries, and machine shops. But the town, though small (about 2,000 at the mid-century), absorbed and profited by these without losing its village atmosphere, or its interest as a trading and banking center for the rich farming region of the Firelands which it served.

Erie County was blocked off from the north end of Huron in 1838. A dozen families chose the location at the mouth of the Vermilion River and settled there above the winding lagoons between 1808 and 1810. David Abbott, an eccentric and public-spirited man from Massachusetts, a Yale graduate, bought 1,800 acres along the Huron River in 1808, and came out with his family in 1810. John Beatty of New London, Connecticut, visited the Firelands in the same year. He liked what he saw, and acquired about 40,000 acres of land. He brought his family out in 1815. He became a Methodist preacher, holding service for his neighbors in a log schoolhouse. He built out of his own pocket a church on the Public Square at Sandusky, five miles from his own home. Almon Ruggles, also of Danbury, Connecticut, surveyor of the Firelands, chose Berlin Heights for his home and settlement. John Hoak and John Fleming brought some fruit trees over here from Canada in 1812. The trees flourished in this soil and temperate climate and were the beginning of the extensive fruit orchards and gardens which, to this day, profitably occupy many of the citizens of these townships.

Many of these people had to leave the Firelands during the War of 1812. But when the dangers were over, most of them returned, and emigrants in considerable numbers began to come into this desirable portion of the Firelands. Ebenezer Merry of West Hartford, Connecticut, became proprietor of the area on the high banks overlooking the Huron River eight miles south of Lake Erie. An Indian village had been perched on this site in 1804, with a Moravian missionary working among them. The Indians migrated to Canada when the first Connecticut settlers began to enter the Firelands. Merry constructed a flour mill and a sawmill, as usual, and laid out the pretty village of Milan in 1816 with its pleasing, offset rectangular green. It became, as we have seen, the great grain port of the district and a shipbuilding center in the 1830's and 1840's. Its growth was arrested during the railroad era and its population has declined. But it still retains in decay suggestions of its glory of a century ago in its Square, a few fine houses, and the river. Its citizens of 1847 did not, of course, know that their village would be of interest to our day chiefly because in that year Thomas Edison was born in the little redbrick house that almost leans over the steep bluff of the Huron River north of the Square. He lived there for seven years, and afterward remembered the Square filled with farmers' teams, the wagonloads of oak barrel staves, the wheat elevators, and the launching of new boats before crowds of spectators on the high ground known to him as the Hogback.

While the enterprising citizens of Milan were building their canal to Lake Erie and trading vigorously in grain, Huron, the natural port town on the lake, slumbered as an inactive village. But as the village was by-passed by the railroads, and the canal lost its usefulness in the late 1840's and early 1850's, Huron revived again. It dredged its harbor and built a lighthouse in 1847. It began to build ships and its little fishing fleets put out to the fishing grounds in the lake. Its houses clustered along the river and around the Public Square which was placed on the lake front and commands a fine view of the Lake Erie waters.

Sandusky, the county-seat town, has already been under our view at various times as we have considered the banks, stage roads, and railroads of the era, and the vigor with which its citizens strove to secure for their port a full share of the trade which the advantages of Cleveland and Toledo were threatening to divert. Its setting on its wide bay, almost encircled by Cedar Point and Marblehead, and with the low-lying islands in sight to the north, was the most attractive prospect on the entire lake front. It had been the terminal for the Indian trail across the Reserve from Youngstown, and a trading post since the first entrance of white men into the west. It was not settled, however, until 1817 when another Danbury man, Zalmon Wildman, and Isaac Mills of New Haven purchased tracts of land here and laid out a town under the name of Portland. Three log houses were put up that year. The name was changed to Sandusky City.

When the Reverend Mr. Read visited Sandusky in 1834 he was impressed chiefly by the stumps in the streets, the leaky, unclean inn where he spent the night, the "worn and dirty aspect" of the two unpainted churches, and the "very low" state of "religion and moral feeling" displayed in the grog-drinking, swearing, Sabbath-breaking habits of its lower-class inhabitants. A dozen years later Charles Dickens thought it looked "something like the back of an English watering-place, out of season." Henry Howe visited it a few years after Dickens was there. He praised its "pleasant situation" and was particularly impressed by its "large and handsome public square on which, fronting the lake, are the principal churches and public buildings. . . . The town is now very thriving, and promises to be, ere many years, a large city." Five hundred lake ships were calling and leaving the port with passengers, emigrants, and produce of all kinds. These ships connected with the two railroads into the interior which Sandusky had just built. Irish and Germans were entering to place their peculiar cultural stamp on the town and its environs. It was already a fishing port, and it was beginning to make barrels, wagon wheels, and lime; it had two furnaces, an oil mill, and machine shops. The population was then about 3,000.

Howe's drawing of the harbor and lake front in 1846 shows a bow-heavy side-wheel steamer pulling away under clouds of smoke from the long dock and wharf, a half-dozen sailboats and some smaller craft on the bay, and an impressive panorama of towered buildings, commission and forwarding houses, and other business houses along the shore line.

CHAPTER EIGHTEEN

ЄMERGENCE OF ϹLEVELAND

IN THE Public Square at Cleveland in 1840, cows leaned against the new, whitewashed fences which the city fathers had erected to keep them out of the grass. The railings divided the Square into four sections. The little trees which had just been set out along the fences were protected by rails stood on end, wigwam style. The freshly whitewashed brick courthouse, two stories high, with a railing around its cornice and a big Ionic wood belfry rising high above the roof, looked out over the trees toward the lake from the southwest quadrangle of the Square, where the statue of Moses Cleaveland now surveys his city. The Old Stone Church, on its present site on the north side of the Square, faced the courthouse. The nice dwelling houses of Doctor Long, C. M. Giddings, Elijah Bingham, William Lemen, John W. Allen, and other prominent citizens also faced the Square or spread about the corners on Superior, Ontario and Euclid streets. Both Superior and Ontario streets crossed the Square, though the early maps indicate that these ten acres were to be a green with traffic flowing around, not across it. The Cleveland House, a center of social life, stood on the site of the present hotel of that name.

The region east of the Square was still mostly forest with few houses. Leonard Case's homestead was one block away on Superior Street. The little one-story building near by, which Case had used for many years as an office, had been given over to his son William. He called it the Ark. A picture of it hangs in the Western Reserve Historical Society Library. William Case gathered about him twelve of the young men of the town who were interested in hunting, in mounting specimens of Reserve wildlife, and in reading and conversation. It was the club center for the social and intellectual life of some of Cleveland's most gifted second generation sons. Out of their interests in the Ark grew the Case Institute of Technology, the Case Library, the Kirtland Society of Natural Science (named for Dr. Jared P.) and other cultural monuments in Cleveland.

The city itself all lay between the Square, the river, and the lake, in the present old "downtown" district. Here were markets and hotels—the American House, where Presidential candidate General Harrison addressed the citizens who gathered in the street under the balcony cheering the Log Cabin and Hard Cider campaign of 1840; the Eagle Tavern, the pretentious Cleveland Center House, Belden's Tavern, and the Franklin House from which the stagecoaches departed for Buffalo, Pittsburgh, Columbus, and Detroit. Here were Trinity and other churches and the Cleveland Academy, opened in 1822, and headed for several years by Harvey Rice. Along wide (132-foot) unpaved Superior Street were rows of mercantile houses: Alexander Sackett's, Baldwin and Weddell's, Raymond and Clark's dry goods, Griffith, Standart & Co.'s forwarding house, Worthington's hardware, Crittenden's jewelry, Butler's bookstore, Doctor Strickland's "incorruptible teeth," the banks, the four newspaper printing shops.

Most of the 6,000 inhabitants in 1840 lived in this area, with the better homes on Water (West Ninth), St. Clair, and Lake streets. Their appointments were those of a country village rather than a growing metropolis. They had not changed very much since Alfred Kelley, as a rising young lawyer, built for his prospective bride a new brick house on the winding path known as Water Street in 1816. Some of the houses were substantial and spacious, each in its yard behind a paling fence, many with charming flower gardens and neat walks. The families got their water from their own wells and cisterns, and used outside toilets because there were no waterworks or sewage systems for many more years to come. They threw their garbage on the back ash heap or on a collective dump where the village pigs still rooted. The streets were not lighted at night. The citizens got their mail, which came in with uncertainty, from the postmaster after paying the postage due. They read the daily *Herald* or the *Advertiser* which, two years later, they would buy as the new *Plain Dealer*.

Out near the point overlooking the river and the lake the light-house was a landmark on land and water, and dominated the panorama as viewed from across the Flats on Brooklyn Hill: iron foundries, soap and candle factories, breweries, carriage works, a pottery, a millstone-cutting plant, and other manufactures spread along the river and in the Flats; the docks and wharves, the canal basin at the foot of Superior Street, busy with canal-boats coming in, unloading, turning; and the coming and going of 2,000 ships a year with hundreds of visitors and immigrants and produce, which kept the Cuyahoga under the bluff swarming all day and most of the night with activity. The Weddells, the Cases, the Mathers, the Huntingtons, the Handys, the Otises, the Allens, and their friends, colleagues, and competitors were discussing banks, railroads, schools, extension of the city boundaries east of the Square, water supply, street improvements. The Cleveland Greys, the newly reorganized City Guards, drilled and paraded about the Square in their gold-trimmed uniforms with "glittering bayonets" and staged precise military drills on the Fourth of July. The men of the fire-department companies, dressed in the coats bought for them by the city, were organized under the colorful names of the Eagle No. 1, the Neptune No. 2, the Phoenix No. 4, the Forest City Hook and Ladder No. 1, the Hope Hose No. 1, and the Cataract No. 5. They drilled and practiced their art of tapping cisterns and wells to be ready when the bell on the Baptist Church warned that another fire had broken out in the wooden city. The 260 members of the Cleveland Temperance Society held meetings, while the Shakespeare Saloon assured visitors that this "agreeable retreat" would pay every attention to "their comfort and convenience." Nicholas Dockstader, the leading hat, cap, and fur dealer of the city, was mayor. Former Mayor John W. Willey, a prominent lawyer and state senator, had just ascended the bench as Judge of the Court of Common Pleas of Cuyahoga County.

Moses Cleaveland's city had come a long way in the fifteen years since the first earth for the canal was turned in 1825 when it was a dormant, sickly village of only 500 people almost overshadowed by Newburg, its contender for the honor of being the county seat. Every visitor had, however, confirmed the founder's judgment, whether he liked the present condition of the village or not, that it was potentially the right site for a great city, and that in due time the hopes of the general would be fulfilled. Harvey Rice, who came out in September 1824 to become classics teacher and principal of the Academy, set down his impressions on arrival. After coming into the harbor over the sand bar in a jolly boat and walking up Union Lane to spend the night at Michael Spangler's tavern, he

took a stroll to see the town, and in less than half an hour saw all there was of it. The town . . . was proud of itself, and called itself the "gem of the West." In fact, the Public Square, so called, was begemmed with stumps, while near its center glowed its crowning jewel, a log courthouse erected in 1812. . . . The dwellings were generally small, but were interspersed here and there with a few pretentious mansions.

Milo H. Hickox arrived in 1831. He was a mechanic and became one of the sturdy volunteer fire fighters of Cleveland. He wrote that

Cleveland . . . is the pleasantest sight that you ever saw. The streets are broad and cross each other at right angles. The courthouse is better than the one in Rochester. [This was the new one, built in 1828, and freshly whitewashed at the beginning of this chapter.] . . . I get nine shillings and six pence per day and board myself. . . . Now for the morals. There are between fifteen and twenty grogshops, and they all live. There was one opened here last week. . . . There is a temperance society, with ten or a dozen male members. The Presbyterian Church has four male members, Baptist six, Methodist about the same, the Episcopal is small [there were two male members]; they have a house, the others have not. The court-house is used at this time for a theatrical company, and is well filled with people of all classes.

Mrs. Rebecca Rouse, who had come to Cleveland the year before as a missionary to the Western Reserve, confirms this analysis of the church attendance. Church meetings were feminine gatherings. When Mrs. Rouse inquired of her landlord at Merwin's Tavern on Sunday morning where there was a church service, he directed her to an upper room in a house opposite the tavern where a few Methodists had gathered for a prayer meeting. Her cottage was a women's headquarters for religious work, and the distributing center for the American Sunday School Union and Tract Society publications which were piled high against the front windows. The frequenters of the twenty grogshops were wont to declare that "there is more religion in Rouse's windows than in the whole village besides."

John Stair, a visiting Englishman, came to see the city in 1833. He wrote that Cleveland is, "for the size of it, the prettiest town I have ever seen in America." He was impressed by the good taste of the people, and observed that "a person who understood drawing, music, etc., so as to teach it well might make money apace there." He noted the pressing need for money and banking in the Reserve; "frequently men who are possessed of a good farm and considerable stock are weeks and months without a cent; they barter, or as they call it, trade for almost everything."

Maximilian, Prince of Wied, saw the town on a clear, sunny June day in 1834. He had come up from Portsmouth on the Ohio River by the newly opened canal. He had been impressed by the heavy walls of forest that still lined the canal most of the way between Akron and Cleveland. He went at once to gaze fondly and appreciatively on Lake Erie, and he wrote:

The sea-like expanse of Lake Erie was very striking when emerging from the wooded village. . . . The dark blue lake stretches to the far horizon like the ocean; the eye is attracted by the white sails and the smoke of the steamboats. . . .

He observed the boats in the basin, the breakwaters, wharves, and lighthouse; and, as he steamed past the city at noon aboard the *Oliver Newberry,* he prophesied the future greatness of this city linked by waterway with the markets of the world.

James D. Cleveland, jurist, and a leading trustee and founder of the Western Reserve Historical Society, the Cleveland Library Association, and the Museum of Art, arrived in Cleveland in 1835. In his review of "The City of Cleveland Sixty Years Ago," he described his walk up Superior Street past the stores and houses which we have mentioned, the town pump on the corner by the Commercial Bank of Lake Erie, the pigs and cows roaming the streets, and the "groves of fine black oaks and chestnuts on Erie Street between Superior and Prospect Streets and a good many in the northeast part of the Public Square." Then he added that "with its scattered houses, its numerous groves, its lofty outlook upon the lake, its clear atmosphere, as yet unpolluted by smoke, Cleveland was as beautiful a village as could be found west of New Haven."

Several of the finer houses were built by Jonathan Goldsmith, the New Haven architect who settled at Painesville, his son-in-law Charles W. Heard, and Simeon Porter. Heard and Porter were for many years partners as architects and builders. Heard was Goldsmith's son-in-law. He had served as his apprentice in Painesville and learned his style. He moved to Cleveland in the 1830's to look after his father-in-law's building there. He was one of the early volunteer firemen. He became wealthy and built and owned the Heard Block in Cleveland. Simeon Porter had learned his trade from his father at Tallmadge and Hudson. After his father's death, he took over and completed the contract for the academy buildings at Hudson. Unlike Hudson and Norwalk, Cleveland's booming manufactures and trade brushed aside all these early homes around the Square and in the first blocks along Superior and Euclid, and no examples survive. Photographs and drawings show them to be of the same design and proportions as those which still stand in other portions of the Reserve, and enable us to see in our mind's eye their setting in the village which so charmed James D. Cleveland.

The Samuel Cowles House, on Euclid, built in 1833, was said to be the most beautiful Cleveland example of Goldsmith's work.

Near it was another, almost its equal, built for Cowles' law partner, Sherlock J. Andrews. Andrews, a native of Wallingford, Connecticut, had come out in 1825 along with John W. Allen, to practice law. He became another of those remarkable public-spirited citizens with whom the village was blessed. He helped organize Trinity Church and erect the building. He was a member of the committee for celebrating the opening of the canal in 1827. He was the first president of the Public Library Board and first president of the Cleveland Bar Association. His house had to come down for Euclid Avenue business, but we owe to him a debt for preserving so much of the material on which we must draw to recreate the early life of the region. It was he, along with Harvey Rice, John W. Allen, and others of the pioneering generation, who organized the Early Settlers' Association of Cuyahoga to perpetu-ate, as Harvey Rice explained, "the kindly feelings for which pioneer life was proverbial, and to secure the preservation of much of the unwritten history of our county and its vicinity." They published the priceless *Annals,* and transferred their collections to the Western Reserve Historical Society "for preservation and for the benefit of the present and future generations." We thank them for the rich legacy.

William Lemen's (or Lemon's) house, erected in 1829, was on the south side of Superior at the Square. It was of one-floor plan, particularly attractive with its low-pitched roof hidden from the street by a high, solid balustrade of Greek design, and its long porch with six Doric columns projecting almost to the paling fence at the street's edge. It was strikingly similar in design to the house built in 1840 in the Firelands south of Vermilion for Joseph Swift, except that the porch on this house was recessed like so many of that period in the Reserve. It too has disappeared, not by invasion of business, but by fire.

The city must have been pleasing in those years to elicit from Charles Dickens' disgruntled pen, on the occasion of his brief stop-over in 1842, the adjectives "pretty" and "beautiful." He had read at Sandusky an article in the newly established *Plain Dealer,* edited by the redoubtable J. W. Gray, which, Dickens felt, insulted his country by threatening to whip England a third time and to sing "Yankee Doodle in Hyde Park, and Hail Columbia in the scarlet courts of Westminster." It was, indeed, a bit of gratuitous and irresponsible jingoism and Dickens had a right to feel hostile toward Cleveland where the article had been reprinted by the *Plain Dealer*. He arrived on the *Constitution* at midnight on April 25, and lay over until nine the next morning. The *Herald* ran a short article saying that

while the boat was in port this morning Mr. D. took a stroll about town with a traveling friend, returned to the boat and immediately retired to his stateroom. The gentlemen and loafers gathered about the dock got a sight of "The Dickens"—and that was all!

Dickens wrote his own account in a letter for his biographer John Foster. He said:

We lay all Sunday night at a town (and a beautiful town, too) called Cleveland; on Lake Erie. The people poured on board in crowds by six Monday morning to see me; and a party of "gentlemen" actually planted themselves before our little cabin, and stared in at the door and windows *while I was washing and Kate lay in bed*. I was so incensed at this, and at a certain newspaper published in that town . . . that when the mayor came on board to present himself to me, according to custom, I refused to see him and bade Mr. Q. tell him why and wherefor. His honor took it very coolly and retired to the top of the wharf, with a big stick and whittling knife, with which he worked so lustily (staring at the closed door of our cabin all the time) that long before the boat left the big stick was no bigger than a cribbage peg.

He missed, by this ill humor, seeing the distinguished and greatly beloved Dr. Joshua A. Mills, the mayor of Cleveland, and proprietor of a drugstore on Superior Street.

On his brief walk through the town, Dickens was most concerned to see the *Plain Dealer* office. He wrote in his *American Notes:*

I found [Cleveland] a pretty town, and had the satisfaction of beholding the outside of the office of the journal from which I have just quoted. I did not enjoy the delight of seeing the wit who indited the paragraph in question, but I have no doubt he is a prodigious man in his way, and held in high repute by a select circle.

For years afterward Editor Gray relished the Dickens compliment to him as a "wit" and "prodigious man" for a paragraph which he did not write, but only reprinted with a credit line which Dickens either did not notice or failed to remember. This pretty town, this most beautiful village west of New Haven, had come along amazingly since its first sickly years when its people burned with fever and shook with chills and wondered if they should move out to Newburg. After 1825 there was no longer any doubt about its future. The rapidity of its commercial expansion after 1827, still further accelerated after 1833, proved the predictions of those who labored in season and out to improve its position. Henry Howe observed in 1846 that

the Erie canal constitutes the principal source of its vast advantages; without that great work, it would have remained in its former insignificance.

He added his own superlatives to those of other visitors:

It is one of the most beautiful towns in the Union, and much taste is displayed in the private dwellings and disposition of shrubbery.

In addition it was

the great mart of the greatest grain-growing State in the Union, and it is the Ohio and Erie canals that have made it such. . . . The natural advantages of this place are unsurpassed in the West.

In the six years since 1840 it had grown from 6,071 to 10,135. About 1,300 of them had come over from Germany. Within a few years they had two German newspapers—the *Anzeiger* and the *Wächter am Erie*—and nine other journals printed in German. In 1850 Cleveland's population was 17,034.

By that time it was no longer the village described at the beginning of this chapter. It was moving almost too fast to chronicle. On the west bank of the Cuyahoga was separate and independent Ohio City with a population in 1840 of 1,577. Norman C. Baldwin was its mayor. It was incorporated in 1836, simultaneously with Cleveland, as City of Ohio. It was an ambitious place, on the road to Medina and Wooster. It had a good hotel where, it was hoped, travelers on the road would stop. It had its own business houses which competed with those in Cleveland, three churches, and it published its own newspaper. It felt a keen rivalry with its neighbor across the Cuyahoga. The ambitious City of Ohio got authority to construct its own slips and canal basin, and in 1837 actually did proceed to build a canal and attempt to assess the cost to the abutting property holders. The scheme, of course, failed, but fifteen years later the abandoned canal bed furnished a good right-of-way approach for the railroad tracks to the river and into Cleveland.

In the 1840 presidential campaign, which brought General Harrison to the balcony of the American House, Ohio City, as it was always called despite its official name, erected a cabin, completely furnished with rifle, dried pumpkin strips, and pioneer furniture to pay tribute to the Ohio candidate. It had given up hope of surpassing Cleveland in size and quantity of business, but Warren Jenkins could write in the *Ohio Gazetteer* for 1841 that

this town has, perhaps, grown more rapidly for the past few years, than any other in the state; and great enterprise has exhibited itself by the grading of streets, and numerous other public and private improvements. Many elegant mansions, and extensive blocks of warehouses, stores, shops, etc., etc., have been recently erected. . . . It bids fair to outstrip its older and richer sister and rival . . . in enterprise and present improvements.

Ohio City continued its aspirations for a decade and a half. It even resisted with force the construction of a good carriage and wagon bridge over the Cuyahoga because it would induce the teams coming in from Elyria, Medina, and the grain farms of the area to cross into Cleveland to trade. The "Bridge War" that

EDISON'S HOME IN MILAN

ONE OF THE FACTORIES THAT HAVE MADE AKRON THE
NATION'S RUBBER CAPITAL

AIR VIEW OF YOUNGSTOWN

resulted became one of the much-written-about and retold stories in the annals of Cleveland. The Cleveland men won the battle, the big bridge stood, and, though Ohio City may have lost some trade immediately, the predictions of disaster were never fulfilled. Both sides of the river prospered. The *Directory of the Cities of Cleveland & Ohio for the Years 1837-38* listed 275 names in City of Ohio along with 1,339 in Cleveland. A union of the two cities had been advocated for years. The new *Plain Dealer* urged it, saying that if the annexation could be effected "without war" it "would place us in the catalogue of 'big cities' and make us a great city." The union finally took place to their mutual profit in 1854. The first mayor of the combined cities was William B. Castle, who was president of the Cuyahoga Steam Furnace Company.

The outlying Cuyahoga County towns were already becoming in fact suburbs of Cleveland. Newburg in the pioneering era was a healthier place than Cleveland, and several of the early settlers deserted the mouth of the Cuyahoga for this higher ground. For some years it far exceeded Cleveland in population. There was a saying common in the day that Cleveland was "a small village six miles from Newburg." Kingsbury had gone to Newburg in 1797, and had built his gristmill there. The settlement contended for the county seat in 1809, but lost to Cleveland. Newburg did not give up, however. When Cleveland decided in 1826 to tear down the old log courthouse and erect the new one on the Public Square, Newburg made another strenuous effort and almost won the honor from Cleveland in a close election of county commissioners. Newburg did get the State Hospital for the Insane.

By 1840 the township had a population of 1,342. Some of the first iron works were set up in the township in the 1850's, and Newburg, like Ohio City, continued to assert a sturdy independence. It did not yield until 1872, when the village decided that its need of the benefits of a city could no longer be ignored and that the best way to get them was to unite with her ancient rival, now a giant city approaching 100,000, ahead of Detroit, and sixteenth in size in the nation.

Sixteen miles southwest of Cleveland was the land purchased

from the Connecticut Land Company by Gideon Granger and named Berea. It was known for two industries—Josiah Holbrook's globe and school-equipment factory which flourished until 1852, and the great stone quarries which are still in operation.

John Baldwin of Connecticut settled at Berea in 1827. His Yankee eye saw the possibilities for utilizing the smooth, grayish-white sandstone which, it is said, he first discovered while digging a cellar for his house. He acquired an extensive holding of land and went into the quarry, grindstone, and building-stone business. He improved the methods of cutting grindstones which went to almost every farm on the Reserve. The building stone was shipped to various parts of the United States and Canada. It was used for the Garfield monument in Cleveland's Lakeview Cemetery, and over two million cubic feet went into the magnificent Superior Street viaduct which for years after 1878 spanned the Cuyahoga River and Flats from bluff to bluff. Baldwin laid out the town with its small triangular green and narrow winding streets. The population grew up around the quarries where the old pits may still be seen scattered about the town. In those early days of quarrying the workers in the pits were a pathetic sight as they breathed into their lungs the dust that hung over the quarries, weakened, labored to breathe as their lungs filled up, and died young of what they called "grindstone consumption." Baldwin invented a blower to carry off this flourlike dust and give protection to his workers. This generous and religious man in 1845 gave to the Methodists land and building for the Baldwin Institute which later became Baldwin University and, united with German-Wallace College in 1913, Baldwin-Wallace College at Berea.

Brecksville was far enough out in the county to develop more in the slow, leisurely manner of the other Reserve towns around its green, pending the motor day and arterial U.S. Highway 21 into Cleveland. Bedford had a few decades of quiet life after it was setttled in 1810 by Benjamin Fitch. He began making chairs immediately and that interest still dominates what is now one of the residential villages of Cleveland. Chagrin Falls was not settled until 1833 when Noah Graves was attracted there by the possibilities of the 150 feet of waterfall. A drawing of the village on the slopes in 1846 shows a considerable settlement spreading around three dams, each with a millrace and a substantial mill on the banks of the river.

The other township villages surrounding Cleveland—Brooklyn, Parma, Warrensville, Mayfield, Euclid—were small, quiet places with a rather stable population and an occasional industry in the midst of a farming, dairy, and fruit-growing region. They would in the industrial era of Cleveland become incorporated units or satellite towns closely tied with the capital city of the Reserve.

The panorama of this capital city of Cleveland in the early 1850's was still a pleasant sight: The riverside under the bluff is an almost solid row of wharves and three or four-story commercial houses. Cleveland Center, in the Flats, encircled by the canal and the huge oxbow loop of the Cuyahoga River, is likewise almost filled with mercantile houses, manufactures, and lumber yards. The river itself is lined with canal barges, schooners, and steamers, all the way down to the Government Pier on the west and Stockley's crowded pier on the east point. Primitive trains are puffing along past the Ashtabula Railroad Shop adjoining Stockley's. A single row of houses struggles up Union Lane. The steep bluff along River Street (West Eleventh) from the lane to the lighthouse is without trees or shrubs and is eroding badly. The foot of Superior Street is congested with buildings of all kinds. From the top of the bluff to the Square its wide expanse, without sidewalks, easily absorbs the carriages and pedestrians. The spires of the new church buildings, the courthouse, and the Academy rise above the groves of trees which still gave point to Cleveland's designation as the Forest City.

By 1850 the city has swept on east past the Square. Fine new homes are going up on Euclid Avenue. The Marine Hospital is on Lake Street out at Erie (East Ninth) facing the lake where the tracks of the Cleveland & Erie and the Cleveland and Pittsburgh railways run under the bluff below Wall Street. The Medical College is at Erie and St. Clair, and the Catholic Cathedral at Erie and Superior. It has some gaslighted streets. The telegraph wires reached the city in 1847, and in 1854 the *Plain Dealer,* the *Herald* and the *Leader* proudly receive through the New York Associated Press news fresh from the wires and print it simultaneously with the New York papers. The newly appointed Water Works Commissioners (Payne, Spangler, and Hilliard) have located the site on the west side of the river for a waterworks for Cleveland; and a reservoir on Kentucky Street and pumping house down by the lake are under construction to replace the cisterns and wells in the back yards. The city has the authentic look of the unquestioned and proud metropolis of the Western Reserve. And it is filling up so rapidly with new people, a heavy percentage of them European, that the original New Englanders are meeting at the Weddell House to form themselves into the New England Society to perpetuate the memory of the day when the Cleveland papers printed marriage and death notices from the old towns back in Connecticut.

The Society, after a period of activity, we may observe, lapsed for a time. But it has been re-formed and is now actively perpetuating the fading memories of strictly New England days. They hold luncheon meetings in the summer on the lawn of the Western Reserve Historical Society Museum under the great elm trees across the wall from the library.

CHAPTER NINETEEN

IRON AND STEEL

THIS quick sweep across the Reserve emphasizes once more the rural pattern of life that was developing there in the first half century or so. Dominantly the Reserve continued for another generation to retain these characteristics. It was a grain, fruit, sheep, and dairy region, still markedly Connecticut in appearance, and steadily improving in the comforts of living. On revisiting the Reserve in the 1880's, Henry Howe was impressed with the advancement which the rural population had made since his first tour on horseback in the 1840's. He said:

I was continually reminded of the Connecticut of that time by the large number of red houses, red barns and little district school-houses by the roadside, also red. Gone are these red things, and gone mostly are the people, and gone the country taverns with their barroom shelves filled with liquor bottles. The boys and girls of that time now living are largely grand-parents. Now the farmhouses are white or a neutral tint, many of them ornate, the creations of skilled architects; all of those hereabouts have porches either upon the main building or upon the addition. . . . Most families have representatives in some neighboring city or on farms farther west, and they often visit the old homestead, bringing their children, and renew the old ties.

These were the mid-century sons who had gone on west, particularly to Iowa; their migration accounts in large part for the fact that so many of the townships remained stationary or actually declined in population. But the ties with the Reserve homestead were so strong that in some instances the married daughters returned long enough for their children to be born on Ohio soil.

229

The county-seat towns had just enough small industries—flour, lumber and woolen mills, ax and scythe factories—to supply the local demands and give employment to the urban population. The new roads, railroads, and lake commerce linked the area at last into some unity and joined it to New York and the markets of the East. It could readily exchange its agricultural products for manufactured articles and ship them economically. The Reserve as a whole still held firm as a portion of Connecticut set down in northeastern Ohio.

It was different in the capital city of Cleveland, in Akron, Warren, and Youngstown, and to a considerable degree at Sandusky and Ashtabula. Lorain was to become another of the industrialized communities, but that would wait for the later years of the steel era. We have seen in passing how, almost from the beginnings, these towns seemed destined to be the manufacturing, commercial, banking, and shipping centers of the Reserve. Some of them did not easily lose their New Connecticut bent and background or leadership, but the pattern of the first half century was heavily overlaid with a cosmopolitan industrialism that made it increasingly obscure. The industrial towns of America were all very much alike, whether they were in Massachusetts, Connecticut, New York, Ohio, or Michigan. The older regional and colonial characteristics became rarer, and were never understood by the increasing number of immigrants who found employment and homes in the industrial towns. By 1870 two out of five of the 92,829 citizens of Cleveland were foreign-born, many of them direct from Germany, with much the same cultural ties to their fatherland that the older Reserve people had to New England.

Behind this profound shift of character was the stupendous and far-reaching force of industrial development based primarily upon two products—iron and oil. Neither was abundant in the Reserve. There were just enough bog iron and oil in the region to arouse a few imaginative leaders to sense the possibilities of these products. The iron ore was of good quality and processed into tough metal which found a ready market. There were fair deposits scattered about the Reserve, particularly in Geauga,

Trumbull, and Mahoning counties. Several charcoal furnaces were built to utilize them. The Cuyahoga Steam Furnace Company began operation at Cleveland in 1835 at its plant on the corner of Detroit and Center streets on the West Side. This company made cannon for the government and built the first locomotive west of the Alleghenies for the Detroit & Pontiac Railroad in 1842. It manufactured the engines for the C.C. & C. and for the Cleveland & Painesville Railroad. It made the machinery for the first successful screw propeller on the lake—the *Emigrant*. Whittaker and Wells also had a small furnace down by the pier in 1839. Over near Painesville the Geauga furnace, set up about the same time, did a good business. There were others at Poland, Youngstown, Niles, Akron, Madison, Elyria, Perry, Sandusky, Medina, Mentor, Conneaut, and Ashtabula.

In 1846 Wilkeson, Wilkes & Company of Poland discovered that raw Ohio bituminous coal could be used in furnaces like those operating in England and Scotland. The product was iron of splendid quality. The discovery solved the problem of fuel. No longer would acres of fine forests have to be chopped down and burned into charcoal to feed the furnaces. Right at hand in the Trumbull and Mahoning county mines was coal in abundance. This new type of furnace sprang up in the Youngstown region in the late 1840's and spread to a few other centers. The region abounded in coal and skilled laborers, but where was the ore to come from in large enough quantities to supply the increasing demand?

Incredible as it would have seemed to the early founders, skeptical as were the industrialists of 1840, the answer was that it lay in vast deposits around the rim of the bowl of faraway Lake Superior. It was then known only to the Indians who traversed the rough and unexplored hills and wove legends around the outcropping mineral deposits and the iron mountains where the lightning crackled and danced in the storms and the roar of the thunder was like the voice of angry gods. Certainly one of the great sagas of our times is the story of iron and steel and of the fortuitous circumstances which made the New Connecticut villages along Lake Erie the central link in the manufacture of steel and steel products for the age of steel. And around that saga are woven the lives of a few leading organizers and men of business, and of uncounted thousands of humble and now nameless men, lured hither from all parts of the world by the magic words "job" and "home."

The discovery by white men of these ore deposits around Lake Superior was accidental. Michigan had reluctantly acquired its Upper Peninsula in 1837. Douglass Houghton, a young geologist, was commissioned to survey the wild territory. He tramped over the rough terrain along the south Superior shore from 1841 to 1845. He discovered the immense copper deposits of Keweenaw and in his reports mentioned cautiously the possibility of iron ore south of Marquette. Actually he came upon the ore near Teal Lake in the autumn of 1844. He was drowned in a storm on Lake Superior on October 13, 1845. His notes were recovered. The tragedy further publicized his work and his findings.

In the meantime, surveyor William A. Burt was running township lines in this region. On September 19, 1844, he accidentally found himself and his party standing on a mountain of iron ore with chunks of it actually scattered about on the ground at present Negaunee, fourteen miles from Marquette. These surveyors did not fully understand what they had found, but they did record it in their notebooks, and talked about it at the Sault. They were overheard and the report circulated. It reached Philo M. Everett of Jackson, Michigan. Everett went up there in 1845 to explore. A half-breed took him part way. A superstitious Chippewa chief named Marji Gesick led him to the vicinity of the iron mountain. Everett went on, and investigated the place. He reported that it was "a mountain of solid iron ore, 150 feet high. The ore looks as bright as a bar of iron just broken." It smelted easily and produced good iron. He staked out a claim one mile square and formed the Jackson Mining Company to exploit it. It struggled along for several years trying against heavy odds of access and transportation to utilize the ore and get it to market.

The word about this treasure chest reached Cleveland men at

the moment of their prosperity and eagerness for extending their enterprises. Their city had been much advertised as a "commercial" town with little manufacturing. Its position on Lake Erie seemed, indeed, to relegate it to a place inferior to the more strategically located Buffalo and Detroit. The leaders of the city could plainly see that a wider base was imperative for the kind of prosperous development which they envisioned in an era of expansion. Lake Superior minerals seemed to offer the key.

Agents of Cleveland interests were among the first on the still unexplored mineral grounds along Lake Superior. A group of Cleveland men, including some of those who formed the Cleveland Iron Company, organized the Dead River & Ohio Mining Company with W. A. Adair as president, and George E. Freeman as secretary, to exploit the copper and silver resources of upper Michigan. Dr. J. Lang Cassels went into the region now known as Cleveland Mountain and Ishpeming for this company. He had been a leading member of the faculty of the Willoughby College of Medicine and one of the moving spirits who helped organize the Cleveland Medical College in 1843. He was a noted chemist of his day. From the Sault he want on into the wilderness by canoe and on foot, accompanied by Indian guides, to do pioneering work in mineralogy and geographical location in 1846. W. A. Adair went with him to the Dead River location. Cassels brought back specimens of the rich copper and silver ore, one of the samples containing one-half pure silver. He made statements and promises about the wealth of this region which were received by most Clevelanders with smiles of incredulity. But Cassels, as a scientist, had calculated conservatively, and events fully backed up his reports.

So did the investigations of other scientific men. The great Charles Whittlesey went up to examine the region. He was one of the leading geologists of his time. We have already met him on various occasions in this study of the Reserve.

Born in Southington, Connecticut, in 1808, he had come as a boy with his father to Tallmadge. He was a nephew of Elisha Whittlesey of Canfield. He attended the academy at Tallmadge, went on to West Point for his education. He was assistant geologist of Ohio in 1837-1839. His fine studies of the Indian mounds of Ohio were published by the Smithsonian Institution. He was with a party of Detroit explorers in the Upper Peninsula in 1845—hot on the heels of Houghton's and Burt's discoveries. He published many scientific papers on the geology and mineral resources of Michigan and, in 1846, his interesting account of "Two Men in the Copper Region." He was employed by the U.S. Government 1847-1851 to survey the Upper Peninsula for mines and minerals.

Whittlesey's work further stimulated interest in Cleveland in the potentialities of the newly found resources. He gave free public lectures on the subject at the Apollo Theatre. In announcing a lecture on the Lake Superior Copper Region on March 7, 1846, the *Herald* wrote: "That wild region of our country, rich in mineral treasures, is now attracting no little notice. . . . We hope to see a full house." The house was full.[1]

The interest was country-wide. The *New York Herald* reported "a fever of discovery" from the Sault westward along the shore of Lake Superior. Men from New York, Boston, Philadelphia, and Pittsburgh, as well as Detroit and Cleveland, were excited about it. Maps of the formerly unknown region were published and distributed. The Cleveland papers carried prominent announcement of the arrival at Younglove's bookstore of maps of this region showing the locations of mines in 1844-1845 and the names of persons making the locations. The Dead River Company advertised for fifteen experienced miners to go out to their location in 1846. The Ohio & Isle Royale Mining Company located mines on the big, romantic island in Lake Superior and began shipping copper in barrels to Cleveland in 1846. Blake, Ransom, and others went up in 1847 and soon reported back "satisfactory progress." The fifty-two tons of copper ore which young James A. Garfield hauled from Cleveland to Pittsburgh in August 1848 had come in from the Lake Superior mines. In the first ten years these Cleveland people took out millions of

---

[1] We note here that the active, influential Academy of Natural Science was organized in Cleveland in 1845 by Doctor Kirtland, Cassels, S. J. Andrews, Charles W. Heard, and the Arkites.

dollars' worth of copper and silver ore from these rich deposits. This first interest in copper was soon to be displaced by the feverish development of the iron-ore trade. The Cleveland Iron Company was organized in 1849 under a Michigan charter. Its first concern was chiefly exploratory, and its first problem was to get its claims to the ore deposits recognized. Events moved rapidly in the next four years, and the Cleveland men prepared for more active exploitation of upper Michigan ore. They reformed the company in1853 as the Cleveland Iron Mining Company. Several prominent men were back of it. W. J. Gordon, who had come to Cleveland in 1839 at the age of twenty-one and had made money in the dry-goods business, became president of the company. Samuel L. Mather, son of Samuel Mather of the Connecticut Land Company, joined the enterprise as secretary and treasurer. He had arrived in Cleveland in 1845 to begin his long career of leadership in the iron business. He furnished much of the money, and the imagination and persistence which brought the company through the discouraging formative years. H. B. Tuttle, John W. Allen, Selah Chamberlain, George Worthington, Henry Brayton and others joined the group. Dr. Morgan L. Hewitt, a Cleveland physician, was at one time president. His brother Isaac, a commission merchant, and John Outhwaite, a shipping man, also joined. They acquired the holdings of the Marquette Mining Company and laid, rather quietly, the foundations for Cleveland's prominence in the business of mining and transporting ore from the Superior beds to the Lake Erie ports.

This company in 1854 mined 4,000 tons of ore, made it into blooms, or ingots, at the forges on Lake Superior, and shipped it down the Lakes. It did not take them long to discover, however, that it was much better to ship the ore itself and have it processed in the Reserve where the coal, limestone, furnaces and forges, skilled workmen and markets were already concentrated. When this decision was made (it seems an obvious one now) the future development of the Reserve as an industrial center was assured. In the process the original company grew under the leadership of Samuel L. and his son, William G. Mather, into the Cleveland-

Cliffs Iron Company. And another son, Samuel, with James Pickands, formed the separate Pickands, Mather & Company in 1883. The other great companies were organized as the discoveries proceeded around Lake Superior and up into the Mesabi, Vermilion, and other iron ranges in this fabulous vulcan's treasure house of ore.

Henry B. Tuttle, for example, withdrew from the Cleveland Iron Mining Company and established his own firm for mining and shipping about the year 1854. His son, Horace A. Tuttle, interested Earl W. Oglebay and David Z. Norton in the business, and in 1890 Oglebay, Norton and Company was formed.

While these first organizations were being formed, the larger public was expressing its concern over the future of Cleveland. They feared that the great moment of opportunity was passing them by. They saw the Canadian ship *Free Trader* tie up at their docks with sixty tons of Scotch pig iron in June 1848. Despite the long haul across the Atlantic and up the St. Lawrence, the iron was sold below Cleveland prices and still made a handsome profit. During the 1850's mass meetings were held in Cleveland to promote the city as an iron center. Committees were appointed to study and report. In 1856 they reported that iron was the destined industry for Cleveland because of the city's position as the economical meeting place for an abundance of coal and ore. A subcommittee negotiated further, a charter was secured for a blast furnace, and a site for it was donated. The citizens subscribed $60,000 for the venture.

Actually the business leaders were already quietly preparing for this part of the iron era. The beginnings had been made early. Some of them were venturesome.

John Ballard & Co. had put into operation in Cleveland the first small iron foundry in 1828—the same year that Henry Newberry hauled from door to door through the town the first wagonload of coal which the housewives refused to buy for their cookstoves. The foundry would not be worth mentioning except for its novelty as the first to be founded.

The first ironworks of any importance was established in Cleveland in 1840 by William A. Otis. He had come to Cleveland in 1836 when the newly opened canal was focusing attention on the commercial possibilities of the town. He became a deacon in the Second Presbyterian Church, president of the Commercial Branch of the Bank of Ohio, member of the Cleveland Board of Trade, and was prominent in civic affairs. The population in 1840 was only 6,071, and the *Ohio Gazetteer* was generalizing on industry by saying that "manufacturing is not carried on extensively" in Cleveland. In 1852, the year the *Baltimore* brought down some ore in barrels, Otis and J. M. Ford began to manufacture iron castings at their new foundry on Whiskey Island. These operations were successful. They expanded into the firm of Otis and Company which later became the Lake Erie Iron Company and the Otis Iron and Steel Company. It was located on the old river bed near the lake and specialized in boiler plate. Otis also built the first rolling mill in Cleveland in 1859, and his company furnished the Union armies with cannon for the Civil War.

Henry Chisholm entered the iron business in 1852. He had arrived in America from Scotland in 1842 as an almost penniless young man of twenty. He came on to Cleveland in 1850 to build the railroad breakwater on the lake front. He saw the need for iron for the opening railroad era, and founded Chisholm, Jones & Company to manufacture railroad and bar iron. His successful firm was later merged with Mather's Cleveland Rolling Mill Company, which grew into one of the great steel manufacturing organizations of the country. At the Newburg plant the first Bessemer steel was blown in 1868.

Fayette Brown was another of the leading ironmen. In 1814 his father had come out to North Bloomfield, where Fayette was born, the last of nine children. He went to school at Gambier and at Jefferson College, Pennsylvania. In 1851 he went to work in the City Bank of Cleveland. After the Civil War, in which he was a major and paymaster, he caught the contagion of the iron business. He went up to the iron country as agent for the Jackson Iron Mining Company and superintended in the field many of their operations. He became general manager of the company and spent twenty-five years in the business. He took out patents for hoisting devices for charging blast furnaces and for improving the design of the furnaces. He became president of the Union Steel Screw Company, and was active in many other enterprises in the steel business, including his son's H. H. Brown & Company, the firm that developed the Brown Hoist, invented by his son Alexander, for unloading the ore ships. He developed also a fleet of carriers to bring the ore down to the new furnaces and for the steel plants rising along the Cuyahoga Flats and in the Mahoning Valley.

These and other pioneer business leaders laid the foundation for Cleveland's eminence in the iron and steel industry. It was to become a closely co-ordinated business involving mining the ore from the pits around Lake Superior, shipping it over its 800-mile voyage down through the Sault, down the St. Marys River, down Lake Huron, down the St. Clair River, across shallow Lake St. Clair, down the Detroit River, and across Lake Erie to the port towns of the Reserve, and then transferring it to the furnaces and mills in the Cuyahoga and Mahoning Valleys where the coal supply was abundant and skilled workmen were plentiful.

The tempo of this remarkable cycle mounted steadily during the decades following the Civil War. The discoveries of Houghton and Burt, of Whittlesey, Cassels, and the others, sent still more explorers and prospectors into the region to investigate further the extent of this iron rim of Lake Superior. Charles Whittlesey thought that the ridge which extended on to the west of Marquette across Michigan and Wisconsin for eighty miles was probably full of iron ore. John Longyear tramped into this region, going north from Green Bay, and came upon the Menominee and Gogebic iron ranges. By 1885 iron ore, dug by Cornishmen, was coming out of these ranges through Ashland and Escanaba. George R. Stuntz, one of the great explorers of his time, tramped over the rugged terrain sixty miles back from the northwest shore, and discovered the Vermilion deposits. The energic Merritt brothers pushed the exploration on to the southwest, back of Two Harbors and Duluth, where they came upon the most fabulous of all the ranges, the Mesabi. Here the exceptionally pure ore lay in vast quantities

so near the surface that it could be scooped out by strip-mining
processes. The first trainload of ore from this area came down to
the lake in October 1892. Thus the source of supply unfolded as
the demand for iron and steel mounted in the nation.

To increase the flow of this ore to the furnaces of the Reserve
and the Pittsburgh region, the barrier of the nineteen-foot falls
at the Sault in the St. Marys River had to be overcome. We
have noted that the first two small locks were completed in 1855,
and that the two-masted *Columbia* locked through on August 14
with her tiny cargo of ore for the Cleveland wharf. The locks were
only 350 feet long, 70 feet wide, and 9 feet deep. These dimensions seemed large before the Civil War and ample to accommodate the largest ship that was ever likely to sail through to Lake
Superior. They did take care of the lengthening ships until 1870
and the mounting tonnage of ore which reached 830,940 gross tons
in that year. Bigger locks were now required as the volume
increased and the ships grew in size more rapidly than the engineers ever dreamed they would. So the Weitzel Lock was added
in 1881. It was a single lock, 515 feet long, 80 feet wide, and 16
feet deep. It accommodated the new ships while they carried
the gross tonnage on up to 9,012,379 in the year 1890—the year
the news of the Mesabi Range spread to the nation. The Poe
Lock, 800 feet long, 100 feet wide, and 22 feet deep, was opened
in 1896—the centennial year of the Reserve. It carried the gross
tonnage on up to 27,571,121 in 1902. The channels in the rivers
were deepened likewise and the tonnage ran up to 38,522,239 in
1906. The Davis Lock was opened in 1914, in time for the huge
demands of World War I, and the Sabin Lock was rushed to completion in 1919. Each was 1,350 feet long, 80 feet wide, and
24½ feet deep, and again the tonnage mounted. On June 26, 1943,
at the height of World War II, the MacArthur Lock was opened.
It was 800 feet long, 80 feet wide, and 30 feet deep, designed
like the first locks of 1855 to lift and lower the largest ships of
the ore fleet—the super 600-footers carrying over 17,000 tons at
a single load. And the cargo again mounted close to 100,000,000
gross tons.

The discoveries of the ore, the rapid improvements in the

techniques of mining, which do not immediately concern our story, and the opening of the locks, and the widening and deepening of the channels through the connecting waters of the Great Lakes were inextricably linked with the rise of big shipping companies. These were centered in Cleveland. They began in a small way and grew with the business after the Civil War. The story of the Mathers, the Hannas, and of Alva Bradley and Rockefeller illustrates the casual and opportunistic character of their origin.

Samuel L. Mather and his colleagues of the Cleveland Iron Mining Company were smart enough to see the importance of shipping as the link between the iron mines on the north and the coal and furnaces in the Reserve. It was their 550-ton brigantine *Columbia* which brought down the first load of ore through the Sault Canal. They bought in 1867 a half interest in the *George Sherman,* and shortly thereafter went heavily into the shipping business. In 1872, with the post-Civil War boom well under way, and the future of Cleveland as a steel center assured, they acquired a fleet of wooden freighters, of about 1,000 tons each, to bring down the ore. They modernized their vessels from decade to decade—from wood to iron to steel, from sails to steam. Following various organizational changes, this outfit became the Cleveland-Cliffs' great fleet of modern carriers which transport a large percentage of the ore down the lakes. In the procession of ships making the six-day round trip with clocklike regularity their long freighters bearing the letter *C* on the stubby black funnel are conspicuous.

The Hannas, too, were in on the ground floor. The family had settled at New Lisbon in eastern Ohio a few miles south of the Reserve. Benjamin Hanna, the pioneer, a Quaker, owned much land, a large store, a share in the flour mill and other interests. He was something of a local figure in frontier days. During the canal-building period the citizens of New Lisbon worked hard and hopefully to get the commissioners to bring the waterway through their town. They failed. The little town settled back into isolation and decay.

One of Benjamin's sons, Leonard, was somewhat frail and bookish. He was given a medical education, and was known as Doctor Leonard, though he did not actively practice his profession. The other was Robert, a good hard-working businessman. Leonard's eldest son, born at New Lisbon in 1837, was named Marcus Alonzo Hanna. In 1852, when Mark was fifteen years old, his father and Uncle Robert decided to move to Cleveland where the canal, the new railroads, and the smart rise in business activity beckoned to active and ambitious men. With a shrewd trader named Hiram Garretson they formed a wholesale grocery company. Like so many other famous Cleveland names who began in this business, they made money. In 1853 Doctor Leonard made a special voyage of inspection to the Lake Superior region. He was much impressed by what he saw. It was not only the possibility of shipping ore down the lakes, but of sending supplies up to the settlements. As his boat moved west along the south shore of Lake Superior, canoes put out to ask for all sorts of articles which the mines and ports needed. He returned to Cleveland with the idea of putting a steamboat into trade with the upper lake. Hanna, Garretson & Company were soon doing a good business up there. This was the beginning of their interest in shipping.

The driving energy behind the development of the firm was to be furnished by Leonard's son Mark. He had grown tall and muscular. His rather flat face was still freckled and his voice was loud. He was not doing too well at Western Reserve. In 1857 he was suspended from the college for a sophomoric prank. He plunged into his father's business. He put on overalls, hustled goods in the warehouse and on the wharf, traveled on the family ships, tossed unruly stevedores off the deck, and served as purser and salesman. It was good training for the hurly-burly era of big business and boss politics in which he was to play so prominent a part.

Mark fell in love with charming young Charlotte Augusta Rhodes who had just come back to her grand home on Franklin Avenue in Cleveland from a finishing school in New York. Her father, the great coal merchant Daniel Rhodes, had grown rich and was a dominant figure in the coal and iron business. He had taken on all the bluff and barking characteristics so common among successful businessmen in that colorful era of the barons of industry. He did not approve of gay Marcus Alonzo Hanna who danced most of the night, organized parties among the new social set of Franklin and Euclid avenues, and Prospect Street, where the Hannas lived. It was still possible in that day for a father to delay if not actually prevent the marriage of his daughter to a man of whom he disapproved. Rhodes delayed this one during most of the Civil War. But Mark joined the Union Army near the close of the war, took on added glamour thereby, and in the end Rhodes had to yield. His daughter married Mark Hanna in the autumn of 1864.

Mark's first business ventures seemed to justify his father-in-law's distrust. He built an oil refinery which burned down. He launched a fine new steamer named *Lac La Belle* which promptly sank uninsured. But Daniel Rhodes retired in 1867. Mark Hanna, Robert Rhodes, and George Warmington took over. The Hanna and Rhodes interests were united, and from that date on Mark was in coal, iron, and shipping with vigor and considerable imagination. The firm, still known as Rhodes & Company, brought down charcoal iron made in the small Lake Superior furnaces which were still operating at the mines. This iron was used in the manufacture of car wheels, which was one of the big activities at Cleveland. Rhodes & Company also acquired furnaces just across the eastern border of the Reserve at Sharpsville, Pennsylvania. The firm grew and prospered. In 1885 it was reorganized and became M. A. Hanna & Company with a far-flung interest in iron ore and coal mines, furnaces, and lake carriers. Mark immediately placed two steamers, the *Geneva* and the *Vienna,* and two schooners, the *Genoa* and the *Verona,* in the carrying trade, and added each year to the fleet which became the great Hanna line of fourteen ships, distinguished by a white star on the funnel with the letter *H* in red.

Hanna's business interests were primarily in iron, coal, and shipping; he was also a friend of John D. Rockefeller and was associated with him in Standard Oil. In Cleveland he had a substantial investment in the street railways, a connection which brought him soon into conflict with Mayor Tom Johnson in a battle over monopoly and fares. In addition to all these business interests, Hanna was for many years a power in Cleveland and Ohio politics. As United States Senator and as the foremost supporter of President McKinley, he became nationally prominent. To the newspapers and the cartoonists of the 1890's, Hanna was the perfect example of the powerful city boss and great industrialist.

Captain Alva Bradley, at one time the dominant shipping master in the industry, had none of these flamboyant personal qualities or political ambitions. He began modestly as a shipbuilder at Vermilion and a captain-owner on the lakes in the mid years of the century when Cleveland was just emerging as the center of business and industry in the Reserve. He moved his headquarters over to Cleveland in 1859, and a few years later built his shipyards there. When the ore boom got going in the early 1870's, Bradley was ready with a fleet of ships to do the hauling. Most of them were, of course, sailing ships and their acres of canvas taut in the stiff Lake Erie breeze as they rounded the islands and headed for the Reserve ports made one of the picturesque sights of the day. He added six new ships to his fleet in the single year of 1875, so heavy was the demand for lake transportation. By that time it was clear that the day of the sailing ships on the Lakes was over. They were too slow and their cargoes were too small. Bradley began to transform his fleet to steam-driven iron and steel ships. They were so big, so numerous, and so efficient that for years they set the pace for all competitors and Captain Alva set the rates for ore transportation just as John D. Rockefeller set them for oil.

John D. Rockefeller, whose Cleveland story we shall consider in the next chapter, entered the ore and shipping business during the 1890's in his usual stupendous fashion. Moving quietly and speedily, with all his great resources, he acquired from the Merritts for a nominal sum full control of the rich Mesabi iron range.

Rockefeller could not understand the lack of business foresight on the part of the big steel men like Carnegie who permitted the source of supply and the carriers to be owned by companies outside of their own organization. This shortsighted policy made them dependent on others for their ore and placed them at the mercy of the mining and shipping companies. Rockefeller took over and extended the railroad linking the mines with Lake Superior. He constructed long ore docks at Duluth, Superior, and Two Harbors, built out into the lake so that the ore trains could pull in alongside to unload directly into the vast bins and the ships could tie up under the bins to receive a cargo quickly into their open hatches. Loading time was cut to a few hours.

With equal rapidity and decision he ordered a fleet of super-carriers built to transport the ore to the lower lake ports. Characteristically he turned to the son-in-law of Amasa Stone, Samuel Mather, expert on lake ships, and a neighbor and close acquaintance, if not friend, of the Cleveland days. In a few minutes' interview with Rockefeller, Mather accepted an order for three million dollars' worth of new ships to be built immediately in the Great Lakes yards. Without disclosing his hand, Rockefeller got all the companies into competitive bidding to their full capacity, and he secured at reasonable cost twelve steel ships which were ready for operation by the beginning of the next shipping season. He formed the Bessemer Steamship Company with headquarters in Cleveland. His engineers studied the problems of ship construction and operation, steadily lengthened the ships and increased their capacity. The next units in the fleet were 500 feet long. New ships were added season by season as the demand for ore rose to new heights. By the close of the 1890's his fleet of twenty-eight vessels was bringing down 3,500,000 tons of ore in a single season. But that was still not enough, and Rockefeller added thirty more ships to the ore fleet. These additions made Bessemer the largest fleet on the Lakes and the most efficient, and Rockefeller had the power to fix the shipping rates. The potential danger of these operations to the big steel interests was perfectly obvious. Having passed by the opportunity which Rockefeller had seized, they now had to buy at his price. In 1901 he sold his mines to United States Steel for $80,000,000 in stock and his fleet for $8,500,000 in cash.

Carnegie learned from Rockefeller. His operations on the Lakes were small by comparison. He bought a half-dozen vessels to bring ore down to the Lake Erie ports and a railroad to transfer it to his plants in Pittsburgh. This was the beginning of what was to become the Pittsburgh Steamship Company, now the largest on the Lakes. At one time it operated more than a hundred freighters. The number has been reduced to around seventy, but the vast increase in size and carrying capacity has expanded the tonnage which they handle. Their ships wear a black band around the top of their silver funnels. Pickands, Mather & Company developed their fleet as the subsidiary Interlake Steamship Company, with a red band on a black funnel as its insignia. Many of these ships were built by the American Ship Building Company at its yards in Cleveland and Lorain. The company offices are in Cleveland. In fact most of the vessels in this enormous carrying trade are operated by companies with headquarters in Cleveland —so accurately did these early leaders foresee and work for the greatness of the city.

The opening up of the mines and the voluminous flow of ore which resulted were reflected year by year in the astonishing growth of industry in Cleveland and other cities in the Western Reserve. All are parts of one stupendous interlocking and interdependent whole. A glance at the Cleveland directories during these years shows what was happening. In the issue for 1858 the firms engaged in the reduction of ore and the manufacture of iron products could be listed in a short paragraph. Only about 650 men were employed in the iron industry. One hundred twenty-five worked for the Cleveland Rolling Mill, turning out 125 T rails each day for the railroad-building boom. Thirty years later the list covered pages. There were 462 establishments, a heavy percentage of which were working with iron and steel. The Cleveland Rolling Mills employed 5,000; American Wire Company, 465; Ohio Steel Works, 625; Globe Iron Works and Shipyard, 543; Cleveland Malleable Iron Company, 550; Union Rolling Mill, 335; the Central Blast Furnace and the Riverside Blast Furnace, 325—to mention samples of the transformation wrought in these few spectacular years. By 1910, when Cleveland's population had passed the half-million mark, there were 14 large iron and steel works and rolling mills, and 231 foundries and machine shops in the city doing $76,000,000 worth of business annually. Cleveland had become the first ranking industrial city in Ohio.

Statistics of this type continued to mount as the decades went by. Raw materials poured into Cleveland; skilled workmen fashioned them into diverse products, and the refinement of industries marched on apace. As the twentieth century got under way, Cleveland was making about two thousand kinds of manufactured articles, in more than that number of establishments. The overwhelming interest was in iron and steel and their finished products. In those days Cleveland was referred to as the Sheffield of America. Warner and Swasey, who located in Cleveland in 1880 to make scientific instruments and precision tools, were constructing the most delicate mountings for the great telescopes at the Naval Observatory, Lick, Yerkes and elsewhere. They continued to make half of all the turret lathes produced in America. At the same time the Brown Hoisting Machinery Company was manufacturing the giant grab buckets to bite out five tons of ore from the freighters with each opening and closing of their jaws. Everything between has been made in the busy mills and factories of Cleveland.

Cleveland made bicycles for the craze which swept the nation in the 1870's, '80's and '90's and put young men in turtle-neck sweaters on the wheels, and gentlemen in cutaways and top hats, with ladies in full skirts and carrying parasols, on bicycles built for two. The manufacture of clothing, including lace and knit goods, hats, and hosiery, was second in value only to iron and steel. Sherwin-Williams, who had established their first paint factory near Seneca Street down by the canal around 1870, became the leading firm in the paint and varnish business. By 1910 there were twenty-three other such establishments in Cleveland, making it one of the great centers for these products.

Charles Brush had made his home city famous for its electrical products. Born at Euclid and graduated from the University of Michigan, he carried on a lifetime of experiments and inventions. He made his first electric arc light out of lampblack rods, coke, and syrup baked in a kitchen oven. On April 29, 1879, he lighted up Monumental Park with twelve of his arc lamps. Before long he had brought electric lights to the dark streets of the nation's cities. He developed more than a score of important patents for lamps, dynamos, and batteries. His company was merged with Thompson and Edison to become General Electric, with vast plants and laboratories in Cleveland.

Sewing machines, stoves and furnaces, automobiles and parts, furniture, boxes and cabinets, chemicals and drugs, shoe polish, leather goods, brick and stonework, beds and mattresses, umbrellas, tools, knives, forks, and spoons—the list is as limitless as the ingenuity and the demands of modern man. It grew up in a few decades around the village of Moses Cleaveland which had less than 20,000 inhabitants when the *Baltimore* dropped her sails and landed those six barrels of ore from Lake Superior in 1852.

CHAPTER TWENTY

THE ERA OF OIL

Oₙₑ of the many great men on the Ohio frontier who, in our day, would have been notable scientists was Doctor Hildreth of Marietta. He had observed as early as 1819 the oil and gas which annoyed the producers of salt in the Ohio salt wells. From some of the wells oil poured out in quantities considered awkward by men who were trying to supply the demand for salt among the pioneers. Hildreth saw that this oil, when properly burned, made a clear light that was far superior to candles and lard and more economical. He predicted that the day would come when it would even light the streets of cities in Ohio. No one paid serious attention. A few barrels were shipped down the river in the 1840's to be used in St. Louis and New York for medications.

By the middle of the century, petroleum oil was a popular medicine, considered excellent not only as a liniment, but, taken internally a few teaspoonfuls a day, helpful to the liver, and good for bronchitis, consumption, and cholera morbus. Under the labels "Seneca Oil," "American Medicinal Oil," "Kier's Petroleum, or Rock-Oil" it was sold throughout the country in bottles, and benefited patients sent back testimonials to its efficacy. Samuel M. Kier had a bottle of the medicine analyzed by a Philadelphia chemist. The chemist advised that it be distilled and burned in a lamp. By 1858 Kier was selling his distilled oil for lamps. In the 1850's several companies in the Mahoning Valley distilled coal oil from cannel coal. Production costs were high and the product sold at fifty to sixty cents per gallon. Even at that price it was cheap, and people liked the bright glow from the oil lamps.

Then in 1859 an oil boom developed in Ohio and Pennsylvania. The bonanza was centered in and around Titusville, Pennsylvania, on the Oil Creek tributary of the Allegheny River forty miles south of Lake Erie and a few miles east of the Ohio line. Here in August 1859 the first well was brought in. Overnight, almost, the whole area was being leased and probed for oil. Old farms of poor and rocky land suddenly began to pour out fabulous quantities of oil. The fever spread across into Ohio. Much of the Ohio oil lay to the south of the Reserve, but what seemed to be a rich field was discovered in Mecca Township, near the center of Trumbull County. It was easy to reach and it was tapped at from thirty to sixty feet below the surface. The newly organized firm of Bonnell, Woods and Jordan, using a hand-operated drill, brought in the first producing oil well in Ohio in the Western Reserve on William H. Jeffries' farm in Mecca. Mecca immediately became a crowded boom town and its three hotels were jammed with speculator guests. The hack line over the rough highway from Warren was crowded with carriages and wagons hauling in men and supplies, and bringing out high-quality crude oil in barrels. Mecca's experience was repeated in various parts of Ohio, and, of course, across the border in Pennsylvania. It was as portentous as the arrival of the *Columbia* in the Cuyahoga.

Scores of small operators rushed in to lease farms and to drill wells. It was a wild and reckless period in American history at the height of the free-enterprise era unregulated and uncontrolled. Anyone who could get together enough money to finance a lease and the crude drilling equipment necessary could sink holes in the ground. He would advertise his gambling spirit with a sign, "Hell or China," and hope for fortune. Geological science was undeveloped and nothing was known about the subsurface formations and their relation to oil. Many operators relied on a forked hazel limb to locate deposits. They seemed to fare as well on the average as their more scientific competitors. They pumped the oil into all available containers and shipped it by wagon in barrels, at considerable expense, to one of the many small refineries that were springing up at Cleveland and vitiating the atmosphere with the foul odors from their brew. The young industry was a brawling confusion in the fields and an unorganized group of small operators at the distilling and refining center at Cleveland.

Upon this turbulent scene entered a young organizing genius named John D. Rockefeller. He was born in the farming community of Richford in the southern tier of counties in New York State July 8, 1839, the son of an itinerant medicine peddler. The family moved about upstate New York, stopping long enough at Moravia and Owego for young John D. to acquire a sketchy elementary education. In 1853, when John was fourteen, they moved to the Reserve and settled on a farm near Strongsville a dozen miles south of Cleveland. John and his brother Will went to the new Central High School in Cleveland. The high school had been established "for boys" in 1846 in the basement of a church on Prospect Street. Andrew Freese, then teaching in one of the grammar schools and later superintendent of the school system, became principal. Girls were admitted the following year and a cheap wooden one-story building was erected in 1852. It stood on Euclid Avenue near Erie Street (East Ninth). John and Will boarded near by on Erie Street. Young Mark Hanna was in this school at the same time, and he and John D. were close friends. They had for each other the attraction of opposites: Mark, a stocky, robust, aggressive and combative Irishman; John D., reserved, keen, almost taciturn, whose characteristic gesture was to hug his slate to his chest with both hands. They maintained their close association throughout Hanna's lifetime as they went separate ways with the same business philosophy in that fiercely competitive era.

After three years in high school Rockefeller had to go to work to make his own way. He did not regard this as a hardship. Nothing was more native or congenial to him than to work, to save, to plan, and to persevere. He had studied and liked bookkeeping. He got a job with the commission house of Hewitt & Tuttle in 1855. He worked as a clerk and bookkeeper for a fifteen-dollars-a-month pittance and still managed to save a portion of his wage to accumulate capital. He kept a small neat ledger of all his income and expenditures. By 1859 he was ready to enter business for himself. He formed a partnership with Maurice B. Clark, a capable young immigrant, recently from England, who was clerking for Otis & Brownell. At the age of nineteen Rockefeller was energetically in the produce and grain business as a commission merchant.

The firm prospered. The precocious, methodical young man indicated that he had a shrewd, organizing mind, an unusual ability to concentrate it on business deals, a willingness to size up the possibilities and take a chance, and a rare genius as a business executive. His father took some credit for these traits. He said that he used to drive sharp bargains with his sons and try to cheat them in order to develop in them shrewdness and self-reliance. Rockefeller kept these qualities well under control, and cultivated at the same time the ability to inspire confidence in those who could help him with cash when he needed to borrow—and he borrowed heavily when he saw the possibility of carrying through a profitable deal. Truman P. Handy, so prominent in the development of Cleveland, was one of the first and most constant supporters of the rising young businessman.

Rockefeller's entrance into the produce business coincided with the excitement of the discovery and rapid exploitation of oil. The Cleveland papers of the period are full of news about the oil wells of western Pennsylvania, and of the interest of Cleveland men in oil refineries. They visited the fields, saw the immense flow of oil in this isolated region, saw it overflow containers and drain away into the creeks and rivers. They saw also that Cleveland, with its good east-west railroad connections and the open waterway of Lake Erie and the Erie Canal, was a natural center for the refining industry. Rockefeller saw that too. And as he went about his business of buying and selling pork and grain, he observed in 1860 and 1861 two oil refineries being built on the Cuyahoga by the enterprising young men of the companies of Hussey & McBride and of Backus, Williams. They were soon making money. More refineries sprang up and yielded big returns on the investments. For at the time crude oil was selling at the wells for from twenty-five to fifty cents a barrel, but the refined oil brought twenty-five to thirty-five cents a gallon. Since a refinery was simple and inexpensive in those days, and the processing of the oil was cheap, the profits were astronomical compared with buying and selling pork and grain.

The vast possibilities of the new product fired the imagination of the ambitious twenty-two-year-old commission merchant. He had met Samuel Andrews, a newcomer to Cleveland from England, a young man with considerable ability as a mechanic and a kind of practical genius at chemistry. Andrews was interested in the process of refining oil, and he thought he saw great possibilities for improving the methods and the efficiency. Rockefeller, who was an organizer and salesman, enlisted Andrews as his technical man, and formed in 1863 the oil firm of Andrews, Clark & Company. At the same time the Atlantic & Great Western (later joined to the Erie system under Gould) brought their first train into Cleveland on November 3, 1863, giving the city direct access to the oil fields. Young Rockefeller was not among the celebrities—Garfield, Payne, Amasa Stone, Sir Morton Peto—who gathered for the banquet and jubilant ceremonies which were even more elaborate than those welcoming Kelley's C.C. & C. a few years earlier. He was purchasing land and erecting a refinery on the red clay bluff at Kingsbury Run above the Cuyahoga alongside the tracks of the new railroad and on the waterway into Lake Erie—now the site of one of Standard Oil's huge refineries.

The venture was instantly successful. It was the kind of business best suited to Rockefeller, who combined with an imagination that conceived an empire an interest in the smallest detail that would cut costs. While Andrews improved the refining process and utilized the waste products, Rockefeller studied the minutiae of operation. He cut his plumbing costs by hiring his own plumbers. When he found that barrels were selling for $2.50 apiece he built his own cooperage shop in 1864 and brought the cost down to ninety-six cents. He plowed the profits back into the expanding business. Within two years his was the largest among the thirty refineries which had sprung up like spring mushrooms along the Cuyahoga. It was a $1,200,000 business.

By this time Rockefeller was certain of his direction. He was also weary of his old partner Clark, who could not see the vision and objected to Rockefeller's reckless borrowing of money to pursue it. Rockefeller abruptly dissolved the partnership, sold his interest in the commission house, bought out Clark's interest in the oil company, and formed the new firm of Rockefeller & Andrews early in 1865. Rockefeller was head man of the largest oil firm in Cleveland, committed now head over heels to the exploitation of a brand-new industry, one in which he had already made $100,000. He was twenty-six years old, and he knew what he was about.

He saw a fabulous market, world-wide in scope, and far surpassing anything yet realized or dreamed of, awaiting the man with the skill and ruthlessnes to exploit it. The business was in chaos, crowded with small independent and competing operators, and springing up in various centers like Pittsburgh, Buffalo, and the cities in the East. And this stranger to New England, this newcomer to the Reserve, this New York-born son of a "doctor" who peddled patent medicines, sensed within himself the power to organize the reckless and wasteful competition into a harmonious unit, and he chose Cleveland as the center for his operations.

The tempo of those operations increased. He placed an agent in the oil fields to help with the buying. He brought his brother William into the business and opened another refinery on Kingsbury Run. He organized Rockefeller & Company in New York to handle the mounting export trade in oil. He opened offices in the Sexton Block overlooking the Cuyahoga River where his own barges added to the crowded traffic on that narrow and crooked waterway. He added warehouses, tanks and boilers, and raised production to over five hundred barrels a day in 1866. Then he took in Henry M. Flagler.

Flagler, born in upstate New York nine years before Rockefeller, had drifted out to Bellevue on the western edge of the Firelands. He became a grain merchant. He married the niece of Stephen V. Harkness, a rich distiller over at Monroeville on the Huron River. On his travels into this grain region Rockefeller had met and rightly appraised the genius of Flagler. Harkness moved on to Cleveland, made more money in real estate, and became one of its most substantial citizens. Flagler came over in 1865. He took offices in the same building with Rockefeller where he carried on his commission business. He was vigorous, imaginative—and interested in oil. He put up $70,000 in capital and joined Rockefeller's firm in 1867. It was renamed Rockefeller, Andrews & Flagler. Harkness invested a substantial sum without actually entering the partnership. Again the operations expanded and the capacity was increased to at least 1,500 barrels a day. Their size and steady flow put the firm in a superior bargaining position with the railroads to force concessions on rates. Apparently one of Flagler's first contributions to the success of the firm was an arrangement with the railroads handling their oil for a rebate on the freight charge. That was in 1867, and the rebate was apparently about fifteen cents a barrel—enough to stiffen Rockefeller's competition against the other Cleveland refiners and to hold his position against the men in the East. This agreement with the railroads was kept secret. Production rose to 3,000 barrels a day, and Rockefeller could guarantee sixty carloads a day to the railroads. In return they charged him only ninety cents, giving him as rebate about forty cents a barrel on the long haul to the Eastern markets.

Entrenched behind this favored arrangement, Rockefeller, now a tall, slightly stooped, quiet-spoken businessman at the age of thirty, growing each day surer of his methods and his power, pressed forward relentlessly with his plans. He reorganized his firm and incorporated it as a joint-stock company under the now famous name of the Standard Oil Company—a name carried over from one of his Kingsbury Run refineries. The articles of incorporation, dated at Cleveland January 10, 1870, bore the names and the signatures of John D. Rockefeller, Henry M. Flagler, Samuel Andrews, Stephen V. Harkness, and William Rockefeller. The purpose was "the manufacture of Petroleum, and to deal in Petroleum and its products." John D. Rockefeller was president, William was vice-president, Flagler was secretary, and Andrews was superintendent. Its capital was listed as $1,000,000.

With young Rockefeller's sharp, masterly touch and generalship at the helm, and with this hand-picked team of able operatives around him, he proceeded energetically, ruthlessly, and with breath-taking speed to take over and organize the entire petroleum business. They held private conferences far into the night at Rockefeller's big brick house on Euclid Avenue, at present Fortieth Street, which he had bought in 1868. In the morning Rockefeller would climb briskly into his carriage at his side door and drive his fine horses down the avenue to his office to carry forward the plans. The effects of this carefully mapped strategy were soon felt in Cleveland and throughout the industry. With the aid of the railroads and the rebate weapon, Rockefeller or his agents approached one by one the independent operators of the Cleveland refineries and forced them to sell their plants to Standard at the values placed on their properties by Rockefeller's appraisers. The price was low, but those who followed Rockefeller's advice and took stock in the company were handsomely rewarded. The others lost a good portion of their estate. But for the most part they had to sell. Only a handful of independents survived. Among the companies swallowed up by Standard was that of Robert Hanna, who had added oil distilling to his interests in 1869. Until 1872, when he had to sell to Rockefeller at half price, his company made a thirty-percent profit each year. Small wonder that feelings ran so high against Standard in those years, or that Rockefeller's group pressed on so relentlessly for control. Rockefeller took complete charge of the oil business in Cleveland.

The consolidation of the Cleveland business was only a small province in Rockefeller's dream of empire. He moved quickly on to the other oil centers at Philadelphia, Pittsburgh, New York, and elsewhere and, by whatever tactics were required, brought them under his control. He would invite them to consider the advantages of amalgamation as demonstrated in Cleveland and join voluntarily in exchange for stock; if they would not listen to reason, his agents would resort to "turning the screw." In the mid-1870's most of the big companies, from whose refineries came eighty percent of the supply, allied themselves with Standard Oil.

And Standard emerged as the world's largest oil refiner with, in
effect, a monopoly on a product that had become essential to world
economy. Its operations soon spanned the globe. They were so
extensive and so central that they were of vital concern to the entire nation. It seemed almost incidental that Cleveland and the
Western Reserve had been its birthplace and was still its home.
Along with iron and steel, Rockefeller's oil effected a revolution in
leisurely, rural, villaged New Connecticut.

Rockefeller was not for a moment content, like so many other
beginners in this industry, with a mere refinery to process oil
secured from other operators in the field. He must own or control
the entire complex process from wells to consumer, together with
all dependent subsidiary activities. He bought large tracts of potential oil land and timber. He built and operated his own factories for making barrels, bungs, paints, and glue for containing
and shipping oil. His cooper shops used up acres of selected oak
each day to make the staves and heads for the 9,000 barrels turned
out. This alone was a giant activity. The small cooperages in the
villages of the Reserve, which made barrels for flour, whisky, and
pork, considered four or five good barrels a day from one cooper
to be fast production.

Standard proceeded to acquire ownership or control of pipe lines
from the wells—about two hundred miles by 1880. It procured its
own cars for transporting oil, and built its own extensive warehouses, with storage for thousands of barrels of petroleum which
flowed daily from its constantly improving refineries. This bee-
hive of industry centered around the huge plants which spread
along the banks of the Cuyahoga and poured forth, in those early
decades of the business, a vile odor over the entire district. It was
so foul and disagreeable on hot nights that it made Cleveland
people sick. One man sued the company and won a settlement
out of court, on the charge of making his home unlivable, killing
his fruit trees, and making his family ill and sleepless from the
acid fumes and stinking vapors which spouted out of one of the
refineries. By 1884 Standard Oil had eighty-six establishments,
and gave employment to nearly 10,000 people, more than the en-

THE LIBRARY AT HIRAM COLLEGE

CLARENCE DARROW'S HOME AT KINSMAN
The house is built in octagonal shape

STATUE OF TOM JOHNSON IN CLEVELAND

tire population of Cleveland in 1845. Many of them were crowded into the spreading area of cheerless, unsanitary tenement districts. A carpenter in one of these shops received about sixty dollars a month. If his hand slipped into one of the unguarded power saws and he lost some fingers, he was out of work without compensation until he was well again, but the company would pay the doctor's bill.

Rockefeller's company had $27,395,706 invested in the manufacture of oil in Cleveland in the late 1880's. The raw materials being used by the company were valued at $35,000,000. These included 731,533,127 gallons of crude petroleum, and nearly four and a half million dollars' worth of barrels, tin cans, cases, bungs, paint, and glue, besides chemicals and fuel. Illuminating oil constituted about seventy-five percent of the $43,705,218 business. In addition Standard was making gasoline, naphtha products, paraffin, lubricating oil, and other by-products of the refining process. Out of these Cleveland distilleries poured the oil for the lamps of every part of the United States and for Europe and Great Britain. The jerky little carriage trains of the early 1850's, bumping along toward Ashtabula, Pittsburgh, Columbus, and Toledo with a few tons of grain and lumber were now long heavy strings of cars hauling barrels of oil from Cleveland across the continent. The busy wharves were piled high with them and the lengthening lake ships were steaming out of the Cleveland harbor with cargoes of them for shipment down the St. Lawrence and across the Atlantic.

Millions of dollars rolled back into Cleveland in exchange. The enormous wealth created by these operations and the rise in the number of wage earners were reflected in the rapid growth of the banks. The First National Bank was organized in May 1863, and was reorganized in May 1882. The Bank of Commerce became the Second National Bank, also in May 1863. In 1882 it became the National Bank of Commerce, with Jephtha H. Wade as president.

The legislature had authorized "associations of persons to raise funds to be used among their members for building homesteads, and for other purposes, to become a body corporate." The Citizens' Savings and Loan Association was organized in 1868 under this act, with J. H. Wade as president. The Ohio National Bank, with Robert Hanna as president, was founded in 1876. In the early 1880's other banks rose thick and fast. The Savings and Trust Company and the Cleveland National Bank were organized in 1883, and the Union National in 1884. Soon there were twenty banking or financial institutions helping Cleveland transact its huge business and accumulate savings. They included eight national banks and the Society for Savings. Truman P. Handy was president of the Mercantile National and of the Cleveland Clearing House Association; Robert R. Rhodes was president of the Peoples Saving and Loan Association; Samuel H. Mather of the Society for Savings; Marcus Alonzo Hanna of the Union National; and W. P. Southworth was president of the National City Bank. By this time, too, we may note that there were over fifty banks in thirty-five villages and towns all over the Reserve. The little village of Poland, population 452, had one; Mantua with a population of 600 had one; Garrettsville, Wadsworth, Greenwich, New London, Burton, Chardon, etc., each had one; Norwalk had three, Sandusky four, Akron and Youngstown each five; and there were several Savings and Loan Associations in Akron, Elyria, Conneaut, and Painesville.

So much wealth pouring into the pockets of a few individuals out of the monopolistic control of a great natural resource began to arouse public interest and concern. The methods used by Rockefeller and his associates, their rebates from the railroads, their harsh treatment of all competition, their political maneuvers to protect their operations against investigation and regulation—all these matters as they came to light brought at length to an end Rockefeller's singlehanded rule over the petroleum industry. Congress and the courts, which he had successfully dodged for twenty years, finally brought the industry under control. But before that came about, Standard Oil had grown from its original million-dollar capital to a hundred-million-dollar capital in a little over two decades. And as Standard Oil outgrew its Cleveland beginnings and expanded around the globe, it left in the Western Reserve and throughout Ohio a very substantial part of its business which continues today as the Standard Oil Company of Ohio.

Through all the oil investigations and agitations of these earlier years, John D. Rockefeller stuck close to business and the Second Baptist Church of which he was a faithful and supporting member. He thought that churchgoing was good for business as well as for the private nurture of the soul, and the people had more confidence in men who did not neglect the church and the work of the Lord. He taught a Sunday school class and was superintendent of Sunday and Mission schools. He gave generously to church work and to Denison University, the Baptist college at Granville, which turned out many distinguished ministers for the brotherhood. And his millions were behind the organization of the University of Chicago and other magnificent philanthropies.

Rockefeller himself was not ostentatious with his wealth despite the fact that he had climbed in a few years from a poverty-pinched clerk slaving over a ledger for a pittance to the glamorous eminence of one of the richest men in the world. In fact during the earlier days of his rise in Cleveland he cultivated modesty and required his associates to avoid the appearance of men who were piling up fortunes. He did indulge himself in a stable of fine fast horses, and he loved to race them against those of his neighbors along Euclid Avenue. But for the most part he was, outside of business, a patient and attentive family man and a pillar of the church, who scrupulously observed the Sabbath, seldom attended the theater, and preferred an easy chair at home with his devoted wife Laura Celestia and their children to the companions at the Union Club.

The mid-century prosperity of the railroad, coal, iron, shipping, banking, manufacturing, and merchant families had been reflected in the rows of Greek revival homes, as conceived and built by Jonathan A. Goldsmith, his son-in-law Charles W. Heard, Simeon C. Porter, and Warham J. Warner, which extended along the more gracious streets. They lined Franklin and Prospect; they stood in dignified splendor along Superior Street east of the Public Square out to the site of the Hollenden Hotel; and along Euclid out to Halle Bros., and the Statler Hotel. From the Hollenden site you could look west in Civil War days at the neat iron and stone fences and the Greek-columned porches of the homes of James Farmer, Fred Sterling, Philo Chamberlain, and Henry A. Raymond. The row on Euclid east of Erie Street included the homes of Truman P. Handy, Lemuel Crawford, Martin B. Scott, Henry L. Gaylord, Henry Chisholm, Samuel L. Mather, James F. Clark, Henry H. Dodge, S. B. Prentiss, Stillman Witt, Selah Chamberlain, Amasa Stone, and other famous citizens. They still kept some of the flavor of New Connecticut in the expanding metropolis of the Reserve. When Emerson, Beecher, or Melville lectured in Cleveland during this period, they talked to many social leaders whose near relatives had entertained them on similar occasions a few weeks earlier in New Haven. And these fine houses were not very different in tone and appointment from those on Hillhouse Avenue in New Haven, and this Yale-oriented society held to the same ideas and customs.

Visitors from Cincinnati even were moved to acknowledge that Cleveland in these years was "the most desirable town in the 'Great West' to live in." The editor of the *Cincinnati Gazette* who expressed that opinion went on to say that

the town is clean, tasteful, elegant and healthful; for vegetables, fruit and flowers it is preeminent—for groves, parks, ornamental trees and shrubs, it is hardly surpassed by New Haven—and these attractions have drawn, and will continue to draw, hundreds and thousands thither—simply as the most comfortable and desirable place to live in. Her public and private schools are excellent; her medical college superior to any in the West, and the prevailing character of her society educational, moral and religious. It is, therefore, "just the spot" for the man with moderate income, to live and educate his family.

The observation was, on the whole, perfectly true, but a convulsive and overwhelming growth was about to sweep over the districts which the Cincinnati editor was praising. Most of these houses, Cleveland's only examples of one of the great periods in

Reserve architecture, would soon be pulled down to make room
for the rapid influx of immigrants and for the spreading volume
of business, so that we must go out to Painesville, over to Norwalk, or down to Hudson to see surviving exhibits—or study the
old photographs which help to recreate this enviable era.

For in the dynamics of a growing city, a peaceful scene like this
could not long maintain itself. While the editor was writing this
piece, the irresistible forces of change were moving in upon it.

Foreign workers and their families were streaming into Cleveland by the thousands year after year and adding their pressure
on the older and poorer districts. Forty-eight different nationalities, speaking almost as many tongues, jammed into the city. Ten
years after Rockefeller had formed the Standard Oil Company the
foreign population had reached to over 68,000. The Irish were
especially strong in Cleveland beginning back in the canal-building days. They crowded into their own sections near the mills on
Whiskey Island, in the Flats, the Triangle, and on Vinegar Hill
until the expansion of industry drove them out into other, already
congested sections. They were swarming with children and enlivened by the hard drinking and fighting of the equally hard-
working men who tended the mills by day. The tenement district
between West Twelfth Street and the lake and river was known
as Shanty Town. The Irish went to church, voted at the polls,
understood practical city politics in the days of the bosses, and
took their share of the graft. The Germans kept on coming year
after year in the second half of the century. There were only ten
Germans in Cleveland in 1832, but by 1900 they numbered about
100,000. Some of them lived on Dutch Hill along with a colony
of Hollanders where wooden shoes and peasant dress were a common sight. Others were scattered in loose colonies on both sides
of the river. Many of them had left the homeland because they
loved liberty and thought they would find it in the American
Northwest. En route they discovered the opportunities of Cleveland and on impulse settled there. They were generally thrifty,
substantial, law-abiding citizens, some of them men of distinction
in the cultural and professional life of the community. They practiced the crafts which were diversifying the economic life of Cleve-

land—brewers, jewelry manufacturers, tailors, toolmakers, bakers, musicians, and instrument makers. They published their own papers, drank beer in their gardens, gave concerts, and supported their own German churches.

In the 1880's the Poles filled up the tenement blocks around East Thirty-fourth which were soon named Little Poland. The first arrivals were from German and Austrian-held Poland where they had worked in the mines and mills. They were brought over by the shipload to work in the steel mills during a prolonged strike in 1882. They were followed by a steady stream of their unhappy countrymen who were to make the Poles the second-largest immigrant group in polyglot Cleveland—the Czechoslovaks being first in number. The Russians and Croatians filtered into the south side in the vicinity of old University Heights. South of the Public Square, scattered along the bluff overlooking the Flats, were the congested and overflowing masses of Italians, Negroes, and Jews. Their district, one of the worst, was called the Haymarket. Russian Jews gathered in the Ghetto around the street markets in the same vicinity. The Murray Hill and Orange Street region was also a Little Italy, populated by a mass migration from Campo Basso. The Bohemians, a large and thriving group, jammed into the downtown district known as the Cabbage Patch and Little Cuba. The Chinese huddled in their Dopetown, on Ontario Street, keeping themselves behind dirty windows to ward off evil spirits. When the construction of the Mall forced them to leave, they moved as a group to a planned settlement on Rockwell Avenue. Hungarians, Portuguese, Norwegians, Swedes, Finns, Swiss, Turks, French, Greeks, Japs, Mexicans, Irish, Welsh, Scotch, English—from all over the world they came to "the most desirable town in the 'Great West' to live in." And their number was augmented, of course, by the thousands of country boys and rural families who came to Cleveland to find work in the mills and factories at what seemed to them to be high wages.

The city was unprepared to receive such an upsurge in population. Water and sewage disposal were inadequate, the streets were dark, unpaved and filthy, and the housing wretched in the extreme in these teeming slums. Saloons flourished, drunkenness was rife, vice rampant, parks and playgrounds were unknown, and schools were hopelessly unable to absorb the numerous foreign-speaking children. The police were the busiest public servants in Cleveland, with all their patrol wagons dashing about to answer calls and extra buggies hired on Saturdays to help pick up the drunks and maintain order. Fires were frequent and disease spread through the tenements. Indeed the city during the post-Civil War period of its acute growing pains presented in many of its areas a distressed and sorry picture.

It took these pains in its industrial stride, accepting the conditions as unfortunate but inevitable, and subordinated them to the exciting onrush of business and manufacturing development. Benevolent and philanthropic societies, many sponsored by the organized nationality groups, alleviated the misery of hardship cases while the commercial houses, stores, and offices burst out of their confinement in the old "downtown" section and moved on east to replace the quiet tree-shaded residences on Superior and Euclid. Inevitably the dominantly Connecticut pattern of life around the Cuyahoga could not maintain itself against such an overwhelming assault in such numbers by other cultures.

The wealthy families yielded their ground, without financial loss, and moved on to the east along Euclid Avenue. The avenue was already widely known for its rows of trees, its lawns and gardens, and its fine homes. It had in the 1860's caused both the local press and visitors to the city to continue the eulogies which the earlier travelers had lavished on Cleveland. The *Plain Dealer,* with some restraint, spoke of the avenue as "becoming each year more stylish and regal." A New York reporter, covering a convention in Cleveland for the *World,* wrote in 1863 that Euclid Avenue "is perhaps the finest avenue in the west, a double row of charming villas and gardens where one might sigh to dwell." Archer H. Shaw, in his centenary history of the *Plain Dealer,* digs up the prize among the rhapsodies, written by a visiting editor from Wisconsin, who said:

The Forest City! The Fountain City! La Belle City! Cleveland!
—beautiful for situation—abounding in palatial mansions looking

out through a wealth of magnificent foliage, spangled with floral gems—like sparkling diamonds in the flowing tresses of some fair maiden. Of all the western aspirants for the crown of beauty, we adjudge thee Queen. . . .

The new millionaires were adding to her regality. They chose the ridge that extended for a mile or so out beyond Amasa Stone's mansion along the north side of Euclid Avenue. This gentle elevation sloped gradually away toward the lake. It had been a section of farms, and the avenue was still unbroken by cross streets. It was an ideal spot for spacious grounds commanding distant glimpses of the lake, icebound in winter and glittering blue and silver under the sun in the spring. Here, apparently at a safe distance from the invasion of the slums and marts, the Nabobs, as they were called, built the ornate mansions in the new rococo style which in the 1860's and 1870's replaced the dignified simplicity of the Greek revival of Goldsmith's Superior Street days.

Each mansion had large grounds carefully laid out, planted, and tended, with paths and walks among the ponds and shrubbery, and sweeping driveways leading in from the avenue, under the portecochere, and back to the big stables where the fine horses, carriages, and sleighs were housed. Many of the interiors were loaded with rich carpets, beds, lamps, stands, paintings, sculpture, and oddities from abroad, especially from Italy.

Samuel Andrews' mansion, which stood on Euclid at Thirtieth Street, was one of the most notable of the establishments. It took three years to build it. It contained thirty-three rooms, six immense ones on the first floor, and five beautifully equipped suites on the second floor for Andrews' five daughters. It had carved staircases and stained-glass windows. Most of the furniture came from England. The men servants wore knee breeches, velvet jackets, and silver buckles on their shoes after the fashion of eighteenth-century baronial Britain. It was later closed and abandoned by the family and for some years the rich furniture and rugs molded and rotted. They were finally sold to a secondhand dealer. The house was torn down, and during the craze for miniature golf in the early 1930's the children of the intruding families gathered under the garish lights to putt balls on the site of the old mansion. These were the houses which extended and made more lustrous the name of the avenue in the period of its glory when the social life of the gay younger set was much talked of and written about.

Rockefeller moved to the avenue in 1868. The house, which was pulled down in 1938, was on the southwest corner of present East Fortieth Street. The grounds extended to Case Avenue and Prospect Street. It was a rectangular brick structure with the arched windows and mansard roof so common in the sixties and seventies. It had the usual big central hall with the long staircase rising along one side to the second floor. The high-ceilinged parlor, with mahogany woodwork, brownish plaster, and white marble mantel, was on the right; and the big music room, in the same décor, was on the left. The dining room, kitchen, downstairs bedroom, and servants' quarters were in the rear of the first story. There were four large bedrooms on the second floor. It was not so impressive as many of the mansions, and it was on the south, the wrong or "Bob" side of the avenue. But it was large and expensive enough to indicate as much of his rising station in life as Rockefeller cared to reveal to the citizens of Cleveland.

This portion of Euclid Avenue proved to be no more secure in its exclusive privacy against the bulging city than the houses on Superior Street. Business and the foreign population continued their relentless pressure. It would soon be flanked by the Polish section and by successive waves of immigrant groups—Germans, Bohemians, Russian Jews, Italians, and, in the second decade of the twentieth century, by the Negroes—as they, too, moved east before the growth of new business houses and magnificent public buildings downtown. The great houses would become tarnished, the window sashes go unpainted, the lawns go to seed, and the avenue would become a rooming-house district.

Modern city planners point out that the better residential section should have gone south toward Brecksville for beauty of terrain, fresher air, and easy transit to the Square. Perhaps so, but it did not. The Cuyahoga was associated with the grotesque confusion of industry, while the east, toward Doan Brook, was virginal and inviting. Jephtha H. Wade had led the way toward this favored spot. He had made his fortune in banking and railroads, and as one of the organizers of the Western Union Telegraph Company in 1856. He bought a large acreage east of the city and north of Euclid Avenue along Doan Brook. It was rustic and wild, and the meandering brook, with its valley and gently rising banks, made it particularly inviting for the development of a country estate. Wade took a passionate interest in developing it. He brought in landscapers, planted it carefully, beautified the brook, and turned it into a handsome park.

William J. Gordon, wholesale grocer, pioneer in Lake Superior iron ore, and owner of one of the most famous horse and stock farms in the West, bought up large holdings along the lake a couple of miles north of Wade's estate. His acres fronted the lake shore for three quarters of a mile, and extended about a half mile south over attractively contoured land. Doan Brook ran through the middle of his property. Like Wade he hired a large staff of gardeners and turned 122 acres into a park of unexampled beauty.

Rockefeller also began to purchase land farther east. Most of it was acquired for him by the colorful and celebrated editor of the *Cleveland Plain Dealer,* Liberty Emery Holden, the man who built the Hotel Hollenden and was president of the building commission for the Cleveland Museum of Art. Known as Forest Hill, the estate lay six miles out from his offices in the Standard Oil Building at 43 Euclid. It was a natural rolling woodland broken with ravines. The ornate three-story frame house on the hill commanded a view of the lake. Rockefeller loved the place so much that from 1878 until he moved his family to 4 West Fifty-fourth Street, New York, he lived there during most of the year. He kept up his town house as a convenient stopover place on Sundays. He, too, employed gardeners and caretakers to build paths and roads, to plant trees and lawns, and to convert the place into a country estate. He still loved to drive his fine horses about the place or into town. Forest Hill, these horses, and the Euclid Avenue Baptist Church were his primary interests after he had slaved through the day in the Kingdom of Standard Oil.

All these estates ultimately became the property of the citizens of Greater Cleveland. These men, who by one means or another were able in their day to create and to accumulate such extraordinary wealth, were also generous in their benefactions to the city. The same men who resisted the formation of the Interstate Commerce Commission, the Sherman Antitrust Act, the lowering of tariffs, the rise of wages and the organization of trade unions, quietly left their estates as monuments to their public spirit.

Their donations came at a most opportune time. Except for the Public Square, Cleveland itself was without any parks or open spaces for the recreation of its citizens. And the helter-skelter, unplanned rush of its growth threatened to exclude the possibility of such areas. It would have been a great misfortune if the highly praised city were blighted with slums, and isolated from the very considerable natural beauty which the gorges, streams, and varied terrain in the general vicinity afforded. The river was already given up to the mills, and the lake, which had enraptured Melish, was pre-empted and walled in by railroads and manufacturing plants. The donation of these great estates turned the attention of Cleveland toward the creation of the magnificent park system which now virtually encircles the city.

Wade set the first example by donating his Doan Brook park of seventy-five acres to the city in 1882. By the terms of his gift, Cleveland added another $75,000 worth of improvements and opened it to the public. Ten years later he added to his gift the site of the projected art gallery. The extraordinarily beautiful building was completed in 1916, facing toward Euclid Avenue across a large oval-shaped lagoon which serves as a reflecting basin. The Cleveland Fine Arts Garden, a profusion of flowers and shrubs, now surrounds the lagoon.

Gordon died on November 23, 1892. He had willed his estate of 112 acres as a gift to the city of Cleveland to be kept forever as Gordon Park for the pleasures of the public. The public has made good use of its boating facilities, its tennis and horseshoe courts and its baseball diamonds, its greenhouses and its pleasant open spaces.

Off to the southeast along the headwaters of Doan Brook lay the farms and village of the Shakers. The brook on its way down through their farms widened out into two lakes. On this secluded high land, far from the worldly city of Cleveland, the Shakers had formed their colony in 1823, built their mills at the outlets to the lakes, and had become for a time a prosperous community. This strange sect held their property in common, and each worked for the good of all. They agitated themselves in their religious meetings, they kept apart from the world, and they practiced celibacy. They became excellent farmers and fair artisans. Splendid samples of their handicraft are gathered at the Western Reserve Historical Society Museum. Since they had no offspring, they could perpetuate themselves only by recruiting converts. This source of replenishment began to fail after the Civil War as eccentric religious fervor cooled. The colony dwindled away, and in 1892 sold its extensive holdings on the heights for $316,000 to the Shaker Heights Land Company. In 1895 the company donated for public use the area around the brook and the lakes which became Shaker Heights Park, the most extensive single unit in the park system. And the following year John D. Rockefeller gave $300,000 to complete the boulevard up the valley to join the Wade and Shaker Heights parks.

Rockefeller also presented another munificent gift in the Reserve's centennial year. In addition to Forest Hill, he owned the 273-acre strip along the brook between Wade and Gordon. He now donated this land to the city to be known as Rockefeller Park, making the entire Doan Brook Valley from Shaker Heights to the lake a continuous public domain. Rockefeller Park has tennis courts and a generous lake for boating and skating. It is most noted, however, and appropriately so, for its Cleveland Cultural Gardens. They feature the native, Old-World culture of the various nationality groups who flocked into the city, lured by the enterprises which these men had developed. They are arranged on the slope between the boulevards. The German Garden, centering around the Goethe-Schiller monument, the Heine bust, and the Unsterberg Marble Fountains, pays tribute to the great literary figures of the romantic period in Germany. The Hebrew Garden features plants from Palestine fenced in by a hedge of cedars of Lebanon. The Italian Garden has a Renaissance fountain and a bronze statue of Virgil. The English Garden is styled in the Elizabethan manner with a bust of Shakespeare and a huge Shakespeare Open-Air Theater. J. G. W. Cowles, president of the Chamber of Commerce in the centennial year, attempted to voice the appreciation of the city before the great mass meeting held on July 22. "From this hour," he said, "in the honored and noble company of Wade and Gordon, as benefactors of their fellow citizens and fellow men, in our hearts with gratitude, and upon our lips with praise, will be the name of the giver of this princely gift, John D. Rockefeller." The estate at Forest Hill, which soon comprised 870 acres, passed on to John D. Rockefeller, Jr., who in turn gave a large portion of it to Cleveland and East Cleveland to enlarge further the municipal park system.

Also in the same year Patrick Calhoun gave to the city a tract of land extending from Fairmount along Doan Brook to Cedar Glen. This gift made possible the development of University Circle, certainly one of the most attractive street intersections in an American city. The natural beauty of its setting is enhanced by the Western Reserve University and the Case Institute of Technology buildings and campuses on the bluff to the east and southeast; by Severance Hall, the million-dollar gift of John Long Severance and the home of the Cleveland Symphony Orchestra, to the northeast; by the Cleveland Museum of Art facing the flower-bordered lagoon to the north; and the landscaped boulevard leading up the valley to the south.

We note in passing three statues of some interest in connection with this story of the Reserve. One is Augustus Saint-Gaudens' bronze sculpture of Marcus Alonzo Hanna erected just north of the Circle in 1907 as a tribute to the friend of McKinley.[1] East of the Circle is the figure of Louis Kossuth where the Hungarians

---

[1] A statue of his great rival and enemy in the streetcar rate war, the many-times mayor of the city, the celebrated Tom L. Johnson, stands in the northwest section of the Public Square.

gather annually to honor their distinguished countryman. And on a hill just west of East Boulevard in Gordon Park is the statue of Commodore Oliver Hazard Perry. It calls up memories of the Cleveland of Wade's and Gordon's day and the youth of Rockefeller. For on September 10, 1860, the forty-seventh anniversary of the battle of Lake Erie, Cleveland citizens, the governors of Ohio and Rhode Island, and hundreds of distinguished invited guests paraded through the city and assembled at the Public Square to dedicate a monument to Perry. Survivors of the battle and the son of the commodore were there. They cheered as the Cleveland sculptor, William Walcutt, pulled away the flags and unveiled the Carrara marble likeness of the hero. The funds had been subscribed by Cleveland citizens and the marble had been shipped over from Italy. The famous battle was re-enacted on the lake, and the daylong festivities ended with a banquet and more speeches at the Weddell House. The statue stood on the Square until the next generation decided to remove it and place in its stead on the same spot the Soldiers' and Sailors' Monument which is still there, but seldom admired by the passers-by. The Perry statue was then taken out to Wade Park and set up on the present site of the Art Museum. It was moved on to Gordon Park in 1913 when ground was broken for the Museum. The bronze cast of Walcutt's sculpture was set up in the park by the Early Settlers Society in 1929.

CHAPTER TWENTY-ONE

THE NEW URBAN CENTERS

Shortly after the Civil War young Dr. Benjamin
Franklin Goodrich of Melrose, New York, happened to pick up a
glowing advertisement put out by the Akron Board of Trade. It
sang the praise of the Summit City as the ideal spot for industries.
The bold statements were not mere groundless and ambitious
boasts. One of the pioneers of the city, after making a journey
through the industrial sections of the world, came back to his home
town and declared his firm belief

that nowhere on the face of the earth is there so remarkable a
manifestation of industrialism as in the territory surrounding this
city for a dozen miles; for here you find not only every form of
modern industry fully developed, but also populous and profitable
markets right at the door of the manufactories.

Goodrich was impressed and interested by Akron's general in-
vitation to industry. It had come at the most opportune moment
for him.

He was no stranger to the Reserve. Though born in New York,
he had attended the academy at Austinburg and then had graduated from the Cleveland Medical College in 1861. He had served
in the war and had practiced medicine in New York for a year or
so. But he gave up medicine for real estate. And in one of his
transactions he had acquired in 1867 control of the Hudson River
Rubber Company at Hastings-on-Hudson, a company operating
under a license from that great and devoted pioneer of the rubber
industry, Charles Goodyear. Competition in the East was fierce

271

and the company was losing money. Goodrich was looking about for a better location. So he went out to Akron to see for himself. He talked with prominent businessmen and civic leaders in the growing city at the Empire Hotel, he looked at the location, and he liked what he saw. The city was flourishing and its present industries were well diversified. It was spreading over the gentle ridge, it was on the canal, it was well served by railroads, it had abundant water supply, and labor seemed plentiful. He returned to New York to consider. He was followed by Colonel George T. Perkins, the president of the Board of Trade, who in turn inspected Goodrich's rubber plant. He, too, liked what he saw. He persuaded Akron to advance money to help move the equipment to the Summit of the Reserve. A new firm, Goodrich, Tew & Company, was formed on December 31, 1870, a two-story building was quickly erected on what is now appropriately named Rubber Street, and Akron was in the business of making rubber—fire hose, belting, billiard cushions, and other articles.

Rubber, of course, was still overshadowed by other products in great demand in the Reserve, in Ohio, and throughout the nation. Horace Greeley, who had visited Akron in 1843, had been much impressed by its five woolen mills, its big blast furnace, its machine shop, its card manufactory, and its four huge flour mills. Four years later George Barber chose Akron as the site for his Barber Match Company, consolidated in 1881 with the Diamond Match Company. In the eighties the company made in Akron a fifth of the entire output of matches in the nation. It was later centered in Barberton right on the edge of the Reserve to the south and at present abutting so closely on Akron that you can tell only by the signs where one leaves off and the other begins. The high-quality stoneware clay beds in Summit County had made Akron a natural location for the manufacture of sewer pipe at the very moment when the cities were beginning to improve their sanitation. Akron worked out the process of glazing it with salt vapor at high temperature to make a product that would not scale and was impervious to sewer gas. During the 1880's, when Standard Oil refineries and big steel mills were spreading all over the bluffs and the Flats at Cleveland, sixteen fair-sized companies were turning out sewer pipe, stoneware, roofing tile and firebrick on the Summit above the bend and the falls of the Cuyahoga.

Ferdinand Schumacher, a vigorous and imaginative merchant from Celle, Germany, had come to Akron in 1851. He opened a store on Market Street and quickly developed a prosperous business. He thought he could produce oatmeal which Americans might enjoy for their breakfast. He tried it out on a small scale about 1854. He rolled the oats, cut the meal into cubes, packaged it in glass candy jars, and sold it by the ounce. Housewives had to cook it for hours, but they or their families liked it. Schumacher then leased a frame building, which he named German Mill, on Howard Street, and began to manufacture oatmeal and cereal products. In 1863, during the boom of the war when demands for everything were overwhelming, he established the Empire Barley Mill, the first of the mills which were to make Akron one of the nation's largest producers of cereals, and the enormous concrete columns of the elevators a characteristic of its sky line. The Schumacher interests became the American Cereal Company in 1891, incorporated the mills at Ravenna, and adopted their name of Quaker Oats. The extensive Quaker Oats Company plant on Howard Street is on the site of the Old Stone Mill which, in 1833, drew water through a race from the Little Cuyahoga River to turn its wheels—and the race is still used by the old mill's giant successor.

The rapid clearing of the frontier for farmlands and the growing market for grain to supply the mounting populations in the cities called for improved methods of harvesting. Lewis Miller invented the first two-wheeled mower, equipped it with the first folding cutter bar, moved his plant from Canton to Akron in 1863 and began another of the important industries of the city. His Buckeye brand of mowers, reapers, and binders was sold throughout the world. In 1877 he was producing 2,000 machines each year, and in 1888 Aultman, Miller & Co., and J. F. Seiberling & Co., were employing 1,000 men from among the thousands who were converging on Akron in those years.

Other plants were making finished iron and steel products—stoves, hoisting machinery, chains, knives, and hardware specialities; twine and cordage; farm and spring wagons and buggies; electrical supplies, dental supplies, leather goods, dressed lumber, and paper bags. Two of the largest publishing houses in the country were located there. The Universalists had founded Buchtel College in 1870 on one of the heights overlooking the city, and Horace Greeley had come out in 1871 to lay the cornerstone of the first building and make an inspiring address on the subject, "Human Conceptions of God as They Affect the Moral Education of Our Race." The college was taken over in 1913 by the municipality and developed into the University of Akron.

This was the general industrial pattern of the town to which Goodrich, with the aid of the Board of Trade, brought the first rubber plant. The population was 3,266 in 1850 and 3,477 in 1860. It jumped to 10,006 in 1870, to 16,512 in 1880, to 27,601 in 1890, and to 42,728 at the turn of the century. Only one-sixth of the population at that time was foreign-born, in contrast to Cleveland's one out of three. The Irish were especially strong, of course, and they made an impressive display of their number and solidarity when amidst great festivities they dedicated on St. Patrick's Day in 1866 their fine church of Saint Vincent de Paul. A goodly number of German businessmen, artisans and craftsmen, teachers and professional men had settled in Akron, a respected and civic-minded group of substantial citizens. There were two or three hundred Jews who in 1885 bought the old St. Paul's Episcopal Church and converted it into their first synagogue. Only a relatively small proportion of the polyglot invasion of Cleveland spilled over into Akron. And in the second decade of the present century, when Akron became a boom town with a vengeance, and the word spread like wildfire that there was light work at high wages to be had at the rubber factories, although many nationalities of the world trekked in, it was the hill country of West Virginia and Kentucky, of Alabama and Tennessee and the plantations of the cotton belt that sent the majority of the thousands of that mass migration to Akron.

In this setting of cereals, sewer pipe, stoneware, and farm machinery, Goodrich's little rubber plant on the banks of the canal was insignificant. Though Colonel George T. Perkins and eighteen associates who yielded to his importunities had invested $1,000 each in Goodrich's venture, the business group and Akron citizens remained skeptical of it. The plant was soon turning out White Anchor fire hose for the new fire engines which all the big towns were buying to try to cut down the tremendous annual losses in the disastrous fires which swept the old tinderbox houses and stores and the volatile new oil refineries. Goodrich had watched the house of one of his friends burn down because the inferior hose of the fire-fighting equipment had burst. Akron's White Anchor was a superior product and it sold. The company, however, had a hard struggle to keep alive during the first decade. Materials were scarce and the finances shaky. One reorganization followed another until May 1880 when George W. Crouse got its capital on a sound footing and the firm was finally stabilized as the B. F. Goodrich Company. Goodrich was president of the company until his death in 1888. Several of the original backers were so unimpressed by the future of rubber that they sold out their interest at the time of this reorganization. The other more venturesome stockholders soon were rewarded with fortunes.

For the era of rubber lay just a few years over the horizon. The bicycle craze swept over the nation during the last quarter of the century. Experiments with every conceivable design were conducted during the seventies and eighties. The new contraption began to get standardized in the late eighties. The drop frame was introduced to make it handy and respectable for long-skirted and heavily petticoated ladies. The free-wheeling coaster brake was patented in 1880. Everybody seemed to want one of the machines. Cycling clubs were formed in all the towns. Church attendance on Sunday dwindled as the parishioners climbed on bicycles and pedaled out to the country. Ministers preached sermons denouncing the demoralizing influence of the bicycles, but the demand continued to mount and the Peerless and Winton plants in Cleveland, along with many others, manufactured them by the thousands. The tires for these wheels, made by Goodrich in the 1880's, were the old solid-band type bound to the rim with wire. The machine bumped and vibrated on the rough streets. The joy of cycling was immensely enhanced by the invention of pneumatic tires which first appeared on the market about 1890. They immediately became standard equipment, and the next year nearly half of all the bicycles manufactured were equipped with them. Cord tires were first made in Akron in 1892. A million people were riding on the comfortable new wheels on the streets and country roads in 1893. They were geared for faster and faster locomotion. Teams raced from city to city, and by the close of the nineties a famed cyclist named "Cannonball" Baker won a miniature diamond bicycle for riding at the breath-taking speed of a little over thirty miles an hour.

The bicycle created a new and boundless market for rubber, and the Goodrich Company boomed, expanded, and made money. But if rubber tires were good for bicycles, would they not also improve the riding comfort of carriages? The virtues of rubber on buggy wheels were dramatically advertised in 1892. The newspapers carried word to the nation that Nancy Hanks, famous racing trotter, had lowered the world's speed record, held by Maud S, by four seconds, and that her sulky had pneumatic tires on its wheels. Immediately the nation wanted rubber on its carriage wheels, and Goodrich, again expanding, manufactured them.

And in that same decade of miracles on wheels, the first horseless carriage appeared on the streets of Detroit to the derisive amusement of the curious and the fright of the horses. The inventive genius of the Reserve was also at work on the automobile. Alexander Winton of Scotland had come to Cleveland in 1884 to make bicycles. He added many improvements, including ball bearings, and in 1895 built his first gasoline-motor bicycle. The next year he built a two-cylinder horseless carriage, complete with friction clutch, electric ignition, and pneumatic tires. Clumsy though it was, it made a sensational run through the streets of Cleveland. In 1897 he organized the Winton Motor Car Company, and on March 24, 1898, he sold the first motorcar manu-

factured in the Reserve. Winton publicized his car by driving it
from Cleveland to New York in seventy-eight hours and forty-
three minutes of running time.

One of Winton's first cars was bought by James W. Packard
of Warren, an inventor of note in the field of electric lamps. He
designed his own car, formed the Ohio Automobile Company in
1899, and began making automobiles in Cleveland. In 1903 he
reorganized his firm and moved his establishment to Detroit
where, as the Packard Motor Car Company, it survived the
intense competition which swept so many of the pioneers away.

Stearns, Baker, Gaeth, Peerless, Royal, and other Cleveland
firms rushed into the business, and by 1910 there were thirty-two
establishments in Cleveland alone representing the automobile
industry. None of these could cope with the competition of
Detroit where the industry was to be ultimately centered, but
they helped create and meet the demand for motorcars, and they
made Cleveland the center for bodies and parts for the finished
Detroit product.

The automobile created another tremendous demand for rubber,
a demand which has steadily increased during the twentieth
century. Goodrich expanded to supply it. The company began
manufacturing pneumatic automobile tires in 1896. By this time
the future of rubber was assured and other companies moved
in to share the business. They, too, chose Akron. F. A. Seiberling
and his brother C. W. organized a small company in 1898. They
named it Goodyear in honor of the man who had first learned how
to vulcanize rubber. They were the sons of J. F. Seiberling of
the prosperous Empire Mower & Reaper works of Akron. Despite
the rising requirements for rubber, they had a hard time to raise
capital for their company. F. A., a short, wiry, ambitious and
driving young man, finally managed to borrow $3,500 and to get
another $9,000 on his personal notes. He bought an old factory
from the Akron Strawboard works, and began to make rubber tires
for carriages. He followed closely the changing needs of the
industry, experimented with new processes, and developed Goodyear within a few years into one of the Big Three in the world-wide

rubber market, making 30,000 different rubber products, from tiny washers to the rubberized casings of the giant dirigibles of World War I. His company was the first to enter the rubber plantation business. In 1916 it acquired thousands upon thousands of acres of Sumatra jungles and planted a million rubber trees. The plantations were soon extended to the Malay States and other parts of the Far East from which ships and trains brought tons of crude rubber into Akron.

Harvey S. Firestone came in 1900 to enter the competition. He bought an interest in the carriage-tire department of an Akron carriage factory, and with twelve workmen began his famous career. The Firestone Tire & Rubber Company rode forward on the same boom with the others to become another of the huge concerns in Akron. He bought up also several square miles of rubber-producing jungle in Liberia to assure a steady supply of raw material for his factories.

Smaller companies—Miller, Star, Swinehart, Diamond—also came to Akron. And by the time the rush of World War I hit America, Akron was a household word everywhere, the number one rubber city of the world, with vast and growing factories spread all over the Summit and the peculiar smell of rubber permeating the gold-rush atmosphere.

In the midst of all this activity the city burst out of its confines around its center of Main and Market streets, and overflowed in all directions impulsively and without plan. Absorbed by the excitement of its industrial development, it seemed to be concerned only with the problem of where to sleep another worker, where to place a roof over the head of a Southern white and his family. The older homes were turned into rooming houses where men slept in relays. They crowded into jerry-built houses hastily thrown up around and in between the factories. They moved into new districts out toward the Portage Lakes, following the factories. The new rubber wealth and the high-salaried personnel moved out to the beautiful West Hill region and developed it into a handsome community of big estates and comfortable suburban dwellings. The Little Cuyahoga River was bridged by the

North Main Street viaduct to make North Hill accessible. The High Level Bridge over the wild beauty of the Cuyahoga gorge linked Akron with Cuyahoga Falls and made that attractive town an adjunct of Akron in easy commuting distance.

These new developments preserved Akron from complete surrender to the immediate urgencies of its business expansion. This was fortunate for the city. Even with these redemptions, it is a pity that one of the finest natural settings in the whole Reserve for a beautiful town should have come so close to being spoiled beyond repair. But the rugged terrain, the Cuyahoga bend and gorge, the Tuscarawas Valley and the Portage Lakes, the old canal basin, resist considerable spoliation.

Akron, which had had its beginning as a terminal and then a port town on the canal, never had much of the flavor of Connecticut. What little it did have was completely and irrevocably lost, submerged, and blotted out by the scores of thousands from other cultures who came to man the factories. One must bicycle or motor on rubber tires to Tallmadge to be reminded that these noisy, turbulent and restless people of Akron are geographically inhabitants of the Western Reserve.

David Tod, United States Minister to Brazil under President Polk, zealous governor of Ohio during the Civil War, was the man who imprinted on Youngstown the industrial pattern which it retains to this day. His father, already eminent in Connecticut, had come out to Ohio in 1800 where he served as Secretary of the Northwest Territory under Governor St. Clair, then as senator in the newly formed state of Ohio and one of the early judges of the Supreme Court. The family homestead was a farm called Brier Hill which lay just outside the village of Youngstown, two miles to the northwest. David Tod was born there in 1805. The farm later passed into other hands, but when David began to accumulate wealth, he bought it back out of strong sentiment for the home soil and memories of his boyhood. From his front porch on Brier Hill he could look out on the valley of the winding Mahoning River and see the smoke pour from the stacks of the furnaces which his enterprise had helped to build in this favored location. For he had opened up the rich coal veins around Youngstown, he had shipped his coal up to Cleveland and practically compelled the shippers and industrialists there to recognize its value, and he had pushed through the construction of the Cleveland & Mahoning Railroad, of which he became president. He encouraged the manufacture of iron, and it was the Anna Furnace at Lowell, using his raw Brier Hill split coal, that first made iron by the new process in August 1846. He himself erected three blast furnaces at Brier Hill.

Other coal-using furnaces immediately rose in the region to utilize what appeared to be an inexhaustible supply of the essential raw material of coal. Philpot, Morris, Warren & Sawyer brought in the Eagle blast furnace which they had built on the canal not far from Brier Hill in 1846. They leased a vast area of the coal beds at the price of one cent a bushel for the first 25,000, and one-half cent for the remainder. The Youngstown Iron Company built a rolling mill on the canal at the southeast edge of the town in the same year. When Henry Howe visited Youngstown in 1846, this mill was the only one in sight of the town. Howe went down the Pittsburgh road a short distance, climbed over a rail fence and, looking back toward Youngstown from the hill on Homer Hines's farm, he drew one of those priceless sketches which lend such charm to his unique *Historical Collections of Ohio*. It represents an almost pastoral scene. Rimmed by hills on both sides, the Mahoning River sweeps leisurely down the middle of its valley, paralleled by the narrow canal, which, in the sketch, looks like a ribbon of modern concrete highway. Hines's farmhouse is on the right, a few warehouses, looking like huge barns in a meadow, front on the canal, and in the distance farther up is a peaceful village with the spires of the Presbyterian, Disciples, and Methodist churches rising above the trees. And on the west in one of the bends of the river, the lone smokestack of the Youngstown Iron Company's mill rises above the church spires and shoots up a wavering column of black smoke which the wind symbolically scatters over the entire scene.

The following year, when Captain James Ward built his Brier Hill furnace, Youngstown men had what was in that day the huge sum of $200,000 invested in the iron business. Twenty-one blast furnaces were erected in this immediate area during the next twenty-five years, and at the beginning of the new century Youngstown and vicinity were producing one-seventh of all the pig iron and steel made in the nation. The village of 1846, quite naturally, was transformed.

Located as it is in the southeast corner of the Reserve, and linked geographically and economically to Pittsburgh and to western Pennsylvania's coal, iron and steel interests, Youngstown rapidly lost any Connecticut flavor which it may have had at the middle of the century. It was a natural target for the railroads which served Pennsylvania and Cleveland. In the early days of railroad building, a dozen or more lines were built or projected to tap the Mahoning Valley industries. The story of their organizations, failures, and consolidations alone fills pages of Youngstown history. When the story was complete, after the Goulds and Vanderbilts had ended their wars and their speculations, and the roads had shaken down into stability, Youngstown found itself served by four of the great east-west systems—the New York Central, the Erie, the Baltimore & Ohio, and the Pennsylvania—all of which meet and pass and maintain yards here. In addition, the flow of Great Lakes ore and the rise of the big companies encouraged the construction of the Pittsburgh & Lake Erie, the Lake Shore & Eastern, and the local Youngstown & Austintown roads —busy industrial belt lines serving the plants, rolling ore down to the valley and coal up to the lake in stupendous quantities.

With one of its important raw materials lying on its doorstep and under the very foundations of its mills, and with quick, easy, and short transportation to the lake and substantial markets, Youngstown moved forward with giant strides. It wanted to have the distinction of being the county seat. This honor had been held through the years by the quiet, conservative Reserve village of Canfield, located in the center of the county. Youngstown stole it in 1876, though Canfield battled every step of the way and surrendered only after a long, spirited and bitter legal fight which was carried through the Ohio courts and was finally settled in favor of Youngstown by the Supreme Court of the United States. The victory centered the county offices at a new courthouse in Youngstown, and turned the horses of the farmers and farm villagers away from Canfield toward the Public Square at Federal and Market streets where business houses were rising and where the recently erected Soldiers Monument was graced by four cannons presented by their Civil War hero and representative in Congress, General James A. Garfield. The population of Youngstown took another jump when it became the county seat. It was only 999 in 1840, and 8,095 in 1870; it reached 15,435 in 1880. The accretions had come in from the surrounding states and from the British Isles. The Irish had been attracted by the canal and railroad-building opportunities; the Welsh, Scotch and English by the manufacture of iron and the mining of coal. There were a few hundred Germans, and a few score of families from France, Norway, and Sweden. At that time there were no Italians, Slavs, or central or southern Europeans.

The streets of the town were still unpaved and the wagons floundered in a sea of mud. The hills and hummocks in Federal and Market had not even been leveled. The city fathers now, against organized resistance of the citizens, paved these streets and laid a few sewer pipes. Gas was manufactured at a plant across the river and piped into some of the houses in 1872. Electric lights appeared in 1888, and the slow-moving horse-drawn cars from Basin Street to Brier Hill were replaced by electric trams. The *Vindicator,* the Democratic newspaper founded in 1869, continued to build circulation.

Industrialization went on apace, reflecting in its way the same activity which was transforming Cleveland and Akron. Coke from Connellsville appeared in the furnaces of Youngstown in 1867 and soon replaced raw coal because it made a superior product. More furnaces and iron-working plants rose on the Mahoning. The big Brown, Bonnell & Company was employing nearly two thousand men, the Mahoning Valley Iron Company about 1,300 more; and the smaller Hem Rod Furnace, Youngstown Rolling Mill, Cartwright & McCurdy, Brier Hill, Youngstown Steel, and American Tube & Iron were employing all together close to a thousand more. Besides these mills, the Arms Bell Company was turning out bolts and nuts, the Enterprise Boiler Works and Wm. P. Pollock & Company were making steam boilers, George Turner specialized in iron fencing for the large grounds around the fine homes in the Reserve, Youngstown Stamping Company made tinware, the Youngstown Carriage Manufacturing Company built wagons and buggies, William Tod & Company made engines, the Youngstown Stove Manufacturing Company made stoves, Forsyth made scales, Lloyd-Booth engaged in foundry and machine work, and various other concerns turned out finished lumber, sash and doors, flour, ale and beer. And the population rose again to reach 33,220 in 1890.

Then the great depression of that generation and the wave of protracted labor unrest, known now as the Homestead Strike because of its extreme bitterness, magnitude, warfare, and bloodshed in Carnegie's steel plants there, hit Youngstown and spread its pall of bleakness, misery, and starvation over the Mahoning Valley. Hungry families huddled in their chill houses, idle workmen tramped and milled anxiously about the streets and Public Square, the city, usually a volcanic red glow at night, was dark, and the fires of the furnaces were out. Soup kitchens were set up, and charities organized to keep the working families going.

During these months of misery and hopelessness, not unlike those that came upon the area in the 1930's, a thoughtful, civic-minded man conceived the idea of relieving the idleness and at the same time conferring upon the needy city a benefit of lasting magnitude. He was Volney Rogers, possibly the originator of W.P.A. Like Wade, Gordon, and Rockefeller of Cleveland, he saw the need of this grimy workshop city for a park to provide fresh air and recreation for its people. Lying just across the iron-girt river was the Mill Creek Valley, one of the most beautiful spots in the Western Reserve. It was in danger of being engulfed in the spreading tentacles of steel. They had already reached out for the surrounding towns: Girard, Struthers, Powelville, Hubbard, Wheatland, Sharon, and South Sharon. Mills had been erected in the earlier days along the creek to utilize its water power, and a furnace had once stood on one of the beauty spots where it had dumped its slag in a heap by the creek bed. But these first efforts to industrialize the valley had been abandoned and it was still untarnished in its natural rugged beauty. It lay off to the southwest from the big plants, and the prevailing winds blew the furnace fumes and pall of smoke in the opposite direction. Why not, Rogers asked, acquire for the city this entire expanse of Mill Creek and set the idle men of Youngstown to work to beautify it and make it usable? Would it not be a wiser, and dividend-paying, use of jobless and brooding hands?

He pushed through the necessary legislation and persuaded Youngstown to issue bonds to purchase Mill Creek. Hundreds of men were put to work cutting out overgrown brush, clearing and building roads and paths, fashioning picnic spots and building dams. Each man was given three days of work each week at one dollar a day. Out of this difficult period, therefore, was born the park which has rescued the city from ugliness and has conferred grace and distinction to its planless growth. It became the scene of family outings and group gatherings. The Market Street viaduct was built and the car line extended to the park near Lanterman's Falls, site of one of the early gristmills. The park has been improved through the years, and now comprises miles of woods, cliffs, gorges, and waterfalls, Newport Lake covering 500 acres and dotted with islands, Glacier Lake where fishermen gather, and the smaller Lake Cohasset which the Youngstown children favor for winter skating. Grateful citizens erected a bronze statue of Volney Rogers, who had become in their eyes the father of Mill Creek Park.

Neither the strikes nor the depression could discourage the abounding enterprise of this valley. In 1892 a group of Youngstown men organized the Ohio Steel Company. They were encouraged by the city which by council action detached a parcel of land from the municipality in order that they might erect their plant on low-tax property. Their optimism gave some employment to the idle and brought renewed hope to the city. By the middle of the decade things were moving forward again. William Jennings Bryan, thirty-six-year-old "boy orator of the Platte," Democratic candidate for President, came to Youngstown. He was fresh from his electrifying triumph before the Democratic Convention in Chicago and the famous words from that speech on the hot night of June 8, 1896, were still ringing along the Mahoning:

. . . We are fighting in the defense of our homes, our families, and posterity. We have petitioned, and our petitions have been scorned; we have entreated, and our entreaties have been disregarded; we have begged, and they have mocked when our calamity came. We beg no longer; we entreat no more; we petition no more. We defy them! . . . Having behind us the producing masses of the nation and the world, supported by the commercial interests, the laboring interests, and the toilers everywhere, we shall answer their demand for a gold standard by saying to them: You shall not press down upon the brow of labor this crown of thorns, you shall not crucify mankind upon a cross of gold.

"In a coat like a deacon, in a black Stetson hat," he was wildly cheered by tumultous throngs as he drove down Federal Street to address the workers, "speaking like a siege gun."

But Bryan was running against a Youngstown neighbor, born at near-by Niles in 1843, a local schoolteacher, an officer and hero in the Civil War, twice governor of Ohio, elected and re-elected to the Congress for fourteen years, and a respected lawyer in Canton. Amiable, dignified, conservative and safe, McKinley was backed by Mark Hanna's campaign fund of three million dollars or more against Bryan's five hundred thousand. Youngstown supported McKinley. During the celebrated front-porch campaign, the largest single delegation to call on McKinley went over from Youngstown three thousand strong. He assured them in his kindly way that he and the Republican platform would lead them on to better things. He was elected by over half a million votes and became the twenty-fifth President, the sixth from Ohio and the second from the Western Reserve.[2]

The predicted prosperity—and the Spanish-American War—came, demanding the products which Youngstown could produce. In 1899 the Republic Iron & Steel Company was organized under the laws of New Jersey with the stupendous capital stock of $50,000,000. It established a headquarters at Youngstown. It took over many smaller plants, including Brown, Bonnel, Andrews Bros., and Mahoning Valley Iron. It modernized and expanded, and built new plants at Youngstown, New Castle, and Sharon. It installed a new Bessemer plant in 1900 and went right on to become the third largest steel producer in America, covering the Flats of the Mahoning Valley with thirteen blast furnaces, sixty-eight open hearth, two Bessemer converters, and seven electric furnaces. A few more years and the world would be looking up with awe at the Republic-made Enduro steel cap and spire stabbing the blue sky of New York above the Chrysler Building.

The population in 1900 rose to 44,885, and people from central Europe and Italy began to come in to find work at the mills.

The Youngstown Iron Sheet & Tube Company was organized in 1900 with a million-dollar capital. The word Iron was eliminated in 1905. It selected a 300-acre site down the river near the spot where Howe stood to draw his sketch. Like Republic, it grew steadily with the years, lining the Mahoning with railroad tracks, sheds, and tall black smokestacks. It established plants at Brier Hill, Campbell, Struthers, Girard, and Hubbard. It recognized the need to own and control its sources of supply; it acquired forty mining properties, zinc, ore, coal and limestone, and its own shipping, and formed seven subsidiaries. It became the largest of the steel mills in the area, turning out all sorts of products, but specializing in steel pipe and seamless tubing. Besides giving employment to over 7,500 men, it has always taken a keen civic interest in Youngstown and fostered a zealous local

---

[2] Ex-President Taft came out to Niles in 1917 to dedicate the McKinley Memorial on Main Street, a beautiful Greek-styled Court of Honor dominated by the McKinley statue and flanked by wings containing a library and an auditorium.

pride. It is one of the chief contributors to hospitals, libraries, and to Youngstown College, opened in 1927 and centering around the handsome Tudor Gothic building on Wick Avenue built in 1931. It enjoys considerable prestige among the citizens, in part because of its close identity with the town. When the attempt was made in 1930 to merge it with Bethlehem Steel, an Eastern company, Youngstown people were fiercely antagonistic, as though the old home place were about to fall into the hands of foreigners. Thanks in large measure to the battle waged by Cyrus Eaton of Cleveland, and several of his colleagues in the inner circle of the Union Club, the merger was prevented. Sheet & Tube continued to be the measure of Youngstown prosperity, and the glow of its blast and open-hearth furnaces and the smoke from its stacks along the Mahoning the flaming symbol of America's Ruhr.

Still other steel companies came; notably the Carnegie-Illinois, Fitzsimons Steel, specializing in cold-drawn bars, carbon, and alloy, Hynes Steel Products, Sharon Steel Corporation, and Tice Steel Company. The United Engineering Company, developed out of merger of the William Tod and Lloyd-Booth plants, supplies equipment for the mills around Youngstown from its eleven-acre factory.

Other big industries not directly connected with the making of steel also chose Youngstown for their plants. Republic Rubber came in 1901 to make belts, conveyors, hose, and all sorts of molded rubber goods. The Ohio Leather Company came in the same year and developed a vast business in finished leather goods. The General Fireproofing Company came in 1902 and built a twenty-five acre plant. Combined with Federal Bronze Company and International Metal Lath, it became the largest manufacturer in the country of stock metal office furniture—filing cases and desks.

The population took another big jump as more people came into the valley to man these plants. It reached 79,066 in 1910, and 132,358 in 1920.

A heavy percentage of the newcomers was Italian and Slav. The little valley town could not contain all the people. Homes for the workers climbed up the scarred slopes of the valley in proximity to the mills. They are comfortable but drab and monotonous. They abut on treeless, eroded open spaces and gulleys, and they look down on the towering plants where the smoke lies heavy over the valley and blots out the tall downtown buildings and the opposite rim of hills. And since the mills operate night and day in good times, shifts of workers are always coming and going along the bleak streets, streaming in and out of the mills and across the bridges.

As in Cleveland and Akron, the well-to-do, the industrialists and better-salaried families, moved out to the new suburban developments among the hills—the Logan and Warren Road Estates, Glen Forest, Logan Brook, Crandall Park and the especially handsome Mill Creek Park region. The old Mahoning Golf Club, founded in 1898, north of the city, became the sporting Youngstown Country Club; the Poland Club became the baronial Tippecanoe Country Club, the Mahoning Valley Country Club erected a replica of Monticello on its rolling grounds, and the Jews built their own exclusive Squaw Creek Country Club. The Mill Creek Riding Club, organized in 1928, with its riding academy, indoor ring, polo grounds, and Annual Horse Show is as famous among horse lovers and sportsmen as the older Chagrin Valley Hunt Club at Gates Mills.

All this prosperity was reflected in the financial institutions. The First National and the Commercial National were merged to form the large Union National Bank. The Dollar Savings & Trust Company, founded back in 1887, developed into the second largest in Youngstown. And the Mahoning National Bank, with its auxiliary Mahoning Savings & Trust, became the number-three institution in size.

The once beautiful river, serpentining down through its primeval valley, where John Young had spread his deerskin for a night's sleep back in 1796, was fully abandoned to the mills. They lined it for miles with smokestacks, with railroad tracks and sheds, with clanging rolling mills and blazing Bessemers. They built stone retaining walls along its banks and spanned it with small utility

MAPLE SUGAR TIME IN GEAUGA COUNTY

THE CHAPEL AT WESTERN RESERVE ACADEMY
Typically New England in its architecture, it was built about 1830

bridges. They diverted its water into the plants to cool the flames, and sent it back into the channel steaming hot and dirty yellow. It never freezes. It gives off a thin vapor cloud of steam as it rolls by around the bend in the center of town, bridged by Market Street, in the cold of winter, with snow heaped on its banks.

It all seems as remote from old Connecticut as the mill section of Lowell, Massachusetts. And, like Tallmadge in juxtaposition to Akron, one must leave Youngstown and stand on the green at Poland or at Canfield to be reminded that this home of Little Steel has evolved on land that is technically still a corner of the Western Reserve.

Warren, though in the orbit of Youngstown and Little Steel, is no satellite town. It bulges with industry, it is the second steel center of the Mahoning Valley, but it still remembers that it was the capital of the Western Reserve before Ohio became a state in 1803, that it was the county seat of Trumbull County when the county embraced the entire Reserve, and that it was a populous center of life when Cleveland was still a struggling and sickly village on the sand-choked Cuyahoga. The heavily wooded Public Square on the sharp loop of the Mahoning River in the center of the town is, with the exception of the domed courthouse, very little changed from the four-acre plot given by founder Ephraim Quinby in 1800. In the north section of the town the older families, holding onto the Connecticut heritage, preserve their ancestral homes. Off to the south, huddled about the big Republic Steel mills along the river, are the rows of shabby houses where thousands of workers from all over the world find shelter. In between, gathered about the Square, are the new business houses flung up by industrial prosperity. It is an interesting juxtaposition of the old and the new.

The industrial age was slow in coming to Warren. Though it had always had mills, they had been small family affairs of the type natural to a favorably placed county-seat river town in an agricultural community. They were gristmills, carding mills, wagon and carriage factories, and small furnaces. The county raised quantities of flax which was harvested and carted into Warren. The fibers were processed and shipped out, and the flaxseed was ground into meal and pressed to make linseed oil. The soil could not sustain the heavy demands of flax growing, and the whole industry collapsed later in the century.

The oil boom at Dixie in Mecca Township reverberated briefly in Warren. For Warren was near enough to feel the frenzy and to catch some of the overflow of speculators who rushed to the spot known locally as the "Oil Diggings." It was soon discovered, as we have noted, that the oil was limited to a few shallow and scattered pools, and the bubble burst. But in 1883 the Winfield Manufacturing Company built a plant at Warren to make oil cans for the new industry, and to turn out lanterns and fabricate metal.

Then the Packard brothers, J. Ward and William D., descendants of an old Warren family, established in 1889 the Packard Electric Company. In Civil War days their father had been interested in a small forge, and had invested in rolling mills and puddling furnaces. J. Ward had gone to Lehigh University for an engineering education. He was excited over the inventions of Thomas A. Edison. He began working with incandescent lamps, and within a few years he had patented one of his own, a lamp socket, and improved vacuum pumps for making lamp bulbs. His Warren company made cables and fuse boxes, transformers, and other such products. This successful family plant was the forerunner of one of Warren's most important industries.

After dismantling and studying the Winton automobile which he bought in 1898, J. Ward Packard built his own model and drove it down the Warren streets. He kept on tinkering with it and making improvements. He determined to go into the automobile manufacturing business. Warren apparently did not have the capital to support such a venture; Cleveland financiers preferred more substantial business enterprises than the horseless carriages, and in 1903 Packard went to Detroit.

These industries sustained without seriously modifying the life of Warren. In 1900 the population was still only 8,529, and just reached 11,000 in 1910. It still had something of a dignified New

England air with its clean tree-shaded streets, its nice homes, and its leisurely business Square. The young business group thought it was backward and stupid, that it should respond to the times and take its place in the valley of steel along with Youngstown. They overrode the conservative opposition which wanted to preserve the family town. They organized a Board of Trade in 1905 to boost the city and coax industry to come in. They built up a high-pressure campaign. They offered alluring inducements. They bought up land on the Mahoning Flats and then offered free sites to companies which would locate their plants in Warren. Actually they made money on the deal as it turned out, because they sold the surplus, after industry came, at a good profit. The first to accept their generous offer was the Trumbull Steel Company. In 1912 they agreed to erect six mills on the donated land. Despite the flood that devastated the Mahoning Valley in the spring of 1913, steel began to flow from the mill on July 31. Rejoicing over this progress, the *Warren Tribune* reported, "There was no hitch in the operation and Warren's largest industry is well on its way to what is predicted a huge success."

During the next seven years, thirty-three industries came to Warren to make electric goods, tools, fans, tanks, cables, welding machinery, steel barrels. Fifteen new business buildings were erected about the Square. The population jumped 130 percent to 27,050. Three thousand new houses were built to shelter them. An addition to the city rose suddenly on the Flats and around the mills. Slovenes, Croats, Serbians, Italians, and other nationalities who had come to Warren to find work, peopled it, and the sound of their tongues was strange on the village green.

Conneaut and Ashtabula were, we remember, the first locations made in the Reserve by Moses Cleaveland. For more than half a century they remained New England in character and primarily rural in their interests. As Melish and other early travelers pointed out, the system of land distribution and sales favored the developments to the south, leaving the lake shore for many years sparsely populated. In 1840 Conneaut had a population of 2,650 and Ashtabula only 1,711. Forty years later Conneaut had reached only 2,947 and Ashtabula 5,522. Conneaut depended on its shipping. Ashtabula, in addition to its shipping, had a number of small industries which made tools and machinery for farms, carriages and wagons, and rubber clothing, and processed hides and leather. Their development up to this point had been slow and orderly and not materially different from that of the other country towns in the Reserve.

Their transformation was brought about by the coming of ore and coal. They were the natural gateway ports for the Mahoning Valley and Pittsburgh steel. Their harbors were among the best on the lake. The mouth of Conneaut Creek and the Ashtabula River needed only to be cleared of sand and deepened to accommodate the largest lake vessels. With the aid of Federal funds the channels were dredged, lighthouses and markers erected, and thousands of feet of docks on both sides of the rivers were built to receive the ships. Railroads linked them to their east-west lines and joined them to the iron and steel mills to the south. Their destiny was inseparably bound up with Warren and Youngstown, and Pittsburgh, and they have to be thought of as having a common interest with them.

It is possible for the casual traveler to drive through Conneaut and Ashtabula on U.S. 20 without seeing any outward signs of this connection. Nothing could seem more remote from Youngstown's mills than these small towns on the gentle beach slope a few miles south of Lake Erie. They might be almost any urban community in the interior, supported by a few small industries, and serving the business and shopping needs of a dairy, vegetable garden, and fruit orchard area. They lack the distinctive Reserve charm of Painesville, Hudson, or Norwalk, but the public squares and a few of the older houses do at least suggest their origin. One would not, however, make a pilgrimage to them for this reason.

A slight detour down to the lake over Route 531 takes you into the midst of the tremendous transshipping activity and reveals the secret of their importance. Here are the miles of railroad tracks paralleling the harbor streams and abutting on the lake. The cars are arranged in long rows on the spurs. Most of them come up from the south filled with coal which they exchange at

the port for a load of ore. The big ore freighters ease into the
harbor and tie up at their appointed berths alongside the batteries
of Hulett unloaders. From a distance these machines look like
giant grasshoppers attacking a blade of corn. As soon as the ship
is tied up, a half dozen of the nimble monsters insert their heads
into the hatches, bite off seventeen tons of ore each, and spit them
out again into waiting railroad cars or into lorries to be hauled
to the stock piles. Once a minute they repeat the process. And
within four or five hours they have unloaded a 15,000-ton cargo
of Lake Superior iron ore. The busy engines pull the cars away,
arrange them into trains, and shove more empties alongside the
ship under the unloaders. The ore-laden cars are dragged out of
the yards, up the slope from the lake, past Conneaut or Ashtabula,
and hurried across the Reserve over the Bessemer & Lake Erie
Railroad to Warren, Youngstown, and Pittsburgh. Day and
night throughout the eight-month lake shipping season this drama
goes on; and it is repeated in part through the rest of the year
from the mountainous stock piles that accumulate around the
harbor.

The miles of track and docks, the hundreds of railroad cars,
the ridges of red ore, the towering unloaders, and the mills scattered all over the lake front in apparently aimless fashion dom-
inate the scene. They seem to have a kind of subhuman life of
their own, independent of men, so completely do they overshadow
the stature of the workers who move inconspicuously among the
machines or ride up and down on the arms of the Hulett unloader.
But there are hundreds of men at work here, and their families
live in the little houses cluttered around the harbor, stringing
up toward Conneaut and Ashtabula, or in these towns which are
connected with the water front by streetcars and busses. They
are, most of them, foreign-born or second-generation sons, pre-
dominately Finns and Scandinavians, though many Italians have
also settled in the district. They came in the early days of the iron
age when sailing ships massed in the harbors with small cargoes
which had to be unloaded with picks, shovels, and wheelbarrows
operated by human hands and backs. Their toil and sweat heaved
the ore across the gap between the lake ships and the railway

cars. And as the inventions of Brown and Hulett were developed
to ease the burden and speed the process, they, and their sons,
stayed on to man the machines.

Their Old World customs and closely knit social patterns were
transplanted into this part of the Reserve and perpetuated. The
Finns, the largest single ethnic group, continue their native steam
baths and other traditions. To this day the Ashtabula newspaper
carries announcement of the church services to be conducted in
native languages. But the melting pot here, as everywhere else,
is boiling away and the young school generation takes on its own
intense form of Americanization. You may see it in their faces
and hear it in their voices as they leave the schoolhouses or throng
the old Reserve streets of these towns on Saturday afternoons.

Though the harbors are overwhelmingly occupied with this
endless transfer of coal and iron from cars to ships and from ships
to cars, there are a few bits of the early days still to be seen amidst
the general clutter. The taverns where the sailors while away
a few hours on shore are a modernized version of the taprooms of
the stagecoach and sailing ship era. The fishermen still have their
docks, and still take their small boats out to the fishing banks as
they did in the days of the Reverend Mr. Badger and Doctor
Hawley. And on the outskirts of the towns, particularly of Ashtabula, are vast acreages of greenhouses for the growing of vegetables for the Cleveland market, fruit farms and nurseries, and
the Griswold mushroom beds to remind us of the original husbandry of the settlers from Connecticut—now carried on largely
by immigrants from Italy.

The effect of the industrial age on Conneaut and Ashtabula
is less pronounced than at Youngstown and Warren, but one has
only to journey ten miles south of Ashtabula to the untransformed
old county-seat town of Jefferson to see and feel the marked contrast between the old and the new in this portion of the Reserve.

The story of Ashtabula and Conneaut is repeated again at Fairport where the industrialized town of about 5,000 looks out on the
great arms of the breakwaters forming the entrance to the harbor.

It is somewhat different at the other important industrial port town of Lorain on the Black River. This settlement, unimaginatively called Mouth of Black River, and later christened Charleston, was splendidly located on one of the natural harbors on the lake. The river passes through picturesque gorges back on the higher land at Elyria, now the beautiful Cascade Park, and then winds for ten miles through prosperous dairy and fruit country. As it nears the lake it makes a sharp circle to avoid entering the lake too quickly, suddenly widens and deepens, and runs westward parallel to the lake shore for some distance before it actually empties into Lake Erie. In effect it built a natural harbor with the neck of land between it and Lake Erie acting as a breakwater.

The settlement's first enthusiastic hopes for greatness were crushed when it was by-passed as a lake terminal for the canal, and again when the railroads chose a route eight miles south through Elyria. Thus isolated from the interior, it declined while Cleveland, Sandusky, and Elyria prospered. At the mid-century, when Elyria was a growing county-seat town of 1,500 people, Lorain, still known as Charleston, was a ruined and deserted village. But it was too valuable a location to be permanently neglected. In 1872 the Lorain and Wheeling Railroad joined the port to the centers of industry, and the village began a revival which has continued to the present day. With its charter for new life in 1876 it took the name of Lorain.

It is, therefore, not so much an old Reserve town in transition, like Elyria, as a direct creation of the modern industrial age. Even the Black River now looks more like an industrial canal than one of nature's streams. It cuts a transportation route 250 feet wide through the town. It can give passage for four miles to the large freighters from the lake. It is bordered on both sides by various industries and small fishhouses, but it is dominated by the giant shipbuilding yards and the smoking, flaming steel mills. For these are the enterprises which brought most of the 45,000 people to Lorain and supported them there.

The first stable industry was the United Brass Company which gave employment to over 300 men in the 1880's. The Lorain foundry, the usual lumberyards and planing mills, the grain market and the railroad shops furnished work for another 100 families. Within a decade after its reincarnation Lorain had become a busy town of 1,500 people. Then the amazing growth of the steel industry in the 1890's swept in. Tom L. Johnson, street-railway magnate, whose career in Cleveland we shall see later, was surveying locations for his steel interests. He chose this new industrial town and built his plant on the Black River south of the city in 1894. His enterprise prospered. He paid high wages ($1.50 a day), and laborers, hit by the panic of 1893, which had deprived them of their one-dollar-a-day jobs, flocked to Lorain to find work. The new giant of industry, the United States Steel Corporation, bought Johnson's interests when he determined to sell out in order to enter politics and civic administration. U.S. Steel expanded the mills until they lined a long section of the river to the east and south of the town. It erected the vast National Tube Company Plant to make pipe, tubes, and a dozen other by-products. The American Ship Building Co. established its yards on the east bank of the river just south of Erie Avenue to make ships for the expanding lake trade. It developed into one of the largest shipbuilding and repair yards on the Great Lakes.

The demand for labor to man the plants was insistent. It outran the short supply of native workers. Like the cry of rubber at Akron, the cry of jobs in the Lorain mills spread to Europe. As at Cleveland, Akron, Youngstown, and Warren, and under the same urge, men came from all parts of the earth to the shore of Lake Erie at the mouth of the Black River. They came in major numbers from Italy, Hungary, Poland, and the Slavic states of Central Europe. Twenty-five thousand arrived at Lorain during the expansive period leading up to World War I, and another 20,000 had come by the end of World War II. While neighboring Elyria continued its slow and solid growth around an unchanging New England Public Square, Lorain spread west of its river and south of its lake into a burly, polyglot, and vigorous mill town where many races of men, speaking many tongues, slowly and painfully worked their way from segregation in small nationality groups toward a civic community.

They have not created a beautiful city. The big mills with their inevitable smoke by day and eerie glow by night, their service yards, stock piles and aesthetically depressing surroundings, are too close and too dominant to accent graciousness and charm in the city which exists because of them. Most of the streets are monotonous and drab, and the business section is confused and undistinguished. But it is better than it was before the tornado of 1924 snapped at the town and wreaked a $25,000,000 damage upon it. The splendid Lake View Park on the west side is a sample and a symbol of the growing maturity of Lorain toward a life which is not entirely pre-empted by the labor in the mills.

The maturity of its spirit was indicated by its accomplishments in World War II. Night and day its men produced steel for the war and sent forth the pipe for Big Inch to bring oil to the East from the Western fields. They built quantities of ships from landing craft to frigates and lake freighters. And when they celebrated Ship Builders Day to turn over their frigate *Lorain* to the U.S. Navy, the nationality groups marched together in parade, as they had worked together in the yards, preserving semblances of their native heritages, but incorporating them into the civic unit of Lorain, Ohio, home town of Admiral King.

Sandusky had struggled valiantly to hold its place as one of the leading port cities on Lake Erie. Its best assets were its protected eighteen-mile-long bay, its limestone, its salubrious climate, its hinterland of good soil adapted to grain, fruit and vineyards, and the near-by fishing banks. Its natural setting was much more alluring than the site of Toledo on the Maumee River. Every visitor to Sandusky praised its favored position on the bay, and marveled at the beauty of the bay itself. Many enterprising men, like Jay Cooke's father, after surveying the possibilities of the Reserve and forecasting the future, chose Sandusky. We have seen how they fought to get the Lake Erie terminus of one of the canals, and lost to Cleveland and Toledo; how they built railroads in advance of their great rival to the east; and how hard they tried to make it a leading port town for the Reserve. It still had only 594 people in 1830—the same size as Cleveland in 1820.

It became the seat of Erie County in 1838 with a population of 1,500. In 1850 it reached 5,000, against Cleveland's 17,000, though the terrible cholera epidemic of the summer of 1849 had devastated Sandusky. The epidemic left 400 dead. Half the population fled from the plague-stricken city and many did not return. New people came. In 1870 Sandusky had expanded to 13,000 against its rival's 93,000. Sandusky could not compete in the economy of oil and iron.

The city recognized that its opportunity was of a different nature. It adapted itself to circumstance and made the most of it. In a pamphlet of 1888, entitled *Sandusky of Today*, this verse was printed:

> Let other cities boast their iron,
>   Their steel and earthenware—
> Rubber goods—tile, pottery, shoes,
>   Or glass in ample share.
> But fam'd Sandusky leads the van
>   For all that man can wish,
> To lumber, grain—in lime, in stone—
>   And beats the world for fish.

This is wretched poetry, but an exact summary of Sandusky's choice of occupation. And in that choice lay its unique distinction among the Reserve towns.

The Germans had contributed heavily to the population after 1850. They liked Sandusky's marine setting, its parks, and its shaded streets radiating out from Washington Park—the generous Public Square. They were pleased to find soil and climate perfectly balanced for wine grapes, and a lake abounding in fish. They went heavily into both occupations. Over the doorways of the business houses appeared good German names: Simeon Schacht, fish; Fruechtnicht & Nielsen, dealers in fish; Engels & Krudwig, wines; Koegle & Doerflinger, baskets; A. Schwehr, fish and cigar boxes; Jacob & August Kuebeler, brewers; Biemiller's Opera House. German families strolled in the park and along the water front. They organized Sunday picnics to the islands, crossing the bay and the lake on one of the several steamers, built in Sandusky yards, engaged in the island trade. To the horror of conservative citizens of New England background, they took along with them their beer and their bands. They gave to Sandusky an Old World flavor that set it off in sharp contrast from the New Connecticut town of Norwalk a few miles south in the heart of the Firelands.

The pattern over which Sandusky was to develop was clearly shaped immediately following the Civil War. The war itself had come near to Sandusky. Johnson's Island, a 275-acre farm and forest lying in the bay, three miles offshore from the city, had been a prison camp for captured Confederate officers. Ten thousand men were imprisoned there during the war, as many as 3,000 at a time. Rumors of plots to free them ran through Sandusky from time to time. An attempt was actually made in 1864. When the plot was hatched, the city and the surrounding region were thrown into a panic because there were enough prisoners on the island to ravage northern Ohio. But the plot failed, the war ended, and the prisoners departed without damage to Sandusky.

Sandusky had profited by selling supplies to the camp, and by the increased demands throughout the country for its fish, wine, and limestone. These products could support a stable and prosperous economy, but they could never be the foundation for big business like iron and steel, oil and coal. Sandusky agreeably resigned itself to the exploitation of these limited but important resources, and to the smaller population which this resignation implied.

The city went into the fish business and became the leading fresh-water market center for lake fish. Herring, whitefish, bass and pickerel were plentiful around the islands off Sandusky. Herring was first in quantity during the 1880's and white fish second. Bass and pickerel were about even at third place, though the catch was beginning to decline. Each morning during the season the fishing fleets put out from the harbor for the fishing grounds. In the days before the Civil War they were equipped with gill and seine nets—a type still in use on the lake. But around 1856 Captain A. Dibble or J. Spencer of Connecticut first introduced the pound net to these waters. They are efficient traps which lure fish through a tunnel into a big impounding net anchored on the floor of the lake. Captain J. B. Keyes, one of the successful local fishermen, followed the example, and before long the new pound nets were standard equipment on the fishing fleet. By 1880 between seven and eight hundred were in use.

They brought in enormous hauls. In a good season the catch would run from 500 to 1,200 tons in a single day. About 1,500 men were employed, and by the close of the 1880's Sandusky had $1,000,000 invested in the industry.

The bay harbor was jammed with fishing boats and the water front was lined with fishhouses. H. C. Post, who became State Fish Commissioner, 1881-1884, operated one of the larger houses. He had left the business on the Connecticut River to come to Sandusky in 1856. He dealt heavily in herring. He sold a third of the catch fresh in the markets which could be quickly reached by the four railroads serving Sandusky. He packed his product in Lake Erie ice, sprinkled it with salt from Syracuse, New York, and loaded it on the trains. A third of the herring was smoked, and the other third was frozen.

A. J. Stoll, J. A. Hosmer & Co., Caspar Voigt, Arend Bros., Simeon Schacht and others all had prosperous fishhouses which sent out the immensely popular whitefish to supply the mounting demand. Fruechtnicht & Nielsen specialized in sturgeon products. In the early days these big fish, from three to six feet long and weighing up to seventy pounds, were considered a worthless nuisance. When the fishermen found them trapped in the nets, they cursed them, as they now do sheepshead, killed them, and tossed them back into the lake. The demand for isinglass, made from sturgeon bladders, led the fishermen to save them for this purpose. Then they discovered that the heads, skins, and other waste parts could be sold to the glue and fish-oil market. Fruechtnicht & Nielsen found a lucrative market for the eggs also. They shipped them in bulk to Europe where they were packed into small cans and jars, labeled, and shipped back to the Eastern cities to be sold as Russian caviar. Served on bread with chopped onion and lemon juice, it appeared on saloon lunch counters and in restaurants; it

proved to be a popular dish. Before long it was sold directly from
Sandusky without going to Europe and back. Sturgeon jumped
in price from 10 cents apiece to $1.00 in 1888.

Fishing is carried on extensively all along the lake, but Sandusky has continued through the years, in its own words, to "beat
the world for fish." The equipment has been modernized. The
launches are driven out to the fishing grounds by gasoline motors
and the nets are raised by the same power. Electric machines
scratch off the scales, and modern quick-freeze units preserve the
fish for later marketing. But the weather-beaten men who scan
the skies over Lake Erie for signs of sudden storms, who take the
boats out, who lift the nets, who gut and sort the catch, are the
descendants of the earlier fishermen and they bear the unchanged
stamp of their trade on their browned faces and their stooped
shoulders. And the big and thriving houses of the Lay Brothers,
the Post Fish Company, and the Bickley Fish Company keep
Sandusky in the forefront of this romanticized industry.

The breweries were likewise flourishing. They had come into
prominence in the 1840's. In the 1880's they were big local business. J. & A. Kuebeler's, founded in 1867, covered thirteen acres
with breweries, icehouses, and malt sheds. They had branches in
Elyria, Bellevue, and Monroeville. Frank Stang's "Old Dauch"
Brewery produced a famous beer which was popular in all the
flourishing taprooms along the Reserve roads. The big Cleveland
& Sandusky Brewing Company in the early days of this century
were shipping out 150,000 barrels of malt beers each year. The
clomp-clomp of the hoofs of the brewers' heavy horses, drawing
long rattling drays, piled high with thick barrels, over the Sandusky streets was as much a part of the city's peculiar color as
the sound of fishermen's voices on the bay at the foot of Wayne
Street and the odor of the fishhouses along the water front.

Icehouses also had a brief period of great prosperity at Sandusky.
The waters of the bay were clean and pure, and they froze into
thick ice from December until spring. In the days before artificial
ice there was a brisk and extensive demand for ice cakes sawed
from the Sandusky Bay. John McKelvey organized a company to

exploit this business. He engaged a large force of men to saw the ice into blocks. Elevators carried the blocks up to the big 50,000-ton storage bins, specially built and insulated to preserve the ice when the hot weather came. It was then sold to the fishhouses and breweries, to the citizens of the town, and was shipped in boxcar loads to Cleveland, Cincinnati, and other cities.

Another distinctive industry centered at Sandusky with the discovery that this region was especially well favored for the growing of wine grapes. The lake tempers the climate and prolongs the growing season for two or three precious weeks after the frosts have hit the regions farther inland. Sturdy, disease-resisting vines in the dry loam soil produced grapes of distinguished flavor. Grape culture was begun experimentally at the middle of the century around Sandusky and on the islands. Success was immediate. Catawba grapes were exceptionally well adapted to the district. Year after year more acres were cleared and vines planted. The yield soared. The incoming Germans found viticulture a congenial occupation here on the frontier of the Reserve in the heart of a new continent. They established wineries which gained for themselves international repute for the quality of their product. Link's winery, the Sandusky Wine Company, Edward R. Moos, and John G. Dorn were among the earlier wine makers. The John G. Dorn Company, founded in 1869, is still one of the big and famous cellars, and is still operated by the founder's family. In its deep, cool cellars underneath the three-story stone and brick building on East Water Street are rooms full of good-smelling barrels, stacks of bottles, and some of the old wine casks used at Cincinnati by Nicholas Longworth in the early years of the last century when he turned the hills around Cincinnati into vineyards.

Engels & Krudwig, both native-born Germans, established their presses and cellars in 1878 as the industry continued to expand. Their winery, standing near Dorn's, continues to make some of the finest American wines. They gather in grapes from the vineyards on the mainland, and they have their own extensive plantings on South Bass Island. M. Hommel, a native of France, began his

cellars out on Clinton Street in that same year—1878. He specialized in champagne and sparkling Burgundies. His wines have
taken first prizes in European exhibitions with the best foreign
growers. The damp, high-ceiling cellars—a series of intercom-
municating rooms deep in the limestone below the rambling stone
building housing the presses, vats, and bottling works—are a bit
of old Provence set down on the shore of Lake Erie. They are
filled with wine-soaked casks, and with vast stacks of cobwebbed
bottles aging the good vintages. Though the ownership has
recently passed into other hands, Hommel's continues the tradition of its famous founder.

Meier, with large vineyards on North Bass Island, Heineman
at Put-in-Bay, and Lonz on Middle Bass add their vintages to
those on the mainland to enrich the singular economy of the Sandusky region. If the versifier whom we quoted had penned his lines
a decade or two later, he would certainly have added a few words
about the city's pre-eminence in wine as one of the products "for all
that man can wish."

The breweries, wine cellars, and fishhouses stimulated other
industries. Cooperages sprang up to make casks and barrels—
hoops, staves, and barrelheads. A. Schwehr made fish boxes.
Koegle & Doerflinger made from 35,000 to 45,000 dozen baskets
a year to supply the grape pickers in the vineyards. Machine
shops were founded to make wine and cider presses and pumps.
The Jarecki Chemical Works were founded to supply fertilizers
and sulphuric acid. Again these were relatively small plants compared with the growing giants of oil and steel in the eastern part
of the Reserve, but they were substantial and distinctive in the
economy of Sandusky.

Less picturesque but equally solid as a foundation for Sandusky's steady, unspectacular growth were the lime and stone of
the region mentioned by our versifier. The vast beds of marl in
the vicinity produced high-grade cement. Big plants rose west
of the city to make cement, their thin gray dust settling like an
early morning fog over the bay. Kilns at Sandusky burned lime.
The Ohlemacher Co., J. B. Johnston & Co., Johnson, Kunz &

Company were engaged in this business. The blue limestone was particularly desirable as building stone. It was uniform in color and it was resistant to moisture and to frost. It was in great demand for business houses and public buildings. Across the bay at Marblehead and over on Kelleys Island were the rich limestone quarries. The quarries, forty feet deep, sent forth year after year mounting quantities of stone for building piers and breakwaters at the port cities, and flux for the hungry furnaces of Pittsburgh, Cleveland, and the Mahoning Valley. The Kelley Island Lime & Transport Company bought up the quarries in 1891. They extended their holdings until they covered over a thousand acres. By 1907 they had $8,000,000 invested and advertised their company as the "largest of its kind in the world." They imported foreign workers from all parts of Europe—Italians, Slavs, Greeks, Hungarians, Portuguese, Poles, Macedonians, Bulgarians, and Germans. A large group of them lived in the isolation of Kelleys Island, others in the vicinity of Marblehead. In the 1930's the workings on the island were closed down, and the industry was concentrated at Marblehead.

The American Crayon Company was one of the early industries of Sandusky, dating from 1835. The company supplied the schools with white and colored chalk. It made wax and oil crayons and water-color paints. The Hinde & Dauch Paper Company also developed into one of Sandusky's largest industries. It gave employment to 300 people in the 1900's making corrugated paper specialties of all kinds. The Woolsey Wheel Company and the Sandusky Wheel Company turned out more carriage and wagon wheels than the factories of any other town in the Reserve and gave employment to over 400 men in the 1880's. Lumber companies and planing mills flourished. Add to these a few tool companies, elevators, railroad repair shops, engine works, spoke lathes, "Hero" binders and reapers, the State Fish Hatchery, and we have a fair picture of the small, diversified activities which supported Sandusky and added each decade two or three thousand people to its population. It reached 15,838 in 1880 and about 30,000 in 1945.

The town, therefore, went through no such revolutionary growth as swept over Cleveland, Akron, Youngstown, Warren, and Lorain to change their appearance. The main business district, including the Sloan Block and the Sloan Hotel, overlooking the Square, the courthouse, and school opposite it still stand almost exactly as they were in the 1870's. For that was Sandusky's one period of major expansion. It built a waterworks in 1876, taking water from the bay and distributing it through a standpipe system. For many decades the huge water tower was a landmark on the sky line. The new houses went up along the shaded streets radiating out from the Square. Small parks at triangular intersections graced the design. Cheap cab service furnished transportation until the streetcars began to clang from the Square to the suburbs. The advertisements in the papers announced prominently and somewhat mysteriously in 1883 that "Herdic No. 5 is used to call Herdic. In this coach persons will be called for and delivered to any part of the city for ten cents." The *Sandusky Register* founded back in 1822, brought the news, as it still does, to the citizens. It was owned and operated for years by the Honorable John T. Mack, trustee of the Ohio State University, and his brother, who made it an important Republican organ in the western section of the Reserve.

Sandusky also became, and still is, a resort town in the sense that applies to no other city in the Reserve. It reached this prominence immediately after the Civil War. Special excursion trains ran up from Cincinnati and the South bearing thousands of holiday pleasure seekers. Pictures of Sandusky in the 1880's and 1890's show Railroad Street filled with passenger trains, the water front and docks swarming with gaily dressed men and women, and the harbor alive with craft of all kinds. Many of the visitors merely stood on the bay shore to watch the coming and going of the ships—614 vessels entered the harbor in a single year, 1887, from foreign ports, 594 cleared for foreign destinations; 3,315 came in and 3,321 went out to domestic ports. For inland people it was a sight worth coming to see: the vast bay rimmed with a fringe of gleaming beach and green forest, and these vessels passing in and out of the narrow channel formed by Marblehead and Cedar Point, with glimpses of the lake off to the north.

The physical setting still preserves the same attraction, but the activity on the bay has changed. The tonnage in the ship channel is still great enough to make Sandusky number eighteen among the nation's shipping ports, but it is borne in the big lake freighters, not in the thousands of small sailing craft of seventy years ago. Most of it goes to the Pennsylvania Railroad Coal Docks at the foot of King Street. They stick out into the bay for more than a half mile. And the visitor who now looks out over the harbor sees a high-riding freighter put in at the docks, sees the giant mechanical loader pick up a car of coal and dump it into the ship's hold in one quick operation, and, if he stays for a few hours, sees the laden ship put out again through the dredged channel for the open lake and the cities of the upper lake region.

In addition to Sandusky itself, with its own attractions, its water front, its fishhouses, its parks and restaurants, there was the lure of Cedar Point and the beautiful islands offshore in Lake Erie. Cedar Point became a great summer resort in 1882. An enormous hotel was erected near the protected beach to accommodate the excursion crowds and to handle the big conventions which were held there during the summer months. For the past seven decades the ferries have been kept busy during the season carrying visitors back and forth across the bay from Sandusky to the Point.

The islands, less closely geared to the city than Cedar Point, have always had a close relationship to Sandusky. They were a unique, almost forgotten part of the Western Reserve. Geographically they lie within the area reserved by Connecticut. But they were not very accessible. Many people were drowned or driven back when they attempted to cross over from the mainland to explore them. They were heavily timbered, and were said to be swarming with rattlesnakes. With so much good land readily available in the Reserve, why bother about the islands? Kelleys Island, the largest of the group, containing 2,888 acres, remained uninhabited until 1833 when Irad and Datus Kelley acquired it and began to cut off its thick stand of red cedar. Much of it was stoked into the boilers of the lake steamers. After 1850 it became a vineyard and fruit orchard and then a quarry. A few fishing villages grew up at the better harbors, and summer visitors discovered the charm of the island as a vacation center.

The Bass Islands fell to the lot of Judge Edwards of Connecticut, one of the larger stockholders in the Land Company. At the various drawings he was allotted tracts in different parts of the Reserve. One of his allotments was on the contoured shore of Lake Erie in Lorain County, and he was given the Bass Islands as a kind of bonus to make up for the acreage covered by the lake waters. He himself never visited his holdings. He deeded them to his sons John and Ogden and they took them over in 1811. They put managers and caretakers on them, cleared the land, raised wheat, sheep and hogs, and made them profitable. The islands developed very slowly, however, with a few hardy settlers, many of them German, moving in to cut timber, farm, fish, and later to grow grapes. From 1860 on the islands were primarily vineyards. Thousands of people came over during the picking seasons to help harvest the grapes. A festive air settled over them. Visitors who came to the islands, particularly to South Bass, to see the vineyards and the lovely Put-in-Bay where Perry had harbored his ships, were entranced by the prospect for both summer and year-round homes. Jay Cooke, who was born at Sandusky, acquired Gibraltar Island in 1864. He built a fifteen-room Victorian castle on the ridge overlooking the harbor and the lake, and made it a quiet summer vacation spot to which distinguished people from all over the country came to visit. José DeRivera St. Jurgo, who bought the islands in 1854, gave the five acres on the harbor for Perry Park in 1868. He induced many enterprising people to come to the islands. Joseph W. Gray, owner and publisher of the *Cleveland Plain Dealer,* bought the big Manor House and spent much of his time on South Bass. J. B. Monroe, a railroad magnate from Toledo, built a fine home at East Point.

Overnight steamers from the big cities came in for the day,

turned their passengers loose on the islands, and picked them up again for the return voyage. Hotels, restaurants, saloons went up around the harbor to cater to the trade. The tourists came in such droves that J. K. Tillotson built the Hotel Victory at Stone's Cove to accommodate 2,000 people per day. A streetcar line ran down to it from Put-in-Bay. A procession of boats from Sandusky carried over conventions, vacationists, and sight-seers. The annual Interlake Regatta brought, as it still brings, thousands of visitors to witness the sailboat racing during the first week of August. This activity reached its height near the turn of the century and then receded. The Hotel Victory burned in 1919 and was not rebuilt. The region is now remote and lonely. But the crowds still come to the islands from Decoration Day to Labor Day to climb the great Perry monument, tour the islands, loll in the park, and patronize the resort spots around the harbor, and the boats still ply back and forth across the lake from Sandusky which is still the chief embarkation port for the islands. Their connection with the Reserve is as tenuous as an afterthought.

CHAPTER TWENTY-TWO

METROPOLITAN CLEVELAND

THE dynamic forces which we have seen operating with pronounced intensity in the urban centers brought about a striking alteration in the whole appearance and nature of life in the Western Reserve. The center of population, formerly converging along the Ohio River, now shifted to the Lake Erie shore. It became polyglot and cosmopolitan. Its density and character, the tremendous economic, industrial, and financial power concentrated in these cities, particularly at Cleveland, gave a new direction to the development of the region. Even the smaller towns that did not entirely lose their old Western Reserve family traits—towns like Ravenna, Kent, Medina, and Elyria—were still modified to a noticeable degree by these forces. Henceforth the direction of growth would be toward the more standardized American pattern and away from the colonial Connecticut style of the original towns and villages.

We have already said that if a man were suddenly dropped down on the northeast corner of the Square at Hudson, he would think he was in an old Connecticut town. But if he were set down in Akron, Youngstown, or, perhaps, Elyria, he would think he might be in the corresponding city in almost any portion of the Republic. This new direction has now been clearly foreshadowed. It remains to follow with some selected detail its rapid unfolding in recent years to see more completely how the Reserve has acquired its present characteristics. They show up plainly in the dramatic onward sweep of Cleveland as the capital city of the Reserve. And we begin with Mayor Johnson, the figure who now symbolizes the first phase of this new direction because of the influence he had on it.

Tom Loftin Johnson arrived in Cleveland in 1880 at the age of twenty-six. He was attracted by the opportunity which this rapidly expanding city seemed to offer for electric streetcars. With industry tending to concentrate along the Cuyahoga and in the Flats while the population scattered over the West Side and moved on east of the Square, streetcar service had become a rich investment and a subject for heated controversy. Thousands of people had to be transported back and forth across the city every day. They were keenly interested in the quality of the service and the fare they had to pay.

Mark Hanna was the most powerful man behind the already established lines, the most important of which served the West Side. They were not interconnecting. If a passenger needed to continue his trip from one section to another, he had to pay another fare. Transfers were not issued. This system, coupled with high fares and the willing co-operation of the city council, made the streetcar business in Cleveland enormously profitable to the owners. An old and well-established Clevelander like Mark Hanna quite naturally resented fiercely the intrusion into this arrangement of an outsider like Tom Johnson.

Hanna's concern was well founded. Johnson proposed to block off for himself a large share of the business. And this bumptious radical, as Hanna regarded him, proposed further to upset a solid order by advocating lower fares and free transfers. From 1880 until Hanna's death in 1904 the two men were poles apart on every issue and waged unceasing warfare on each other.

Johnson was a vigorous and tireless fighter. He had come up the hard way. Born at Blue Spring, Kentucky, in 1854, he had seen his father lose his property during the Civil War, he had sold newspapers at Staunton, Virginia, when he was eleven, he had had a few years of schooling at Evansville, Indiana, and at the age of fifteen he was working in a rolling mill at Louisville. The next year he got a job with a small street railway in Louisville, and while still only sixteen, became secretary of the company. He invented a new fare box which soon yielded him $30,000. With this capital he bought into street railways in Indianapolis and made $500,000. Having attained this Alger-like position, he looked about for other fields to conquer. He invested in street railways in Detroit and Brooklyn and in steel at Lorain, but the opportunities in Cleveland challenged him most and he moved in personally on this city. He battled hard for a foothold and persevered in his assault on Hanna's interests. He managed to unite some of the small companies on the East Side to form the Cleveland Electric Railway Company. He improved the service and counted on increased traffic to offset reduction in fare and free transfers. The responsive public named his system the "Big Consolidated." Hanna in response formed the Cleveland City Railway Company on the West Side, which the public called the "Little Consolidated." In the long ensuing struggle, Hanna had to yield by popular demand to Johnson's fare-transfer scheme. Johnson sold his interest in Big Consolidated, Hanna united Little Consolidated with it, and the system operated, still warring over rates and franchises, as the "Concon."

Johnson did not sell out his interests in order to retire. Instead he went into politics to continue his war on Hanna, on all forms of what he considered special privilege, and for the betterment of Cleveland as a whole. He was led to this decision by a conversion as dramatic for him as the transfiguration of Saul on the road to Damascus. He boarded a train in Cleveland in 1885 to make a trip to Indianapolis. The newsboy offered him a copy of Henry George's *Social Problems,* to the indignation of Johnson. The conductor overheard his scornful rebuff to the newsboy, and quietly recommended the book. Johnson, who had read little, bought it, was captivated by it, and became from that moment a reformer and disciple of Henry George.[1] He read also *Progress and Poverty,* an earlier book by the same author. He made the acquaintance of George, attended meetings on tax reform, and learned to make speeches to the populace. George urged him to enter politics.

---

[1] He was buried near George in a Brooklyn cemetery.

Johnson, a Democrat, ran for Congress in 1888 from the Cleveland district, a Republican stronghold. Theodore E. Burton defeated him. Two years later, in his persistent way, he tried again against the same opponent and won. He won again in 1892. He was so much under the spell of George's ideas that he circulated a million copies of his *Protection or Free Trade* at public expense by having it printed in the *Congressional Record*. Burton defeated him again in 1894.

Tom Johnson began to cast his eye on the mayor's office. In this demanding transition period the office was an old-fashioned and hospitable clubroom, equipped with a carved walnut buffet, a decanter, and good cigars, where friends might call and be taken care of. There was no push or fuss, no worried concern about the development of the city, no eagerness to alter the good old system of "bosses and boodle" so familiar to all American municipalities. The cry of "the shame of the cities" was just beginning to be heard in the journals. John H. Farley held the office at the turn of the century. He was a fine, honorable, old-line Democrat and friend of Hanna's. As his term neared its end, the street-railway franchise came up for renewal. Farley wanted to continue the old arrangement for a period of twenty-five years. This was Johnson's opening. He ran for mayor, simplifying all issues into a simple slogan: "Three-cent fare on the streetcars." He inflamed the voters, and rode into office on the wave of their enthusiasm. He rushed downtown and burst into the office to take over on the morning of April 4, 1901. He was in a hurry because Mayor Farley was about to sign that morning an ordinance which would have turned over to the railroads the city's rights to lake-front lands. Johnson got a temporary injunction restraining him from signing. The injunction expired at 11:00 A.M. Johnson was dreaming of the future when the Mall and an improved lake front would beautify and lend dignity to downtown Cleveland.

For the next decade the activity of Mayor Tom Johnson was a national sensation and of international interest. Now a stout, portly figure of middle height, bubbling with energy at forty-seven, he never permitted himself or his associates or Cleveland to relapse into easy ways. The thin lips above a strong chin might flash a winning smile, or they might snarl into a brusque outburst. He could amuse his constituents with good stories or stir them with a blistering attack on greed. He was quick, alert, always on the move, always fighting for improvements for the city. He gathered about him a devoted young brain trust. Its leader was the brilliant young Newton D. Baker who had come to Cleveland in 1899. He was slight of build, a little stooped like a scholar, carefully tailored, and always quiet-spoken. He idolized Johnson. He once said that there must be a special heaven for men like the mayor. For six years he worked around the clock, carrying on the legal battle against the street railways, which he finally won, helping the mayor through his entanglements, and making speeches about the reform program.

In marked contrast to this dreamy-eyed young lawyer was the new city clerk, Peter Witt. He had been an iron molder, and a member of the labor union, and he was an evangelical socialist. He had struggled through poverty; he had been cold and hungry. His experiences seemed to sharpen an already harsh tongue. People flocked to hear him lash privilege and monoplies, and attack the inequalities in the tax structure. He made a special map of the city to show the unequal distribution of the tax burden and to point out ways of increasing the city's revenues. He did not seem to mind the bitter attacks which these measures provoked. The workingmen were behind him. They crowded into the big tent which Johnson set up for meetings, and cheered Peter Witt when he launched a verbal assault upon the men of the "Onion Club." He became an institution in Cleveland as a one-man town meeting, and long after his patron was retired from the mayor's office he continued to be Cleveland's most colorful speaker. He filled, year after year, first the Hippodrome and then the Auditorium with audiences who paid admission to hear him scold the wrongdoers and advance his own ideas on what was good for Cleveland.

Johnson had promised Cleveland more paved streets, more bridges, elimination of the grade crossings, improved sewers and waterworks, a new city hall, a market house for the West Side,

better lights for cleaner streets, hospitals, public bathhouses,
police and prison reform, as well as the three-cent fare. He meant
to deliver. He persuaded "his preacher," Dr. Harris R. Cooley,
to take over the Department of Charities and Corrections. Cooley's
program was sensational in its day. He completely reformed the
department. He established the Farm Colony on a 2,000-acre
tract to replace the wretched poorhouse. Here man and wife, instead of being separated and institutionalized, were housed in their
own comfortable cottage on the farm. Prisoners from the idle
workhouse were sent to the farm where they worked in the open
air with a minimum of supervision. Delinquent boys were sent to
a corresponding Boys' Farm, operated on the same plan. It, too,
was successful. He developed the Outdoor Relief Department to
give work to the unemployed. The program was so unusual, so
forward-looking in the early days of the twentieth century, so
bold an attack upon the problems besetting the overgrown industrial cities of the nation, that social workers from all over the
world came to study it at firsthand.

They were impressed also by the work of two other men among
Johnson's helpers. One was his new police chief, Frederick Kohler,
who, with firm but humane hand, cleaned up the dives, brought the
"social evil" under better control, and made a national reputation
for himself. The other was the equally notable Dr. Martin
Friedrich, health officer for the city. Epidemics were rampant in
crowded Cleveland. Smallpox and other contagious diseases
scourged it. Previous health officers had made little headway
against the evil. German-born Doctor Friedrich went to work
with the same vigor as the other young men in Johnson's band.
He inspected the water, meat, and milk supply, he disinfected
buildings, he supervised sewage, he examined schoolchildren, and
he stamped out filth diseases. By 1909 Cleveland was noted for
having the lowest death rate of any of the larger cities in the
country.

Johnson also won, for a brief period, his cherished ambition of
giving to Cleveland the three-cent fare. He relieved the peddlers
and hucksters of the heavy license fees which they had formerly

to pay. He got better wages for city employees. He extended and improved the parks and encouraged the poor to use them. He educated the people to a fuller understanding of the problems of a big city and fostered in them a high degree of civic-mindedness which is still felt in Cleveland. As Brand Whitlock said, Johnson tried to conduct "the business of Cleveland in the interest of those who own it, namely, the people of Cleveland." And he earned from Lincoln Steffens in 1905 the much-quoted citation, "the best mayor of the best governed city in the United States."

After nearly a decade of unremitting excitement Cleveland tired of Tom Johnson, of the railway fight, and the mounting municipal debt. They turned him out in 1909. It was a blow to him, but he took it with a philosophic outward calm, saying, "I had been mayor for so many years that many people lost sight of conditions as they existed before that time." He remained a controversial figure long after his death in the spring of 1911. To many people who loathed his advocacy of municipally owned streetcars, he was an irresponsible charlatan. When he ran for the governorship of Ohio against highly respected Myron T. Herrick, successful attorney and officer in the Society for Savings, he had been soundly defeated. He took his big tent out into the state to campaign among the people, but they failed to respond. The opposition called him a circus clown. Hanna blasted him at every opportunity, and went to his grave believing him to be an anarchist and a demagogue, bad on general principles, a monopolist and city boss, an interloper who created unrest and emptied the dinner pails which the Republicans had filled.

The inner circle and a substantial proportion of the common citizens stood loyally by him, unswerving in their admiration. They believed that he had arrived on the scene at a critical moment and that by his zealous administration he had brought Cleveland forward into a new and happier period. They erected the statue on the Public Square to him in 1915. It bears this tribute:

> He found us groping leaderless and blind
> He left a city with a civic mind.

And you will still see an occasional citizen pause in the busy Square to look up at the seated figure of the mayor and take time to read Peter Witt's inscription:

Erected by popular subscription in memory of the man who gave his fortune and his life to make Cleveland, as he often expressed it, A happier place to live in, A happier place to die in. And located on the spot which he dedicated to freedom of speech.

No single leader with such vivid color rose to succeed Tom Johnson, but the city moved on, in the usual cycle of advance and retreat, in the succeeding decades. The most notable projection of Johnson's dream for the city was the realization of the Mall plan and the rebuilding of the section southwest and northeast of the Public Square. This design laid the foundation for permanently beautifying the heart of Cleveland. The whole area along East Third Street between Superior Avenue and the lake front was cleared of its heterogeneous collection of buildings and developed into a generous Mall way after World War I. Though still a bit barren and immature, it does effectively join the congested Public Square region to the lake and affords splendid glimpses of the magnificent expanse of Lake Erie which many Clevelanders had almost forgotten. About the Mall are grouped the handsome public buildings which give it a solid air of dignity and distinction.

The great Public Library on Superior Avenue between Third and Fourth streets stands on the south end of the Mall, and its long, pleasant history room on the north side looks out across the spacious greensward to the glittering blue lake. This French Renaissance structure of gray marble, five stories high, sets the stately, but not forbidding, tone of the entire grouping. Completed in 1925, it was the realization of the hopes of Case, Whittlesey, Kirtland, and that great generation who formed the Cleveland Library Association in 1848 and organized the Public Library of 1867. Its size and its dominating location bear witness to the central place in the cultural life of the community assigned to it by leading Clevelanders. Its sister institution, the Western Reserve Historical Society and Library, born in the same year, was housed for some time in the old Society for Savings Building on the northeast corner of the Public Square. Later it was moved to the two adjoining mansions in the opulent residential section around Wade Park.

West of the Library the Federal Building forms the southwest corner of the Mall and ties it to the Public Square. It was the first unit in the group, begun during Johnson's days as mayor and completed in 1910, the year after he left office. To the east is the Federal Reserve Bank Building, the ten-story headquarters of the Fourth Federal Reserve District, built in 1922 by the same architects who designed the Library—Walker and Weeks. The home of the *Cleveland Plain Dealer* is also grouped with these buildings on Superior to form a harmonious unit. Just north of them, forming the east side of the Mall, is the Board of Education Building, also a Walker and Weeks creation. Farther north is the Public Auditorium erected in 1922. Facing the Library, the *Plain Dealer*, and the Reserve Bank, each representing an important activity of the city, the Auditorium furnishes seating capacity for 11,635 people to hold meetings for public discussion, political conventions, events of all character, and for the presentation of the Metropolitan Opera once a year. Thanks to the imagination and drive of Mrs. Adella Prentiss Hughes, typical of the energetic leadership of the city, the Opera draws its audience from all over the Reserve and closes its Cleveland season with a profit.

To the north on Lakeside Avenue is the beautiful City Hall, another of Johnson's dreams. Curiously enough, Cleveland had never had its own city hall. For years the city government was quartered in leased space in the five-story mansard-roofed Case Building, completed in 1875 and typical of the courthouses, poorhouses, college buildings, and state institutions of that decade. Finally in 1916 this Renaissance building of Vermont granite was completed at a cost, expensive for its day, of $3,000,000, and Cleveland at last had a respectable home and another handsome building for its Mall. The County Courthouse, in the same general style though lacking the same simplicity, flanks it to the west on Lakeside. The Stadium and the Horticultural Gardens, constructed in the early 1930's, pushed the Mall development right out to the lake and converted a garbage dump into a unit of civic pride. The lake front which Johnson fought so hard to preserve for the people of Cleveland now belonged permanently to them.

Around the southwest corner of the Public Square a different type of transformation was under way. It was engineered by the fabulous Van Sweringen brothers, Oris P. and Mantis J., certainly as strange a pair as ever made a contribution to the development of the Western Reserve in all its history. The brothers, who were inseparable, began their amazing career as real-estate operators while they were striplings. In 1905, when Johnson's star was at its zenith, they got control of Shaker Heights and proceeded to develop it into the model suburb for the affluent. They laid out the vast circular common with its inn and its stores in colonial design and they built a rapid transit south of congested central Cleveland along Kingsbury Run to connect their village with the Public Square. To carry out their scheme they had to buy the Nickel Plate Railroad. Then they planned a campaign to locate the Union Station in the proposed group of new buildings on the southwest corner of the Square. Johnson had opposed this plan in favor of a site upon the lake front. He delayed the Van Sweringen design for years, but failed to win support for his own, and in the end the brothers won.

They had pyramided their interests into a $190,000,000 empire. They completed on January 26, 1930, the Terminal Tower Building, flanked by the interconnecting units of the Higbee Department Store on the east and the Hotel Cleveland on the north and west. The Tower, rising 708 feet above the Square, became the dominant landmark of Cleveland, visible for miles along the approaching highways and flashing its light far out on the lake to the passing ships. They incorporated in the unit the Union Station and brought the main railroads and their own rapid transit into it. They provided an aesthetic and handy solution to the problem of getting trains into the heart of the city without accepting the ugliness inherent in railroad tracks. Few cities in the nation are able to debark passengers right into the center of things with such convenience and such grace. The cost of the development had reached

$119,000,000. Adjoining this unit on the south are office buildings and the mammoth Post Office, completed in 1934, which connects directly with the Station.

This impressive south group bore no architectural relationship to the Mall. It was strictly modern American skyscraper, appropriate to the day and in keeping with the character of the promoters who envisioned it. They went on their individual way driving upward their speculative spiral. They built for themselves a sprawling castle east of the city on their Daisy Hill Farm. It contained enough rooms to accommodate several families comfortably in the later years of the depression, but the Van Sweringen brothers lived there more like hermits than emperors, shared the same bedroom, collected books and manuscripts, and kept their own counsel. The depression pulled their kingdom down about their heads and buried the hopes and fortunes of thousands of people. All that was left was the ruins of a financial structure so complicated that no one could disentangle it—and the Terminal Tower group, set firmly on a caisson foundation reaching down 200 feet to bedrock, and physically independent of the worthless paper which had created it.

Lest we lose touch with the pre-Johnson, pre-Van Sweringen era, we emerge from the vast concourse of the Terminal and look north across the Square where, only so short a time ago, the cows were grazing at their leisure. There we note the old Chamber of Commerce building, erected in 1898. Since 1925 it has been the home of Cleveland College, the downtown branch of Western Reserve University, where, in their own way, thousands of students carry on the basic tradition which brought the Arkites together a few blocks to the east. On the west corner we see the ten-story brown-stone Society for Savings Building which has stood there for nearly sixty years. And west of it the Old Stone Church, built by the Presbyterians in 1855, blackened by almost a century of smoke, contemplates with venerable serenity all the fever and the fret of restless Cleveland.

While these developments were going on downtown, the city was rapidly moving in all directions, except north, to cover most of

Cuyahoga County. We have already examined at some length the direction of this expansion, the mounting congestion of foreign groups in the earlier residential districts, and the flight of the better-income families to the attractive suburbs. They developed the beautiful section around Wade Park and University Circle. They spread over Cleveland Heights, which in Rockefeller's Cleveland days was a crossroads known as Turkey Ridge because wild turkeys roamed about among the scrub. This neighborhood began to build up in 1905, and in 1921 became a municipality. Its population of around 60,000 spread over eight square miles of attractive country, falls apart, quite naturally, into many small communities. They spread more recently over the rolling region of Shaker Heights, developing this restricted community into a nationally known residential suburb of over 25,000 people. A few of the wealthy chose the lake shore and developed Bratenahl. Others went farther east to Chagrin Falls, Hunting Valley, and Gates Mills, and to country places in the same region.

The population spilled over also to East Cleveland, which in 1911 became an independent city, and now has a population of over 40,000. It filled up Euclid to 20,000 and continues to spread along a network of boulevards into once open country between the towns. It has flowed south to form present-day Warrensville, Maple Heights, Garfield Heights, Cuyahoga Heights, Newburgh Heights, and Brooklyn, and to embrace Brecksville, Parma, and other outlying communities in the Cleveland orbit. It has expanded westward to form Lakewood, the largest residential suburb, a community of over 70,000. Lakewood has no industries and its people commute to Cleveland offices where their business interests are centered. Rocky River and Bay Village, also beautiful towns on the lake front, repeat the pattern of Lakewood. There are, in fact, a dozen cities and forty-two villages in Greater Cleveland, all dependent upon the metropolis itself, but all technically separated from it and from one another as independent governing units. They have a combined population of about 450,000, one half the size of Cleveland itself which is estimated at 900,000.

ST. JOHN'S CATHEDRAL IN CLEVELAND

One of the newest and finest of the downtown buildings, it was dedicated in September 1948

A REGATTA ON THE LAKE

GENERAL MOSES CLEAVELAND'S STATUE
In the Public Square with the Terminal Tower in the background

These smaller population units satisfy a natural American wish for local independence. They reflect a little of the original New England sentiment for the town meeting where the people immediately affected can discuss their civic problems, control their own schools, elect their own mayor and council, and hire their own police. They carry with them the serious problem of over-all city planning, of public services, of taxes and the support of the city itself, and of welding all the diverse communities into a reasonably harmonious metropolitan area.

With a third of the total population living several miles out in these suburbs, the transportation problem became as acute as it was in Johnson's day, though for a different reason. Clevelanders still complain, as a matter of civic privilege, about the streetcars and busses and the congestion around the Square. The opening and improvement of more boulevards, and the construction of new bridges over the Cuyahoga have been notable accomplishments, but the city has grown so fast that these outlets barely keep the flow of traffic in the same relative position. Like Alice, they must run hard to stay where they are. The one achievement which indicates that at last Cleveland is catching up with itself and its opportunities is the redemption of its magnificent lake shore and the construction of the Memorial Shoreway eastward from the Mall to Gordon Park and westward over the Cuyahoga and along Edgewater Park on the lake to Lakewood.

Johnson's regime had given great impetus also to the social consciousness of the growing city and to the adjustment of the racial groups to their new environment. This side of Cleveland life was developed at the same time that the physical improvements were being made. The Reserve had been traditionally hospitable to the cause of the Negroes. Its ports had received fugitive slaves from the south over the Underground Railway and had slipped them across Lake Erie to safety and freedom in Ontario. A professor and a number of students at Oberlin rescued some slaves held at Wellington by Federal officers in September 1858. The rescuers, twenty-seven in number, were in turn arrested and tried before the United States Court at Cleveland. Two of them were convicted, and the sensational court battle which followed rocked Cleveland and the whole country. During the trial business stopped, mass protest meetings were held in the Square, and salutes were fired to honor the prisoners. One of Cleveland's lawyers was sent to defend John Brown when he was on trial for his life. When Brown was executed, the Cleveland bells were tolled and the newspapers appeared with black borders.

These were samples of the temper of the Reserve. Negroes, however, did not come to live here in large numbers until World War I when they began a migration from the South to the North which has not ended. They gradually spread over a slum area south of Cedar Avenue and east from the river to One Hundred and Fifth Street. During the depression days of the 1930's two Federal projects were developed to help remove some of the wretchedness and provide good housing for the increasing colored population. World War II and the acute need for more workers for the war industries attracted additional thousands, and further intensified the housing shortage and the congestion.

Despite unfavorable conditions the Negroes have made a distinct contribution to the cultural life of their community and the city. They have been encouraged by the fine leadership of Rowena and Russell Jelliffe, directors of Karamu House at Eighty-ninth Street and Quincy Avenue—a settlement-house project established in 1915 by the men's group of the Second Presbyterian Church. Karamu House has fostered particular interest in the drama and dance. In the same community are the Gilpin Players and their theater which have achieved a high level of distinction.

The ethnic groups from abroad, whose arrival, settlement, and first slow adjustment we have previously noted, have molded themselves into the fabric of Cleveland life. Beginning with the inevitable tight cluster of peoples clinging to their native ways and to one another in special districts, they have, in the truest and best sense known to America, melted into the larger community which is the city itself. They comprise two thirds of the total population. Different nationality groups still are concentrated in certain localities. East of the business district and north of Euclid Avenue the

Lithuanians and the Yugoslavs are thickly congregated. The Russians and the Greeks are gathered about East Fourteenth Street south of Prospect Avenue. Poles and Czechoslovaks are settled heavily on the South Side with Pulaski Triangle at East Twelfth, Superior, and Payne as the shrine of their respect for their native heritage and their allegiance to the America for which they have fought in two world wars involving their cultural homeland. On to the east, beyond University Circle and south of Euclid is the heavy concentration of Italians. The Jews have chosen the district west of Wade Park and around Kinsman Road. The Germans are still dominant on the West Side, and the Irish, Rumanians and other groups fill in the region between the Flats and Ridge Road.

Until recent years most of these nationalities spoke their own tongues, followed customs nearer to their European origins than to the Reserve. Several of them still publish their own national newspapers. But amalgamation, though still far from complete, has progressed astonishingly. With immigration shut off, with intercommunications with their homelands growing more and more difficult, and with the catastrophic upheavals in Europe, destroying the civilization with which they had been linked, assimilation in Cleveland, as at Akron, Youngstown, and Lorain, was speeded up. The school system has done good work. The new generations, born in the Reserve, unfamiliar with the lands of their fathers, are a part of the city where they were born. They speak good English, and they are, in some respects, more American than their American contemporaries. They have intermarried, and their cultures have mingled, creating something new and different, perhaps something more vigorous and alert, with a minimum of friction and conflict. Citizens with all varieties of foreign names, which few have bothered to change or Americanize in spelling, have become leaders in politics and business. They hold offices in the city and county, they sit on the city council and on the school board, and they work in the frame of American institutions for the betterment of the city of which they constitute an overwhelming majority.

Most of the nationality groups have made their contributions to this political maturity. Educated under Johnson, who was de-

pendent on their votes, they have moved on from the era of fla-
grant bossism. Not much is left of the kind of control exerted over
the foreign population by Czar Harry Bernstein, the banker,
saloonkeeper, and restaurant owner who held in the palm of his
hand the Russian Jews, Italians, and Negroes of the old Fifteenth
Ward. The groups became progressively less easy to deliver at
the polls. Maurice Maschke, a German Jew educated at Western
Reserve University and Harvard, was able to do it with less
blatancy than Bernstein. He was an opponent of Mayor Johnson,
and he organized the foreign vote, which had supported Johnson,
to bring about his defeat. He ran Herman Baer against him.
Baer was a German from one of the districts where Johnson had
been strong. Maschke was a controlling power in Cleveland and
the county for the next twenty years. Great respect was paid to
him at the time of his death in 1936.

The Hungarians contributed Louis Petrash to the city council
and various offices, Julius Kovachy to the municipal bench, and
Hugo Varga to Mayor Burton's cabinet and the vice-presidency
of the Cleveland Bar Association. From the Poles came Joseph
Sawicki as municipal judge, Felix Matia as director of parks under
Mayor Davis, Joseph Trinastic as councilman and assistant director of the Citizens Bureau, Rose Laskowski as head of social work
in the Broadway settlement, and W. J. Nowak as publisher of the
Polish *Monitor Daily*.

The Czechs sent John J. Babka to Congress, and from the
Bohemians Joseph Artl went to the city council and the municipal
bench. Frank Celebrezze, appointed to the same bench in 1937,
was the first Italian in an important office. The Slovenians made
the most outstanding contribution to the city, and also to the state,
in the person of Frank J. Lausche, who rose from the municipal
bench to the Common Pleas Court, twice to the office of mayor of
Cleveland and twice to the governorship of Ohio.

These same nationality groups have made extraordinary progress through their hundreds of clubs and their immigrant halls
around which their social life has centered. The Czech Bohemian
National Hall on Broadway, founded in 1896, is used by ninety

Czech societies. It has theaters, dance halls, clubrooms, a library, and like facilities for their interests. Alta House, in an Italian colony of over 20,000, is the meeting place for eighteen Italian organizations. It maintains a summer camp for children, plans day picnics for mothers, and provides playgrounds, gymnasiums, dance halls, educational programs, and health clinics for the colony. Goodrich House, with its farm near Akron, and Merrick House serve the Poles, Lithuanians, Ukrainians, and Slovaks in the same manner. The East End Neighborhood House, also Polish, has a maternity dispensary and organizes folk celebrations. The Slovene National Home on East Sixty-sixth at St. Clair, is the largest of eight Slovene community centers. Seventy-five societies, so fully are they organized, united to build it as a center of Yugoslav culture in Cleveland. In addition to the usual gymnasium, dance floors, library, and clubrooms, it has an auditorium, seating 2,000 people, for concerts, recitals, lectures, and speeches.[1]

Since Johnson's reform days the social conscience of Cleveland has never been at ease. Social workers have continued to find here a rich field in which to labor. Hiram House, Goodrich House, the Tremont Area project in the poorer working district on the high Cuyahoga bluff overlooking the Flats, are notable in the literature of the sociologists. They have enlisted the many service agencies, church groups, businessmen, luncheon clubs, women's clubs, parent-teacher organizations, in concentrated programs to overcome juvenile delinquency, to provide supervised playgrounds, and effect general improvements in the living conditions of the depressed areas. They are making good progress.

If these activities left any doubt about the product of the great melting pot, a visit to a World Series game in the late summer of 1948 would have dispelled it. Cleveland has promoted and followed baseball ever since it organized the Forest City Club in 1869. It had a team in the National Brotherhood of Baseball Players formed in 1885. And it was represented by the Cleveland

---

[1] Wellington Fordyce, "Nationality Groups in Cleveland Politics," OSA & H Quarterly, Vol. 46 (1937), p. 109*ff.*, and "Immigrant Institutions in Cleveland," *ibid*, Vol. 47 (1938), p. 87*ff.*

Indians when the American League revised its membership in 1900. Nearly a thousand spectators flocked to the diamond to see the Indians play. The team had risen only once, in 1920 under Tris Speaker, to pennant-winning heights before Bill Veeck took them over and produced the champions of 1948. There was more excitement in Cleveland during the World Series than had been generated by any single event of any nature in the 150 years of its history. Every available spot in the Municipal Stadium, with permanent seats for 78,189, and temporary capacity for 20,000 more, was jammed, and the world's record for attendance at a baseball game was broken by a crowd of 86,288. And the most vigorous and fiercely partisan rooters, who wept when Robert Feller failed in his greatest hour, and went mad when the Indians won, were the sons and daughters of the men and women who had migrated to America and settled in the tenement groups which we have just described.

Back of all this physical expansion of Cleveland and the material progress of its people are the stability and continuing growth of industry and commerce. They have set the pace. The older concerns have grown with the years, and were catapulted forward by World War II: the White Motor Company, headed by Robert Black; Thompson Products, turning out hundreds of parts for automobiles and airplanes, headed by Frederick G. Crawford, formerly president of the National Association of Manufacturers; Warner & Swasey, toolmakers, headed by Charles J. Stilwell; Republic Steel, headed by President Charles M. White and Chairman of the Board, fighting Tom Girdler; American Steel and Wire, headed by Clifford F. Hood, and employing 7,000 in Cleveland; Standard Oil of Ohio, headed by W. T. Holliday.[2]

Scores of sensational newcomers have added their contribution

---

[2] In 1944, when war production was at its feverish peak, the *Cleveland Plain Dealer* published a series of fifty-one interview-articles by Roy Rutherford about the men who head and guide some of the industries of present-day Cleveland. He entitled them "Boys Grown Tall." They make informative reading for students of the industrial leadership in modern Cleveland. Rutherford did not discuss another group of leading men like Ralph Bellamy of the *Plain Dealer*, Louis B. Seltzer of the *Press*, Walter I. Beam of the Chamber of Commerce, or the men who guide the destiny of the great banks, stores, and commercial houses which play so central a role in the life of Cleveland. They would be the subject for a companion series.

to the vast workshop which is Cleveland. The Lincoln Electric Company, under the leadership of its president James F. Lincoln, has grown in the past quarter of a century into one of the great electric welding concerns of the world, and has attracted national attention with its incentive labor plan and the resulting high wages earned by its 1,000 employees. The Cleveland Diesel Engine Company of General Motors, managed by Vice-President George W. Codrington, is a relatively new industry employing 5,000 people. The Reliance Electric & Engineering Company, Clarence L. Collens president, has three plants in Cleveland with 2,000 workers. There are Enamel Products; Lamson & Sessions; Ohio Crankshaft Company, which went from 450 to 4,000 workers during World War II; Cleveland Graphite Bronze, which has grown in twenty-five years from 20 to 7,000 workers. And these are only the beginning of an almost inexhaustible list of enterprises which have further congested the Flats, have sprung up farther east between Euclid Avenue and the lake, and spread mills and factories around the outskirts of the city and in near-by towns. They represent the industrial leadership of the present day which corresponds to the Stone, Gordon, Wade, Mather generation of the era of great beginnings. The proliferation is just as striking at the middle of the twentieth century as it was seventy-five years ago. And it would be even greater if Cleveland leaders did not control it somewhat by discouraging certain developments such as the government proposal to locate a forty-million-dollar machine-tool plant there because it would vex the already troublesome problem of importing laborers and finding homes for them.

The accumulating wealth and a potent intellectual ferment, revitalizing the New England tradition with elements from all nations, have produced an extraordinary cultural development in Cleveland which influences the entire Reserve. It created in 1918 and generously supports the Cleveland Symphony Orchestra with beautiful Severance Hall for its home. The moving spirits behind the organization were Arch C. Klumph, famous Rotarian, musician, and manager of the orchestra, and Mrs. Adella Prentiss Hughes, who succeeded him as the guiding genius of the orchestra. Under

Nikolai Sokoloff and Artur Rodzinski it became one of the leading symphony orchestras in the nation, and under George Szell it has maintained its distinguished reputation. Dr. Rudolph Ringwall, associate conductor, has made a great contribution to the musical life of Cleveland through his well-patronized Pop Concerts.

Cleveland has supported the educational institutions which express the same eager spirit. Again they unite the firm old New England tradition with the spirited ambitions of newcomers to the Reserve. Western Reserve University has grown steadily in influence and power as a leading institution of higher learning since it was moved from Hudson to Cleveland in 1882. It has drawn heavily on Cleveland men and their wealth for its support. Adelbert College for men and Flora Stone Mather College for women, together with the distinguished professional colleges and graduate school, send forth each year to the Reserve and to the nation young men and women of the highest competency. Case Institute of Technology emphasizes training on the higher levels in the sciences which support and direct the immense and diversified industrial concerns of Cleveland. On a practical and applied level, the John Huntington Polytechnic Institute, founded in 1918, offers "a free evening polytechnic school for deserving persons of Cleveland," that is, young people, normally of college age, employed in industry, who desire to improve their abilities. Fenn College and Cleveland College bring their resources to serve thousands of students who must work for their living while pursuing, chiefly at night, their course of college study. John Carroll University, near suburban University Heights, with a student body of 500, trains men in a liberal arts tradition under the guidance of the Jesuit Order. Ursuline College, Cleveland, founded in 1871, and Notre Dame College at South Euclid, founded in 1922, provide education under Catholic auspices for almost 600 women. In these institutions Cleveland attempts to educate the largest possible number of its youth on the level of their capacity from applied handicraft to the frontiers of research in science and medicine.

Everybody in Greater Cleveland seems to be interested in drama. The pattern has changed with the years and the changing community. During the third quarter of the nineteenth century John Ellsler was the driving spirit who made Cleveland theater-conscious. This actor-promoter in the post-Civil War years managed the Academy of Music playhouse on Bank Street. He, with his wife and daughters, acted with his stock company, and toured the near-by Reserve towns. He brought to Cleveland all the notable plays and stage personalities of the time: Edwin Forrest, Charlotte Cushman, Charles Keen, Joe Jefferson, Edward A. Sothern, and the rest. He wrote in his memoirs:

Every Opera Company, foreign or domestic, all Burlesques or Opera Bouffe Companies, all the pantomime troupes, every comedian and tragedian that travelled from 1855 to 1875, they all walked the boards of the old Academy of Music while under my management.[3]

In 1875 he built the Euclid Avenue Opera House and opened it with Bronson Howard's *Saratoga* or *Pistols for Seven*. The house did not prosper. Cleveland was caught in the doldrums following the Panic of 1873 and could not adequately support the theater. Ellsler had to abandon his Opera House in 1878. Sold by the sheriff to Mark Hanna, it burned in 1892. Hanna rebuilt it in 1893. All the theaters of the 1880's and 1890's—the Park, Lyceum, Cleveland, Columbia, Star, the Peoples, and the Opera House—have disappeared. The present Hanna Theatre, opened in 1921, is the only surviving legitimate theater. But the theater did not actually die. In keeping with the dispersion of the population, it went out to the people themselves. There are fifteen recognized community theaters in Cleveland, each producing five or more plays a year for a discriminating public, each the expression of more intimate community interests. They are ably directed and maintain a high standard of excellence in their productions. Among them are the Lakewood Little Theater, the Bay Village Players, the Shaker Players, the Chagrin Little Theater, the Gilpin Players, and the

---

[3] His "Stage Memories" are now in the Western Reserve Historical Society Library, MS. 3025. Quoted in Benton, *Cultural Story of an American City—Cleveland*, Vol. III.

Western Reserve University Players. The Play House on East Eighty-sixth Street is one of the leading little-theater organizations in the country. In addition to these firmly established community theaters there are at least two hundred dramatic clubs of one kind or another that cultivate interest in drama and produce plays from time to time. This form of activity is a thousand times more rewarding than mass witnesses at a commercial spectacle.

On January 6, 1874, the *Cleveland Leader*, discouraged by the lag in cultural interest, lectured its public in these words:

If Cleveland people had the enterprise they have credit for, Case Hall, Brainard's Opera House, and Garrett's Hall would be filled with audiences every night. We should have an art gallery where pictures and statues from master hands would revolutionize our ideas. We should have a public library of 100,000 volumes.

What the editor then despaired of has been richly brought to pass.

CHAPTER TWENTY-THREE

THE RESERVE IN TRANSITION

THE rest of the story in other parts of the Reserve is
much like that of modern Cleveland. It differs in details, in degree
and intensity, not in basic pattern. Rubber at Akron and steel
at Youngstown have supplied most of those details. They have
swept these two cities onward until their power and influence are
felt in all the villages for which they have become an attracting
center. Other and more potent migrations have overrun and sup-
planted that first mass movement of old Connecticut peoples to
the new West. Their impact has been so great, both in its numbers and in its character, that it has been felt throughout the length
and breadth of the Reserve. Akron still had only 69,000 people
in 1910 on the eve of its sensational boom. By the end of World
War I it had 209,000, and at the beginning of the depression in
1930 it had risen to 255,000. Ten thousand of them left when the
factories slowed down, but this number and more trekked in again
during the demanding war days of the 1940's.

Three fifths of those who arrived before 1930, over 150,000, had
come from the South, chiefly from the hill country. Many of them
had never been in a large city before in their lives. The roads between Akron and the hills were lined with jalopies filled with
families on their way to find work in the factories or going back
home to see their folks. The rest of the influx came heavily from
the European immigrants. The two elements were alien to each
other, strangers in a strange new land, people who had come not
as colonists to clear a forest and plant a culture, but as migratory
workers seeking a wage while the good times lasted. Eleven thou-

331

sand of them were Negroes for whom a few jobs were opened in the rubber factories. The Southern whites, feeling little identity with their Northern industrial community, sought social unity with other workers who had come from the same state. The West Virginians formed the largest contingent. On the basis of geographical origin they organized West Virginia Day and gathered together for one vast picnic.

Akron had something of the clamorous air created by large numbers of people away from home, temporary sojourners crowded together in a boom town too small to contain them. The best efforts of the officials and civic leaders to bring the town forward to absorb them could not keep pace with the overwhelming growth. The blow of the depression was a painful shock to American towns founded on diversified industries. In restless, impetuous, and unstable Akron, a one-industry town dependent on rubber, it was not a shock but a disaster and an awakening. Signs of impending trouble had not been wanting. In 1913, when the rubber companies were mechanizing their processes to meet the demands for more and cheaper rubber goods, 15,000 workers had struck the plants. The war and the high level of prosperity of the 1920's, with their abundant work and good wages, relieved the tensions. Management fostered a forward-looking program of company unions, workers' associations, educational activities and benefits which lasted out the decade. But it could not endure the heavy battering of the depression.

In the face of cutbacks and unemployment, the workers began to look with favor and hope to the big unions. The A. F. of L. United Rubber Workers' Union was organized in 1934. John L. Lewis himself came to Akron in January 1936 to press the intensive drive of the C.I.O. for unions "that can raise articulate voices." A few weeks later the bitter rubber strike began with a sit-down in the Goodyear plant. Then came the mass picketing and the full-scale strike, involving Goodyear, Goodrich, and Firestone, which rocked the rubber capital for five weeks and left an aftermath of rancor and suspicion. The United Rubber Workers went over to the C.I.O. in April 1937. Favoring New Deal labor legislation held the uneasiness in check until the renewed demands for rubber throughout the 1940's, and the tremendous growth in numbers and power of organized labor brought an interim of peace and relative stability to Akron.

Akron has matured considerably as a city in this decade of prosperity. It is no longer a boom town. It has had another big increase in population, and it still has a large margin of migratory workers. But it also has a strong nucleus of permanent families and a substantial number of second-generation young citizens, born, reared, and educated in the city and completely at home there. The foreign population has worn off the sharp edges of its differences. The nationality groups have come out of their first tight and exclusive little native colonies, and have become citizens of their town. They begin to express themselves in civic affairs. Their sons fought as Americans all round the globe in World War II, and when they returned to their home city, they, with their younger brothers and sisters, helped fill the bulging classes of the University of Akron in the rush toward higher learning and greater technical and professional competency.

The improved living standards, despite the acute housing shortage, are clearly evident in the neat homes with picture windows that have spread over the pleasant terrain of suburban Akron, utilizing the ridges and the lakes; in the air of assurance that has settled over the residential sections developed during the 1920's; and in the business section where the banks, stores, restaurants, and hotels, though crowded, seem somehow less confused. The Central Tower Building, twenty-eight stories high, standing at Mill and Main streets, was completed in 1931. Topped with a beacon that burns through the night, it dominates the sky line and typifies the spirit of the city as the cathedrals expressed the preoccupation of the medieval towns. The Tower looks out over the spreading city, over the rubber factories and elevators, over the Cuyahoga bend and gorge; and it looks down on the well-preserved remnants of the old canal cutting its way like a sharp gash through the ravine in the heart of the city just as it did when so short a time ago it first linked this village in the heart of the Reserve wilderness with Cleveland, the lake, and the markets of the world.

Over at Youngstown we substitute steel for rubber, and a heavier percentage of foreign-born for the native Southern whites, and repeat the story of Akron. During the expansive decade of the 1920's Youngstown's population rose again from 132,000 to 170,000. It was made up of fewer migratory workers and more families who had come to make the city their home. Even in its most hectic days it never had the impatient emergency atmosphere so characteristic of its neighbor during the same period. Through the long depression of the 1930's it lost only 2,000 people. The distress of that period brought the same unrest and the same conflicts to Youngstown that it brought to Akron. The big mills cut back production as orders fell off. Unemployment mounted and bread lines lengthened. The C.I.O. organizers moved in to form the Steel Workers' Union and demand recognition from the companies under the New Deal legislation. On May 26, 1937, they closed the mills with the biggest strike yet seen in the Reserve.

The vast steel plants in the valley, with their fires out and their stacks smokeless, were silent and foreboding. Surrounding them with pickets were thousands of angry, idle men. Other thousands milled about in the city. It was a grim and somber moment in Youngstown's history. Charles P. Taft came in for the United States Mediation Board to try to settle the strife. He failed. Rioting broke out around the plant of Republic Steel. When it was over two strikers were dead, twenty-seven were injured, and hundreds were weeping and retching from the gas bombs hurled into their midst. Youngstown Sheet and Tube tried to open their plants to those who were willing to return to work. State troops were sent in to preserve order. They were met at the railroad station by organized strikers marching with flags behind a spirited drum corps. During the ensuing back-to-work movement under troop protection five more workers were killed and 307 injured. The Supreme Court affirmed the legality of the National Labor Relations Act under which the Union was waging its war, and Little Steel negotiated a contract. Again the world war and the insatiable demand for steel pushed the conflict into the background and brought a decade of unparalleled prosperity to the valley of steel. A new influx of workers poured into Youngstown. The city was now old enough and stable enough to absorb them. It, too, has matured rapidly during these years. An atmosphere of civic enterprise is plainly observable. The Negro population, greatly increased during the 1940's, has been skillfully integrated with the community. They take an active interest in the city, and in the schools where their children are accepted without friction through the wise direction of the superintendent, principals, and teachers. The foreign groups have become acclimatized and their children in increasing numbers fill the schools and go on to college—many of them to the evening classes of Youngstown College. The names on the rosters of the big graduating classes in the high schools are predominantly foreign, but it is hard to distinguish these keen second-generation sons and daughters of immigrant parents from the few remaining descendants of the Connecticut pioneers. They have, of course, no Western Reserve consciousness. The spirit of modern Youngstown is unconsciously best expressed, perhaps, by the muscular murals enshrining the god of steel on the walls of the thronging Open Hearth Room of the Pick Ohio Hotel which are reproduced alfresco and built into the outside wall along the busy sidewalk.

Warren felt sharply the advancing tempo of the 1940's. It had expanded from 27,000 in 1920 to 41,000 in 1930, and had remained stable at that number until 1940. Then the exigencies of World War II taxed the capacity of the steel mills and the plants making cables and parts and lamp bulbs for tanks and planes and automobiles. Workers flocked in, many of them from West Virginia, boosting the population again to an estimated 60,000. The years of prosperity following the war kept most of them there after the reconversion of industry to peace. One sad reminder of the penalty of the war continued in Warren where the steel caskets were made to shroud the bodies of American dead in all quarters of the earth to be transported for burial in their home soil for which they had fought. These years placed a severe strain on Warren, but the city had been stamped so firmly in the mold of the Reserve that it did not entirely lose its identity with its earlier traditions.

Ravenna with its huge war munition plant and Elyria with its numerous smaller industries absorbed the pressures of the war years without undergoing pronounced or permanent change in the orderly pattern of their ways. Both continue to be primarily county-seat towns, attractive, intimate communities of homes on tree-shaded streets with a suggestion of relaxation and leisure. The army of workers at the war plant in Ravenna had come in only for the duration, and they were housed in hastily constructed barracks much like troops at the training camps. When the emergency was over, the temporary buildings were picked up and moved to nearby Hiram and other college campuses to provide cafeterias, recreational halls, classrooms, and dormitories for the masses of veteran students who exchanged their guns for college textbooks.

The other parts of the Reserve were not materially affected by the war years. A few factories were erected at Geneva and Painesville, but Chardon, Burton, and other outlying, peaceful residential towns in Cleveland's powerful orbit were undisturbed. Residents of these communities went in to Cleveland to work. Big busses from Thompson Products, Inc., and other plants made the rounds of these towns and villages morning and evening to pick up and deliver workers at their homes, like school busses gathering up the children to carry them to the township centralized schools. The little towns have remained, with few modifications, much as they were before the rise of big industrial cities. Almost all of them are inextricably geared to metropolitan Cleveland. The rural areas have tended to concentrate on the products for which they are best suited—dairy herds, cheese, truck gardens and hothouse vegetables, fruits and nurseries, and, in some of the more fertile sections around Leroy, Lodi, Greenwich, and New Haven, corn and wheat.

There are a few surviving bits of interest tucked away in the Reserve along the country roads. Phalanx Mill, ten miles northwest of Warren, built in 1813 by Eli Barnum of Connecticut, still stands beside its well-preserved mill race. Though remodeled and turbine-powered, it continues to grind corn and wheat for Trumbull County farmers. Near the old mill is a red granary and cheese factory, relics of the short-lived communal Phalanx Company planted here by 200 colonists on 1,500 acres of land in 1844. In marked contrast six miles southeast of Chagrin Falls is the twenty-five-year-old Czechoslovak village of Taborville founded as a co-operative by Joseph Martinek, leader of the Labor Gymnastic Union. It reproduces a typical village of the upper valley of the Elbe on a 110-acre tract of gardens, fields, and orchards. In the summer, when many families come here for vacation, the town crier rings the village bell three times a day, morning, noon, and evening. The young Czech-Americans speak their native tongue at the meetings in the community house, present plays and native festivals in their outdoor theater, and practice gymnastics in a conscious effort to preserve the weakening ties with the ancient folkways.

The Reserve has continued to be distinguished for the number and quality of its colleges. These institutions testify dramatically to the richness and continuing force of the contribution of the New England settlers. Oberlin College has for over a century led the way in the liberal-arts tradition. It is a remarkable combination of passionate individualism sponsoring radical causes, and of a balancing conservatism which at the same time resists change. It began with a zealous devotion to "the plainest living and the highest thinking" for the purpose of extending "the blessings of education to the teeming multitudes of the Ohio and Mississippi valleys." Its motto was "Learning and Labor." It caused a sensation when it first admitted Negroes at a time when other colleges would not accept them. It admitted women to its classes in 1837. A century later it commemorated this epoch-making act by erecting on the campus a memorial gateway to the women of Oberlin. It has grown rich in its later years from an endowment bestowed by Charles Martin Hall, one of its graduates, who made millions out of aluminum. Its students are drawn from all sections of the nation and from abroad, and their high thinking is no longer coupled with plain living or with work in the founders' meaning of that word.

But the changes which it has undergone are not different from those which have affected Williams and Amherst, and on its beautiful campus near the center of the Western Reserve it still preserves with a high standard the best of the New England tradition.

Hiram College, serene on its hill, was a denominational school founded by the Disciples. It trained ministers for this brotherhood, as it still does, but, like other church schools, it moved gradually away from divinity to a liberal-arts program in which it is strong and thorough. From Hiram has gone out a host of brilliant men into all the professions. President Garfield, historian Hinsdale, and poet Vachel Lindsay, to whom a beautiful memorial room in the library is dedicated, are the most famous if not the most typical. Lake Erie College on its spacious campus at Painesville is the counterpart of the same kind of institution exclusively for women.

The newer demands brought about by the transformation of the Reserve into an urban and industrialized life are reflected in the rise of the state and municipal colleges and universities. Kent State University is a response of the state of Ohio to provide under state support an important undergraduate and professional school serving the northeastern portion of the Reserve. Youngstown College and the University of Akron, as we have noted, serve the needs of these great urban centers. Through their evening classes they carry opportunities to hundreds of employed students who would otherwise be denied advanced training.

This is a long and thrilling development from the day when young Seabury Ford and D. Witter made their way on foot through the forest from the Reserve to Yale College and Joshua R. Giddings tramped across the sparsely settled townships from Jefferson to Canfield to study law with Elisha Whittlesey. The purpose and the dream have never altered; the colleges in their extensive work are but the fruition of the desire for a richer and fuller life for more people which first lured the colonists into this land.

ɛPILOGUE

Across its 120-mile sweep from the Pennsylvania line to the Blue Hole of Castalia, from the lake-shore towns and villages to the cities and farms along its southern ridge, the Western Reserve is brisk and strenuous with continuing growth. This growth has never been interrupted or seriously retarded since that July day in 1796 when Moses Cleaveland with a boatload of his men paddled his way along the shore of Lake Erie in search of the mouth of the Cuyahoga and a likely site for a town. His statue stands today under the shadow of the Terminal Tower in the Public Square which he paced out a century and a half ago. Bareheaded, with a keen explorer's look in his eye, he holds a Jacob's staff in his right hand and a surveyor's compass in the crook of his left arm. He faces diagonally across the Square toward Lake Erie as though he were contemplating the town which he planned and the tremendous changes which the intervening years have brought about. He appears to view them with satisfaction. They are more than he asked for or ever dreamed of. He did not foresee the Tower behind him, the vast mills in the Flats, the coming and going in the Cuyahoga of the giant 600-foot freighters, the swarming busses and streetcars in the Square, the thousands of people from all countries who would find their way to his city, or the million inhabitants who populate greater Cleveland. But he would undoubtedly say that all this is an extension which he did not envision rather than any change in the direction of his purpose.

The extensions have been so stupendous that the original stamp of early Connecticut may seem to have grown somewhat dim. It is like one of the ancient parchment manuscripts where a new composition has been written over the letters of the old without destroying them, and the original may be read by experts in palimpsests. Much has happened, as we have now seen, on these three million acres since the first mass migration of Connecticut people into Ohio. But they did remain homogeneous long enough and their culture was firm enough to make a permanent impress upon the region which no amount of change has been able to erase. There are no trees in the Square at Cleveland, no stumps, no fence; no cattle graze there and no horses are hitched to a railing. It is cluttered with walks and monuments, and the wide, traffic-filled streets have invaded it and reduced it to a turn-around for streetcars and busses. But its mere presence there always surprises the visitor as he emerges from the station under the Tower, and enough of its original atmosphere survives to suggest something of the vision of the man who placed it there. And a visit to the corresponding greens at Canfield, Hudson, Jefferson, Painesville, Leroy, Burton, and a dozen other towns and villages in the Reserve less affected by the changes serves to dramatize the rapid but orderly transition of the region from colonial New England to modern Ohio.

Radical alterations often seemed imminent. The arrival of Joseph Smith and Brigham Young at Kirtland caused trepidation in good Connecticut hearts. Mormonism was an alien doctrine and way of life to New England Congregationalists. They were harsh with Joseph and his devoted band, and they drove them out of the Reserve. But the Temple still stands and the Latter Day Saints who worship there are not recognizably different from the other citizens of the Western Reserve. The massive migrations of European peoples into the Reserve, far overshadowing in numbers the original emigration from Connecticut, threatened to bring about significant changes in the character of the region. But these, too, were contained, absorbed, and conditioned by the firm holding of the earlier tradition. The Reserve retained much of its distinctiveness and continued in its sure direction.

The enterprise and boundless energy which brought Moses Cleaveland and his men to survey the wilderness and sustained the first settlers through the hard years in their clearings among the forests have never lagged or faltered. The same spirit which built the first sawmills and gristmills by the waterfalls also built the giant steel mills, rubber factories, and oil refineries. The same vision which fashioned the first small hulls to sail on the lake, which dug the shallow ditch from Akron to Cleveland, which strung rails across the land, and which founded the first banks for the commercial structure, also designed the giant freighters for moving ore and coal, the network of roads which link the towns to one another and to the nation, and erected the towering monument of modern industry and commerce. The same hope for the future which laid the first logs for a village schoolhouse also created and supports the schools and colleges which now distinguish the Reserve.

It has all been a high and unparalleled adventure projected by one generation and continued by the next. It has been so absorbing and exciting that we have not often paused to examine the road over which we have come. A hundred and fifty years have slipped by, registering their changes. The shattering effect of two world wars on the older civilizations of Europe have startled us into a sharper understanding of what we have been creating here during this century and a half. In the light of our experiences and of our increasing maturity, this achievement seems, despite its shortcomings, a priceless heritage. And the Western Reserve, aware of its background and of its strategic position at the heart of America's basic industries, rich in education, drama and the fine arts, rooted in the past but with its head erect, faces with equanimity the destiny which persistently unfolds before it.

ACKNOWLEDGMENTS, BIBLIOGRAPHICAL NOTE AND INDEX

ACKNOWLEDGMENTS
AND BIBLIOGRAPHICAL NOTE

In my years of travel about the Western Reserve, meditating on this book and accumulating the materials for it, I have met and talked with many people who have contributed to it in various ways. Chief among them have been Robert L. Groves, Henry S. Sherman, and D. James Pritchard, and their colleagues of the Society for Savings. Their interest in the Reserve is alive and deeply rooted, and their knowledge of it is extensive and detailed. I am deeply grateful to them for their substantial aid over the past three years and for their careful reading of the manuscript. The publication of this volume coincides with the centennial of the Society, which has witnessed most of the developments recorded herein. The very nature of the occasion has personalized their interest but has never at any point deflected them from a scholarly detachment in viewing this vital portion of the history of a developing America.

The Western Reserve Historical Society, the Cleveland Public Library, the Ohio State Archaeological and Historical Society, and the Museums at Norwalk and Burton have all given me generous help. Citizens in the various towns and villages have generously answered my questions, showed me old family diaries, written me letters, and have built up the atmosphere where they have not contributed directly to the text. It is a pleasure indeed to recall these experiences: visiting Tallmadge with O. G. Stinchcomb and Jack Fullen; the afternoon at Hiram with President Fall; exploring the old canal with Jim Pritchard; pleasant days at Oberlin with Carl Wittke; studying old houses and churches with Anne Gregory; extended visits to Norwalk, Hudson, and the lake-shore villages; going about Sandusky at various times with Karl E. Whinnery, and discussing the Lake Erie islands with Dr. Langlois, the man who knows most about them; the conversations with New Haven people who have roots in the Western Reserve, especially Mrs. George P. Baker, whose interest in Hillhouse helped me to fill in that neglected chapter in Reserve history.

The source materials themselves are voluminous and varied. Fortunately the surveyors and early settlers belonged to the journal-keeping generations. Their records, most of which have found their way into the libraries and many into publication, are invaluable. Several of them were incorporated into Charles Whittlesey's primary work, *Early History of Cleveland* (Cleveland, 1867). They have been supplemented by memoirs and articles by the older generation which lived through the hard days on the frontier, and by autobiographies and travel notes left by men who spent much of their lives in the Reserve or who made visits of inspection to it. These have been mentioned or quoted in the text. Complete files of most of the newspapers published in the Reserve are available both at the Western Reserve Historical Society Library and at the Ohio State Archaeological and Historical Society Library.

Many of the counties have voluminous histories of their origin, settlement,

345

and development compiled after the Civil War before the materials perished with the death of the older settlers. William Henry Perrin, *History of Summit County* (Chicago, 1881); Samuel A. Lane, *Fifty Years and Over of Akron and Summit County* (Akron, 1892); W. W. Williams, *History of the Fire Lands* (Cleveland, 1879); *The Mahoning Valley,* published by the Historical Society, 1878; and later ones: General Thomas W. Sanderson, *Twentieth Century History of Youngstown and Mahoning County* (Chicago, 1907); H. L. Peeke, *The Centennial History of Erie County, Ohio* (2 vols., Sandusky, 1925); *Centennial History of Akron* (Akron, 1925); Joseph G. Butler, *History of Youngstown and the Mahoning Valley* (Chicago and New York, 1921).

There have been several lengthy, almost encyclopedic treatises on the Western Reserve and Cleveland: Harriet Taylor Upton, *History of the Western Reserve* (3 vols., Chicago, 1910); Samuel P. Orth, *History of Cleveland* (3 vols., Chicago, 1910); Elroy McKendree Avery, *A History of Cleveland and Its Environs* (3 vols., Chicago and New York, 1918); C. A. Urann, *Centennial History of Cleveland* (Cleveland, 1896); James Harrison Kennedy, *A History of the City of Cleveland, 1769-1896* (Cleveland, 1896); W. Scott Robinson, ed., *History of the City of Cleveland* (Cleveland, 1887); Elbert Jay Benton, *Cultural History of an American City—Cleveland* (3 vols. published of several projected, Cleveland, 1943, 1944, 1946).

Briefer, more specialized treatments appear in Alfred Mathews, *Ohio and Her Western Reserve* (New York, 1902); P. P. Cherry, *The Western Reserve and Early Ohio* (Akron, 1921); Harvey Rice, *Pioneers of the Western Reserve* (Boston and New York, 1888); and *Sketches of Western Life* (Boston and New York, 1887); George C. Wing, *Early Years on the Western Reserve, with Extracts from Letters of Ephrain Brown and Family, 1805-45* (Cleveland, 1920); James Wallen, *Cleveland's Golden Story* (Cleveland, 1920); Archer H. Shaw, *The Plain Dealer: One Hundred Years in Cleveland* (New York, 1942); Frederick C. Waite, *Western Reserve University, the Hudson Era* (Cleveland, 1943); *Western Reserve Academy: One Hundred Years of Western Reserve* (Hudson, 1926).

The houses have been given a thorough study by I. T. Frary in *Early Homes of Ohio* (Richmond, 1936), and by Ella Grant Wilson, *Famous Old Euclid Avenue of Cleveland* (Cleveland, 1932-1937).

The surveyors' notes and land records are on file at the courthouses at Norwalk and at Warren, though the Western Reserve Historical Society has several of them, along with much uncatalogued manuscript material. The Mormon material is voluminous, in record form at Painesville, in a library of printed matter, and in the exceptionally fine study of the movement by Fawn M. Brodie, *No Man Knows My History, The Life of Joseph Smith, the Mormon Prophet* (New York, 1945). The Hillhouse material is in New Haven and in Leonard Bacon's *Sketch* (New Haven, 1860). The data on Alfred Kelley is scattered through various documents and partially brought together in James L. Bates, *Alfred Kelley: His Life and Work* (Columbus, 1888). There are good biographies of several of the prominent men who figure in the Reserve: Herbert Croly, *Marcus Alonza Hanna: His Life and Work* (New York, 1912); Allan Nevins, *John D. Rockefeller* (2 vols., New York, 1940); Carl Lorenz,

Tom L. Johnson, Mayor of Cleveland (New York, 1911); Tom L. Johnson, *My Story* (New York, 1911); George W. Julian, *The Life of Joshua R. Giddings* (1892).

Henry Howe, *Historical Collections of Ohio* (in many editions) are unique and priceless. He made extended journeys over the state in the 1840's and again in the 1880's, talking with people, sketching scenes, and recording the passing era. No historian could get along without them. C. C. Huntington, *A History of Banking and Currency in Ohio before the Civil War* (O.S.A. & H.S., Vol. XXIV, 1915) is a fundamental piece of scholarship on the complex subject. The canal is the subject of many shelves of public documents and reports, and has been given rather thorough treatment in *History of Ohio Canals, Their Construction, Cost, Use, and Partial Abandonment* (O.S.A. & H.S., Columbus, 1905).

There are scores of other volumes, old magazines, directories, and guidebooks which I have perused and from each of which I have distilled perhaps a few sentences for my purposes and to enrich the text.

INDEX